IMAGES
of America

SAN BENITO

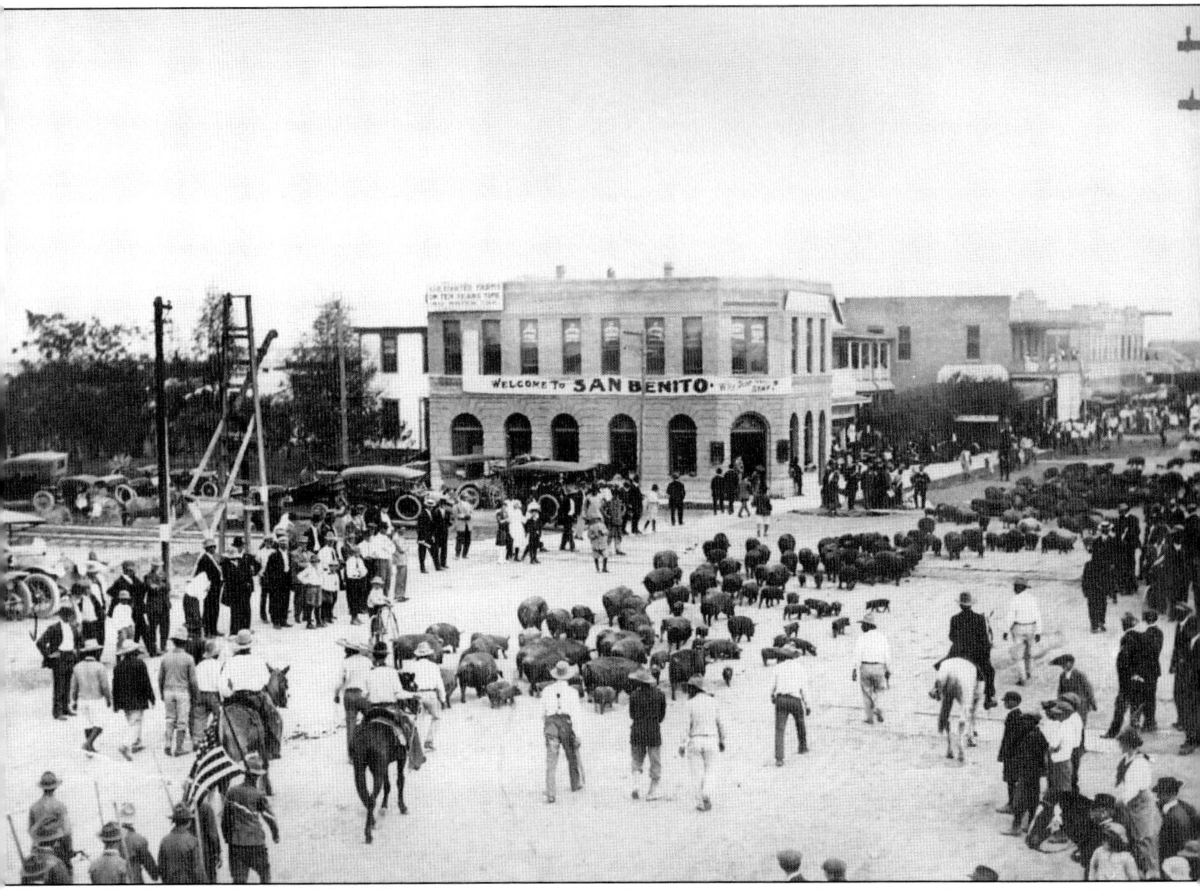

Cabbage Day Parade was an annual event, but Hog Day was something else. Alba Heywood had 2,000 hogs on his farm and decided to stage a hog parade. All the hogs, guided by a swarm of herders, filled the street from curb to curb and stretched four blocks long. They had marched up Sam Houston Boulevard until the head of the parade neared the site of the present city hall when someone fired a pistol into the air, spooking the hogs. With its hoofed participants squealing, grunting, and running in every direction, the Hog Parade ended with most of the hogs taking refuge under houses. It took three days to round up the hogs. This was the first and last Hog Parade in San Benito. (Courtesy San Benito Historical Society.)

On the Cover: Parked in front of the San Benito Irrigation Company, drivers and land agents eagerly escort potential northern buyers to the cultivated crops and land parcels for sale around San Benito. Land-seekers were beginning to come into the area, slowly at first, then in a flood. Robertson's agents once signed up 4,000 acres in small tracts within a single two-week period. John F. Barron said of land developers, "They would charter a train all the way down from Chicago. They didn't have an office. Everybody was involved. You didn't have to have a license, you just got in and put your sign up—you were in the real estate business." (Courtesy San Benito Historical Society.)

IMAGES
of America

SAN BENITO

San Benito Historical Society

ARCADIA
PUBLISHING

ISBN 978-0-7385-8024-1

Published by Arcadia Publishing
Charleston, South Carolina

Printed in the United States of America

Library of Congress Control Number: 2009934873

For all general information contact Arcadia Publishing at:
Telephone 843-853-2070
Fax 843-853-0044
E-mail sales@arcadiapublishing.com
For customer service and orders:
Toll-Free 1-888-313-2665

Visit us on the Internet at www.arcadiapublishing.com

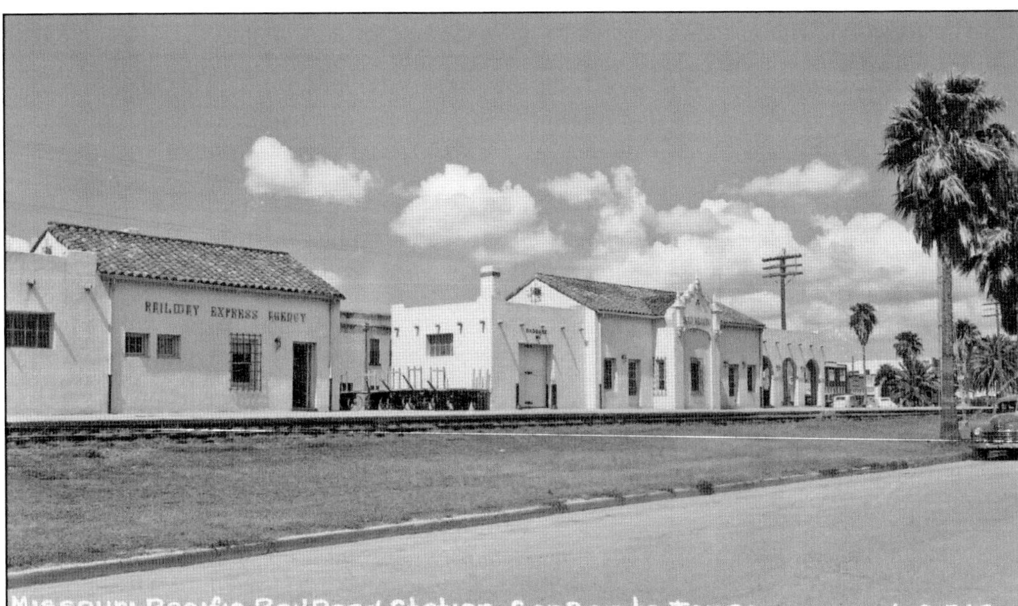

The original St. Louis, Brownsville, Mexico Railroad depot was replaced by the Missouri Pacific Line Spanish revival style depot in 1928, and the rails were also moved from both sides of the building, to the north side only. This depot was demolished in the mid 1960s, a loss still felt in the hearts of locals. (Courtesy San Benito Historical Society.)

Contents

ACKNOWLEDGMENTS

We are grateful to the families and individuals who generously shared photos and stories of their lives in order to make the history of San Benito more complete. Special thanks to Mr. Victor Leal of CyberNation for his technical contributions, which brought our computers and equipment up to date and allowed us to create this book.

To learn more about the history of San Benito, go to www.sanbenitohistory.org and search our research topics. We received over 800 photographs and were allowed only 127 pages with abbreviated captions, so other images with their complete stories may be found on our Web site.

Our museum address: 210 East Heywood
Thursday–Saturday
10am–4pm, $3

To join the San Benito Historical Society:
Meetings third Tuesday of the month,
6:00 p.m. at the museum 956-399-9991
$10 membership fee may be sent to the above address

Introduction

Several factors played into the publication of this book documenting the history of San Benito, Texas. Spatial limitations required us to make numerous hard choices; many topics, covered in depth on the society's Web site, have necessarily been abbreviated or omitted. Any perceived biases were unintentional; our aim was to illustrate events that recorded the growth of the community and its diverse culture, using subjects both sober and lighthearted. Whenever possible, we used modern-day street addresses to help describe the locations pictured. Finally, though early San Benito's downtown was well-photographed by professionals, images capturing the daily lives of its residents were harder to find, necessarily limiting our coverage.

The Rio Grande Valley is actually the delta of the Rio Grande River. It is the southernmost triangle of Texas, formed between San Antonio, Del Rio, and the mouth of the river. In its southeastward movement toward the Gulf of Mexico, the Rio Grande left cut-off riverbeds thousands of years ago in its attempts to reach the coast. These dry beds were called *rios secos* by the early Spaniards; with years of usage, the term transformed into *resacas*.

The semi-nomadic Indians living in southern Texas and northeastern Mexico at the time of Spanish contact were Coahuiltecans. When Spanish colonists arrived to inhabit the delta in the 1700s, they wanted the best grazing land for their cattle, leading them to establish their ranches on or near old Coahuiltecan camps. As the Spanish moved in, disease and deliberate attacks devastated the Native American population, to the point where it was reported that some desperate parents had sold off their children as Spanish slaves. With the decline of South Texas's first people, the Spanish and Mexican settlers of the Rio Grande Valley controlled the land and established their ranches. They called themselves "Tejanos."

The strategy of Spanish administrators was to settle colonial Mexico's northern border called Nuevo Santander with strong people who would serve as buffers protecting the rest of Mexico from hostile Native Americans and encroaching British and French colonists. As a result of a commission by the king of Spain, in 1748 Jose de Escandon, Count of Sierra Gorda and Knight of Santiago, gathered 3,000 Spaniards, including farmers, ranchers, and men with building skills, as well as three thousand Native American Christian converts, to colonize land that later became Texas. Land north of the river nearest the Gulf was reserved for wealthy haciendados (homeowners), generally Spaniards. Such men received huge land grants that stretched northward from the Rio Grande for as far as 100 miles.

On March 1, 1789, the king of Spain gave the 57,269-acre Concepcion de Carricitos Grant to Eugenio and Bartolome Fernandez, Spanish noblemen and distinguished soldiers, for their services to Spain and in further consideration that they colonize the property. Many descendents of *Don* Bartolo and *Don* Eugenio Fernandez still live along the Rio Grande around Las Rucias, Carricitos, Landrum's Ranch, and La Paloma. It was on this land grant that the City of San Benito was later established.

The large herds of Spanish-Mexican cattle brought in by colonists multiplied. Escandon's plan established Mexican cattle kingdoms, introduced the concept of the cowboy in North America, and created land titles protected by Spanish law north of the Rio Grande. For 300 years of Spanish rule, settlers, soldiers, priests, craftsmen, and adventurers streamed north across the river engaging in trade, commerce, and ranching, and by 1846, small farms and ranches dotted the Concepcion de Carricitos Grant. These people "proved to be hardy, resilient, and adaptable to changing circumstances, qualities that helped most of them adjust to a variety of changes," according to Armando C. Alonzo, borderland specialist from Texas A&M University. Fehrenbach writes, "There was an old saying: 'to be a *vaquero* (cowboy) was to be a hero; to be a ranchero was to be a king.'"

According to San Benito founder Sam Robertson, the adults on these ranches were "kind and most hospitable." They raised goats for dairy products and for meat, as well as chickens and pigs. They sold hides to get money for ammunition, coffee, and clothing. For entertainment, they raced horses and held cockfights, smoked corn shuck cigarettes, and played Monte.

When Gen. Zachary Taylor arrived with his troops in 1846 and fought the battles of Palo Alto and Resaca de las Palmas, he recruited many teamsters, bullwhackers, and hunters from among the Mexican citizens who lived on the ranches. Many of these men stayed with his army until the end of the Mexican War. Col. Stephen Powers, an officer in General Taylor's army, became interested in the area and settled in Brownsville when the war was over. As a result of the Treaty of Guadalupe Hidalgo ending the war, all the land between the Rio Grande and the Nueces River was conveyed to the U.S., and Colonel Powers, a lawyer and judge, was employed by descendants of the Fernandez brothers to protect their property, securing title confirmation to their lands. By this treaty, all Mexican residents became American citizens with all rights, privileges, and duties of U.S. citizens. Judge Powers received about half of the grant for his legal services. The Fernandez heirs took their portion in strips from the river to the base line about one and one half or two miles from the river.

At the turn of the century, the St. Louis, Brownsville, and Mexico railroad, connecting Robstown and Brownsville, was being planned. Civil engineer Sam Robertson won the subcontract for building trestles, bridges, and laying tracks. He noticed a peculiar feature of the topography: Land drained from the river instead of toward it. About 1 mile from the river, he discovered an old, dry resaca, heading north about 16 miles to the present site of San Benito. Besides constructing railroads, Robertson had also constructed irrigation systems. Knowing the potential of alluvial soil under irrigation, the gravity irrigation project, which gave birth to the town of San Benito, occurred to Sam Robertson. When his crews were laying the railroad trestles across the dry resaca, he envisioned San Benito's main irrigation canal.

Riding his horse through the brush, Robertson discovered that resaca banks were slightly higher in elevation than the surrounding land, indicating that gravity irrigation could supply water to farm tracts. This discovery, leading to an irrigation system and the coming of the railroad, were the driving forces that led Sam Robertson to plan a town at the intersection of the Resaca de los Fresnos and the railroad tracks.

May 6, 1904, the supply train reached the banks of Resaca de los Fresnos. The crew built a bridge across the channel and set up a supply camp. Originally, the site was to be named "Powers" after Steven Powers, but by May 29, it had been changed to "Bessie" in honor of railroad official Benjamin F. Yoakum's daughter. The U.S. Post Office rejected the application for "Bessie," however, because the name had already been issued. Robertson then submitted the name "Diaz," honoring Mexican Pres. Porfirio Diaz, a man he admired. Coincidentally, owners of the Mercedes tract had named their town "Diaz," advertising heavily in the Midwest, only to change it back to "Mercedes." Robertson, seeing the opportunity to capitalize, decided to retry "Diaz." This attempt provoked a lawsuit by Mercedes. By the time Robertson's application for "Diaz" had finally been granted on April 2, 1907, the irrigation project investors had already named it "San Benito Land and Water Company." On May 11, 1907, the U.S. Post Office Department approved the name change from "Diaz" to "San Benito."

Needing investors for his project, Robertson approached Alba Heywood and brothers Scott and Otho Heywood who had recently struck it rich at Spindletop. San Benito Land and Water Company was established March 1907. Construction of the railroad depot began March 1908.

Texas builder and writer James Lewellyn "J. L." Allhands once wrote, "God built the San Benito canal, and Sam Robertson put the water in it." With this history and plans for the future, the little town of San Benito was conceived.

One

How We Began
God, The King, and Colonel Sam

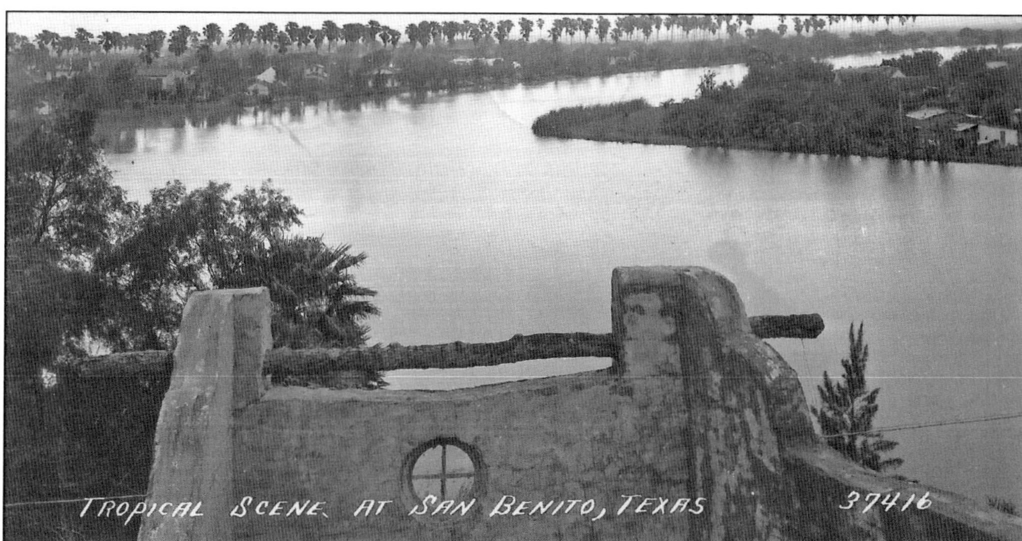

A dry riverbed when Sam Robertson first saw it, Resaca de los Fresnos became San Benito's main canal, providing water for citizens and farmers, and bringing Robertson's vision of a gravity irrigation system to fruition. This picture, taken from atop the Aztec Building looking west, shows the Palm Grove neighborhood to the left and the Fred Booth School neighborhood to the right. (Courtesy San Benito Historical Society.)

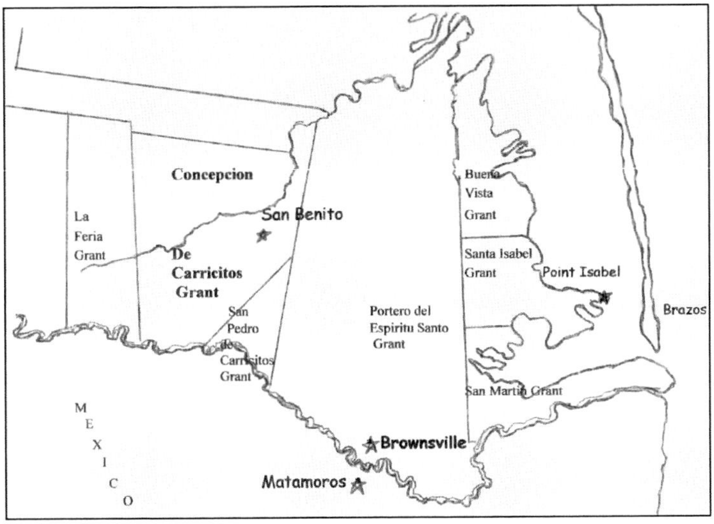

The Fernandez tract followed the riverbank, while the Powers tract was further away from the Rio Grande. Powers later bought out some of the Fernandez heirs and acquired a large piece of land along the river, which became known as Rancho Cipres. The land on which Sam Robertson founded the town of San Benito was donated by the heirs of Colonel Powers. (Courtesy Clare Zepeda.)

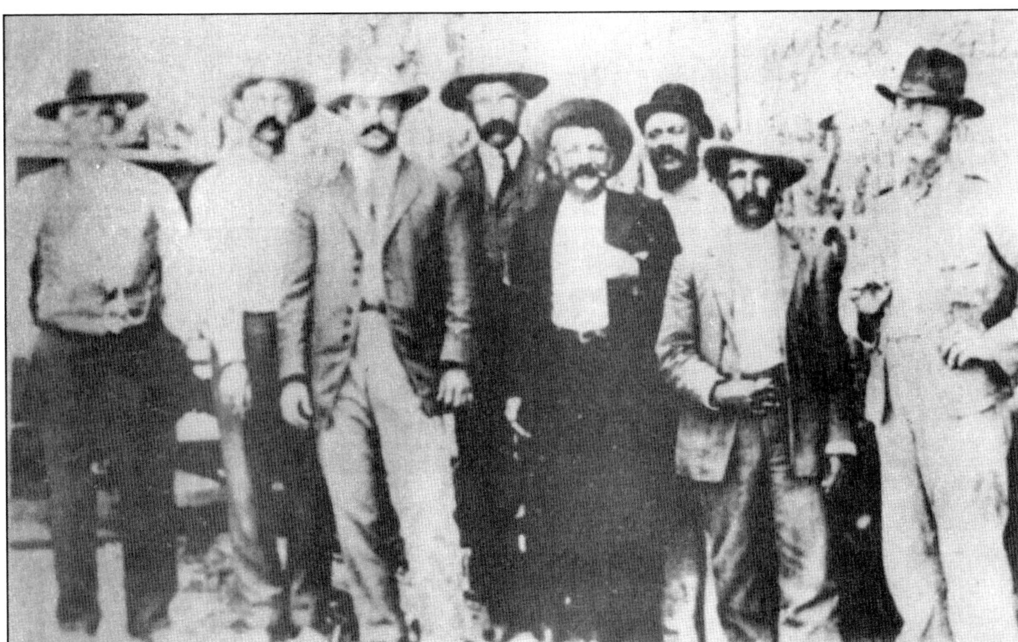

The men pictured here in the first years of the 20th century were descendants of original land grant families. From left to right, those pictured include Jose Esparza, unidentified, John Wood, unidentified, Enrique Zepeda, Dionicio Esparza, Carlos Esparza Jr., and Fred Kowalski. Jose Esparza, a prominent area rancher, also served as Cameron County commissioner of Water Precinct No. 3 from 1882 to 1886. Carlos Esparza Jr. served as a Cameron County deputy sheriff and was murdered in 1919; his killers were never found. (Courtesy Clare Zepeda.)

Sam A. Robertson (1867–1938) epitomized the frontier spirit. He began the irrigation project, the Spiderweb Railroad, and the development of Port Isabel, and served as San Benito's sheriff and first postmaster. From the Brownsville Historical Association's *A Blast From the Past Volume 1,* he said, "From 1903 to 1917, I had a grand time in the Valley, working an average of 20 hours a day, seven days a week. There was not a dull minute, so to hell with money if you have interesting work." (Courtesy San Benito Historical Society.)

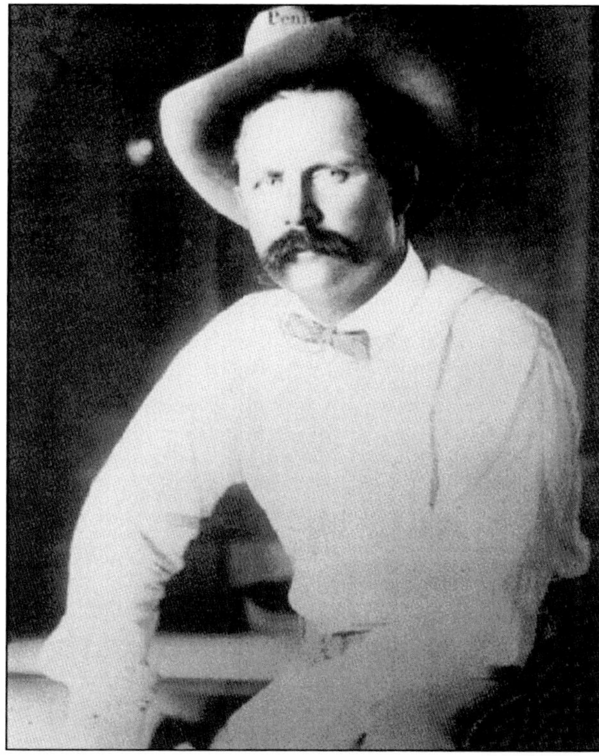

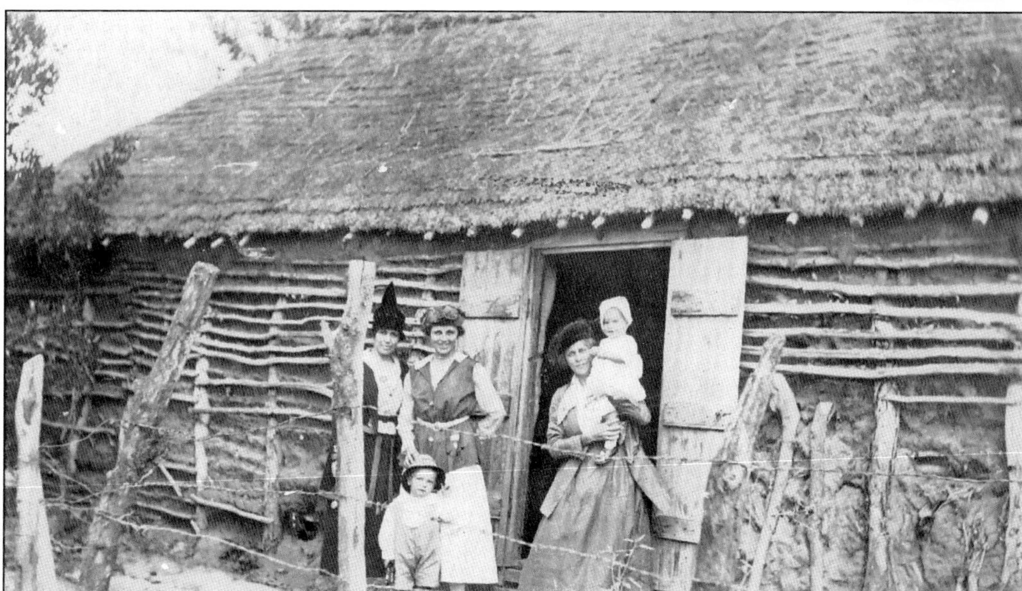

When they first arrived in the area, some families lived in jacals, temporary homes made of native materials like mesquite, carrizos, palm fronds, and mud. The Landrum family lived in a seven-room jacal complex until their two-story brick house by the river—Rancho Cipres—was completed in 1902. But jacals weren't only built by families; anybody who couldn't afford imported lumber lived in a jacal or a tent, including railroad workers, canal diggers, immigrants, and ranch hands. (Courtesy Ernie Agar.)

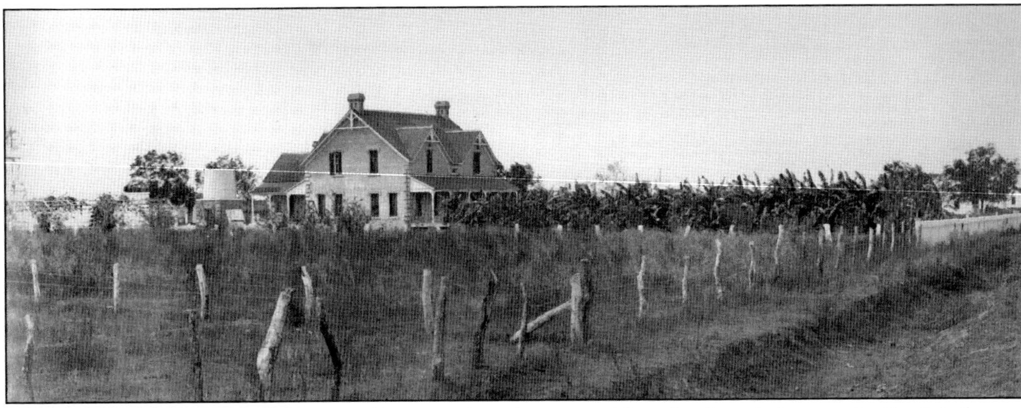

The daughter of Colonel Powers, Frances Landrum and her husband, James, built this home, completed in 1902. Adobe bricks were fired in an on-site kiln. Many families who lived on and worked the Rancho Cipres remember Landrum as a benevolent *patrón*. The ranch workers also lived in well-kept brick homes. The Landrum house still stands at the intersection of Texas Highway 281 and FM 2520. (Courtesy San Benito Historical Society.)

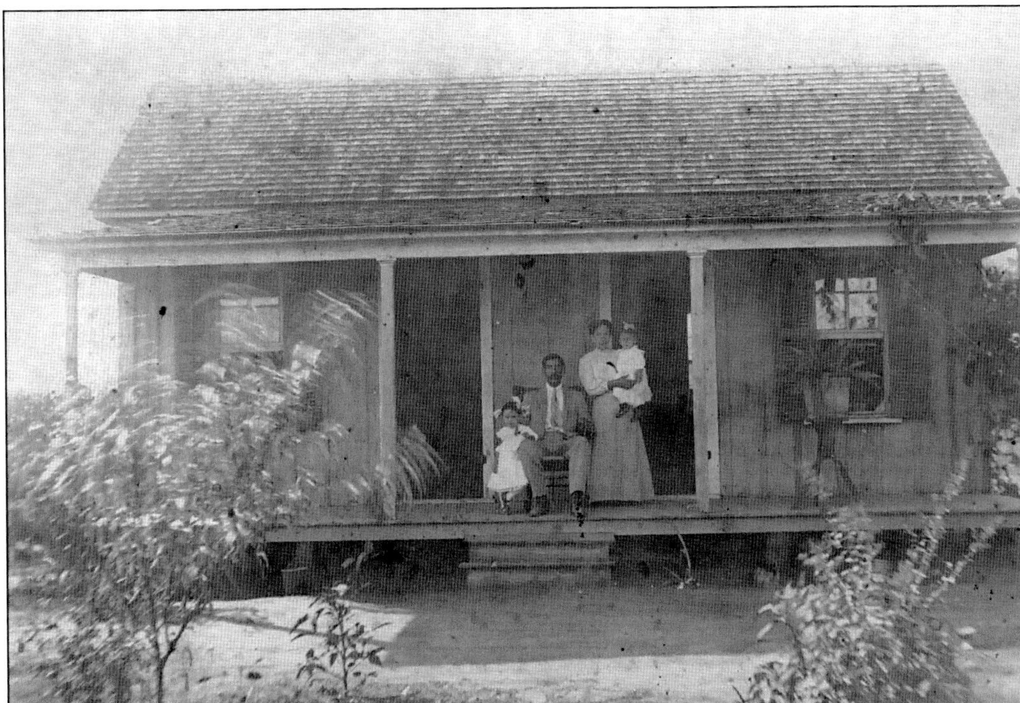

Shown here in 1912, Silvestre and Martina Aguirre and their daughters, Leonor (left) and Rosario, lived near La Encantada before San Benito was settled. Born in Texas, 1880, Silvestre was a farmer and carpenter who built his own home before going on to build many others in town. A bilingual businessman who kept up with the times, Silvestre had an eye for detail, evidenced here in the strict symmetry of his house, with its double front doors and shuttered windows. (Courtesy Silvestre Rodriguez.)

This 1907 postcard is addressed to Mr. Albanus Clemens Purvis of Diaz, Texas, in Cameron County. He is an ancestor of the first postmistress. That same year, the town's name legally changed to San Benito on May 11. (Courtesy Ernie Agar.)

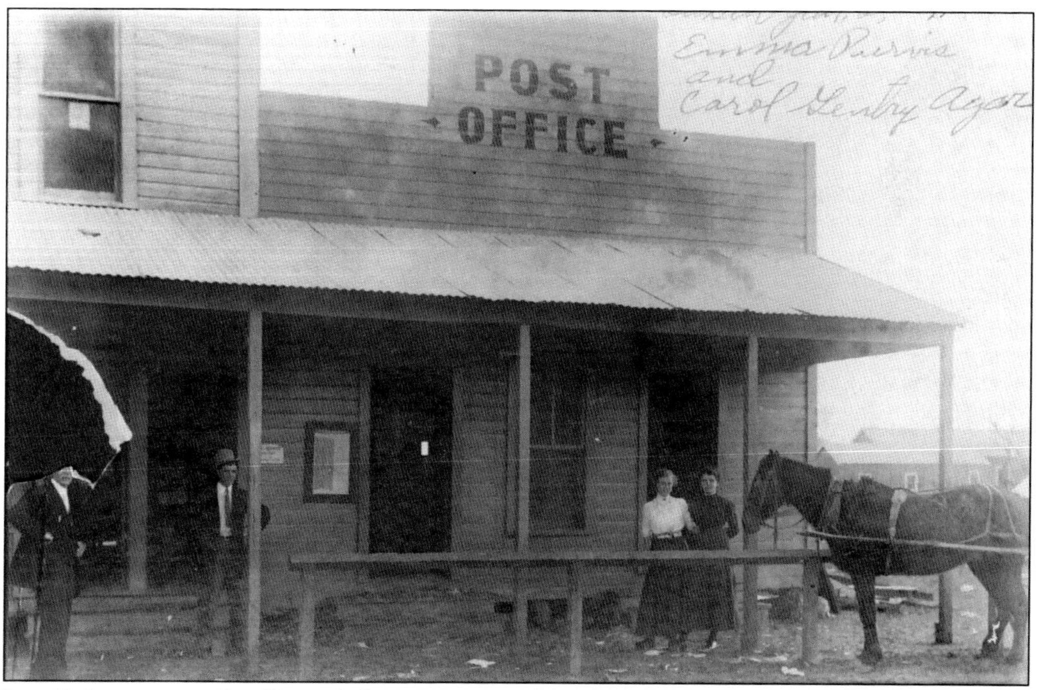

Sam Robertson was San Benito's first postmaster. Later Emma Purvis, 17, became the first female postmaster of San Benito's wooden U.S. Post Office located at 181 West Rowson. (Courtesy Ernie Agar.)

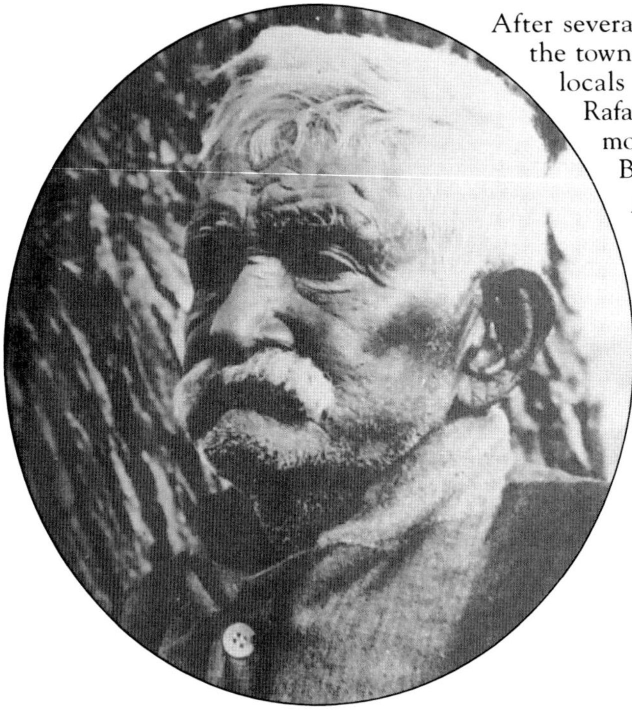

After several unsatisfactory attempts to name the town that Sam Robertson had founded, locals credit former riverboat cabin boy Rafael Moreno, who hit upon the lasting moniker. He suggested the name San Benito, *Saint Benny*, to honor his former *patrón*, Benjamin Hicks. Rafael ended up becoming the camp cook for Robertson's surveyors. His specialties were venison, javelina, and salad of nopalitos (tender cactus). Another theory suggests that he combined the first names of Sam Robertson and Ben Hicks to honor both men. (Courtesy Rey Avila.)

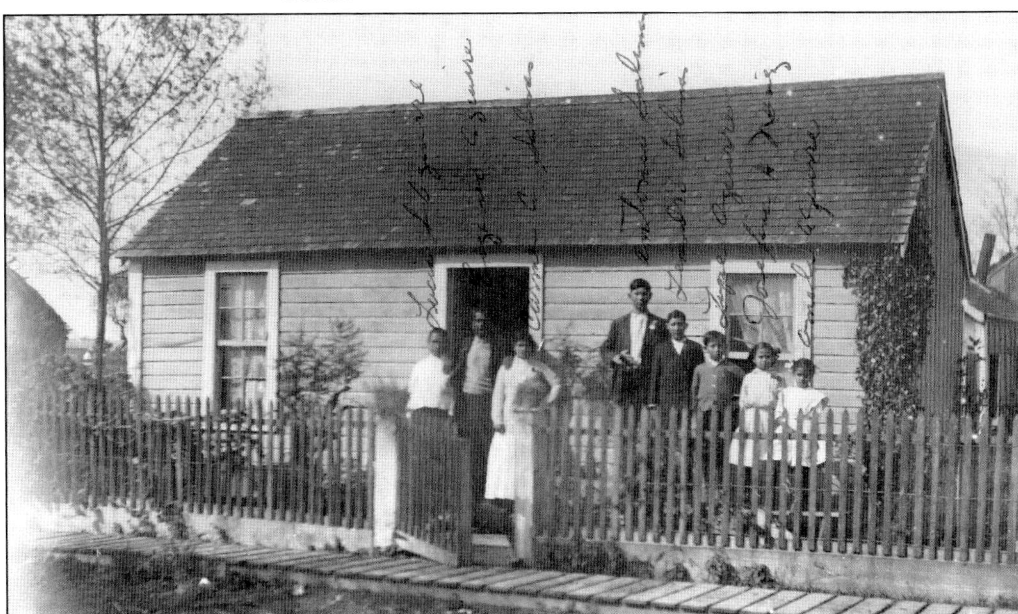

Cameron County deputy sheriff Eugenio Aguirre, purchased the first residential property in today's San Benito: 124 Hidalgo Street. His wooden house and fence were fronted by a wooden sidewalk. Neighbors recalled that Eugenio would bring home drunken prisoners, tether them to the big tree in the yard, and slap them sober. Several members of the family became public servants. Seen here are, from left to right, Lucia and Eugenio Aguirre, their daughter Carmen, Antonio and Leandra Salinas, and Lupe, Josefina, and Ameli Aguirre. The property and home is still owned by granddaughter Maria Robles Nuñez. (Courtesy Maria Robles Nuñez.)

Two

How We Grew
Trestles, Tracks, and Machetes

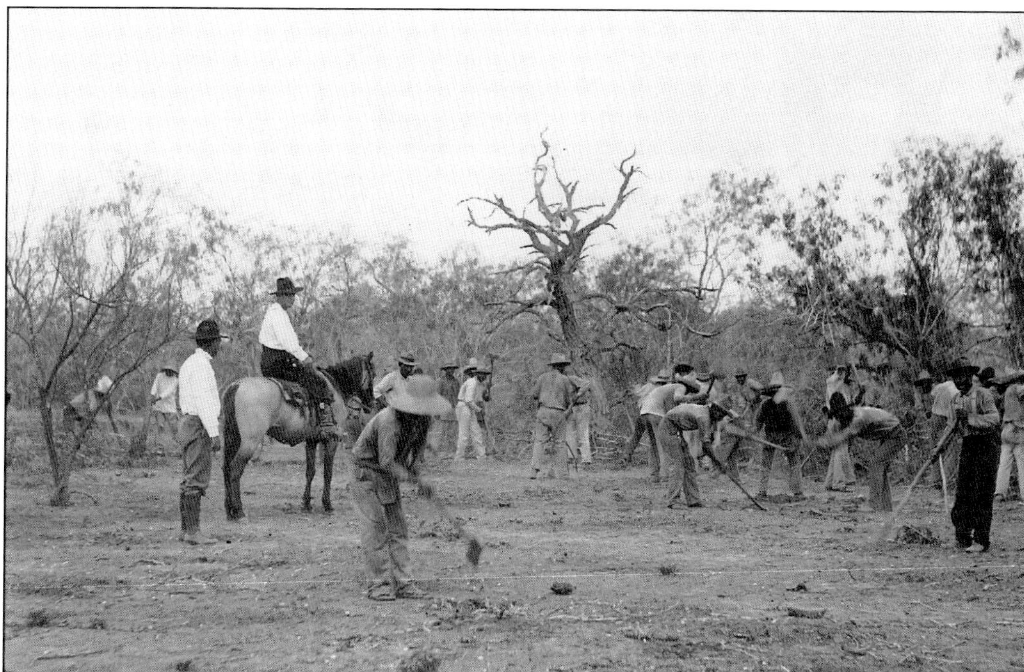

Before the railroad could be built, somebody needed to clear the land in its path. James Franklin Ratliff from North Carolina won the contract. He brought his mule teams down and hired local men, such as Santos Mancillas and his brother Dionicio, who moved from Paso Real to San Benito to do the work. Ratliff married Anita Mancillas of Galveston and raised a family on his land at the place where, today, Carlos and Scott Brown Streets intersect. Ratliff named several of San Benito's streets in his neighborhood after his children. (Courtesy San Benito Historical Society.)

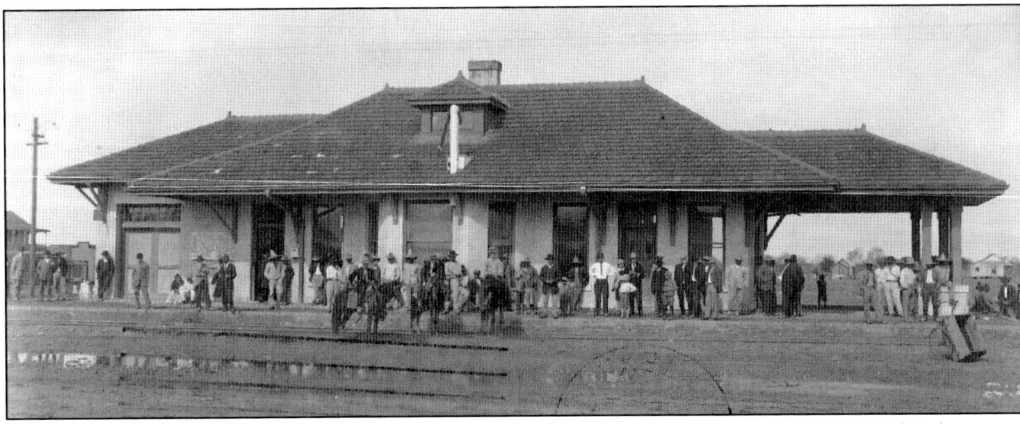

The 1908 St. Louis, Brownsville, and Mexico Railroad depot was the first of two at this location. Early photographs show rail lines on both sides of the wooden building. It was replaced later by the Missouri Pacific Railroad's stucco building. (Courtesy Ernie Agar.)

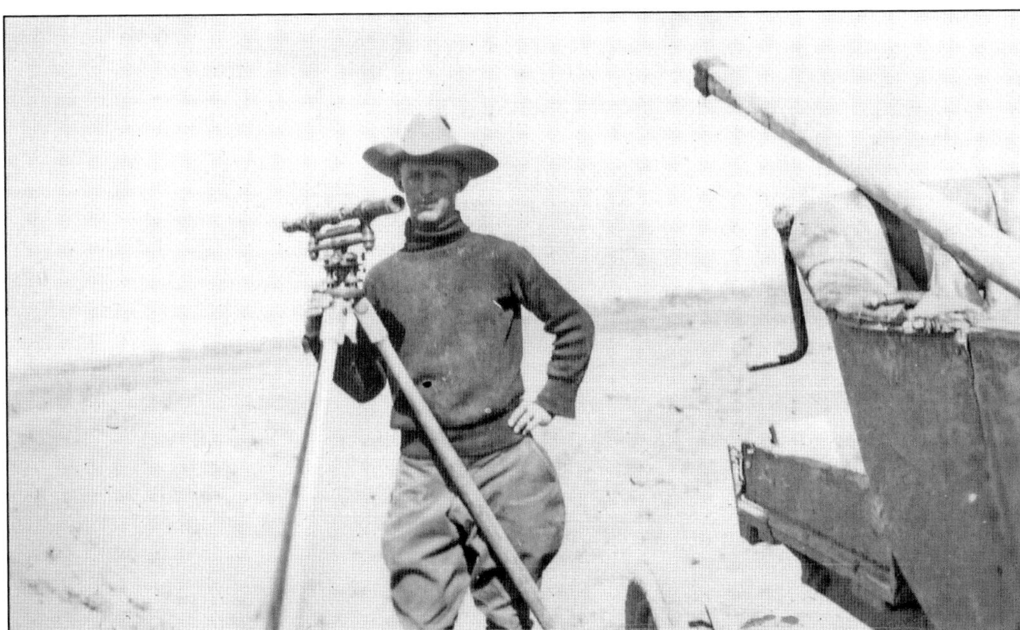

Richard T. Collins surveyed the land for clearing and canal building. He carried his equipment in his truck. He also sold insurance, farmed, was part-time bookkeeper for several small businesses, briefly owned a small café, and served as city secretary and tax assessor during Scott Brown's term as mayor. Collins also sang with the 40 and 8 Quartet. He married Madeline Wolfersberger, and they had two daughters, Mary Catherine and Madeline Jane. (Courtesy Mary Catherine Lovett.)

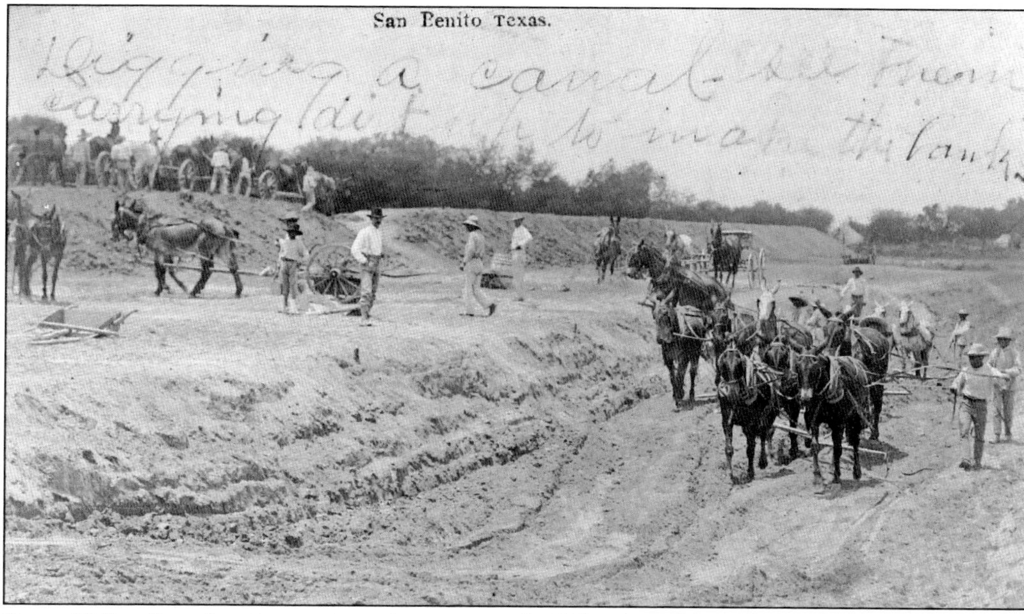

Some 32.5 miles of main canals and resacas and 66.5 miles of lateral canals provided water to 45,000 acres of land in Sam Robertson's irrigation project. Joe G. Ballenger's company dug many of the canals using mules before large dredges were brought in to do the digging. The mules were kept on the 400 block of South Sam Houston Boulevard. (Courtesy Ernie Agar.)

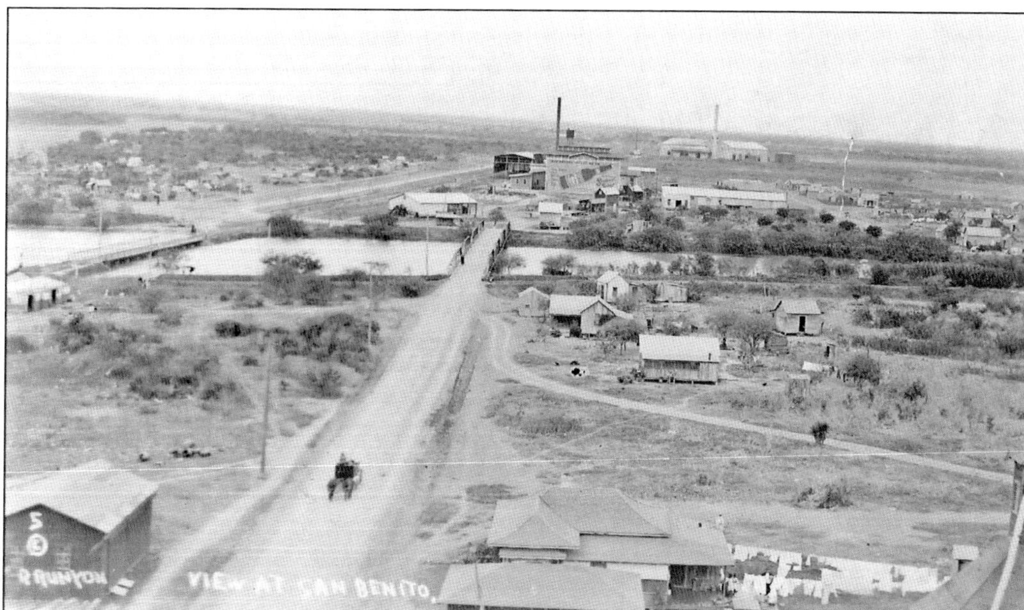

In this photograph, the center railroad trestle crosses the resaca at the very spot where Sam Robertson first envisioned the irrigation-fed city that would become San Benito. The bridge seen here on the left is the Robertson Street Crossing; the Stenger Street Crossing is on the right. The Rio Grande Valley Ice Company can be seen behind the Southern Select Beer sign, and the sugar mill is in the background. (Courtesy San Benito Historical Society.)

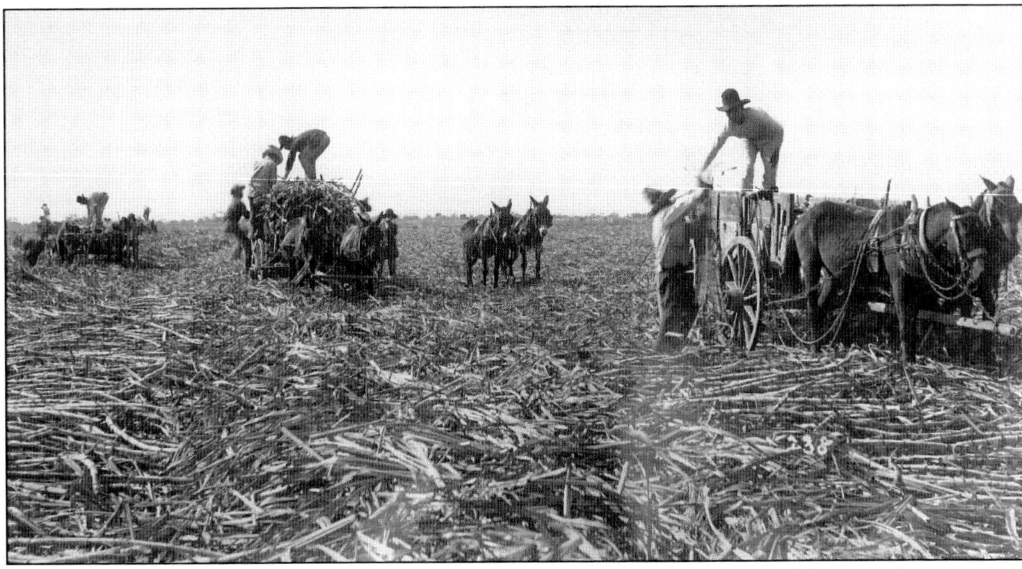

In 1909, local farms produced an average of 1 ton of refined sugar per 25 tons of sugar cane, roughly the amount harvested from 1 acre of land. Five sugar mills, including the San Benito one, were built. Harvesting was done by imported labor and locals who earned 75¢ day. Mexican citizens canoed across the river on a daily basis, eager for the opportunity to earn a living, first by building the railroad, then by working in the new year-round agricultural industry. (Courtesy San Benito Historical Society.)

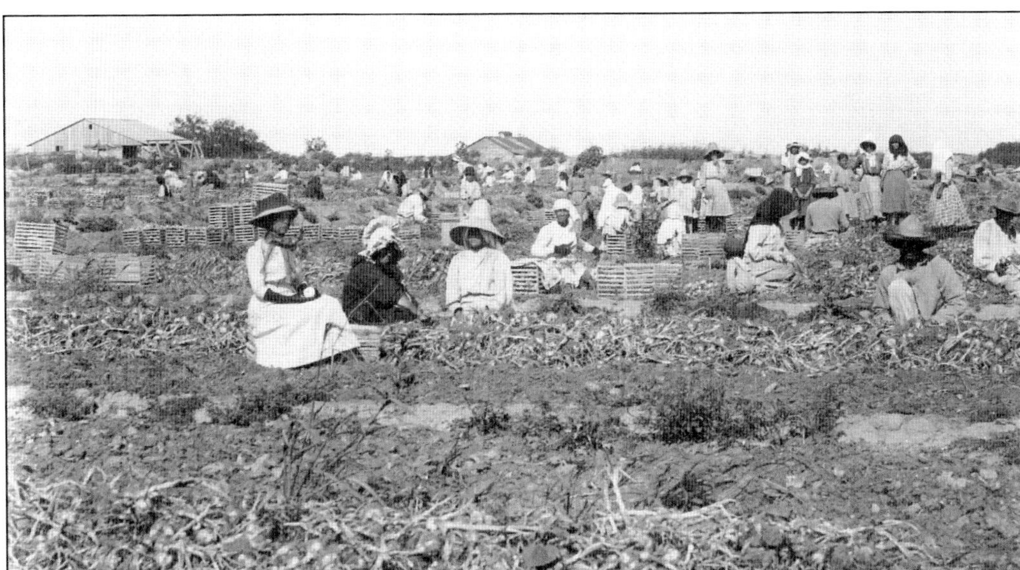

Bermuda Onions yielded 350 bushels per acre in 1909, selling at prices that ranged from 75¢ to $1.10 per bushel. Local farmers also grew cabbage, potatoes, oranges, lemons, peaches, bananas, grapes, figs, dates, cotton, corn, alfalfa, cauliflower, peanuts, lettuce, watermelons, and broom corn. Rice, however, was a failure. (Courtesy San Benito Historical Society.)

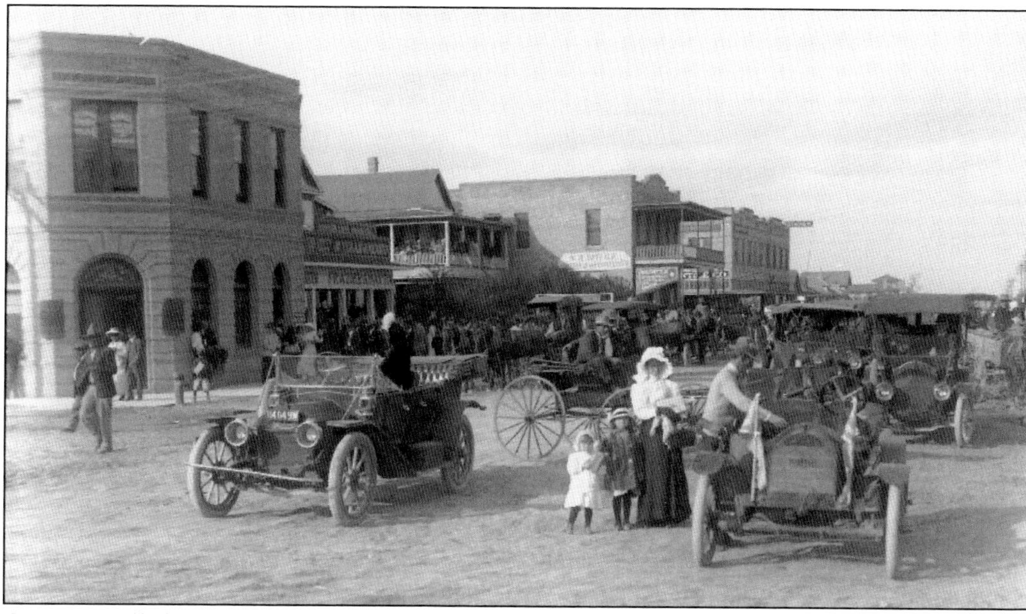

On a typically busy 1910 day, Model T Fords fill the dirt 100 block of North Sam Houston. The cornered Farmers State Bank building adjoins the San Benito Land and Water Company next to the palm-tree-fronted San Benito Hotel and the two-storied building at the corner of Stenger Street and Sam Houston Boulevard. (Courtesy San Benito Historical Society.)

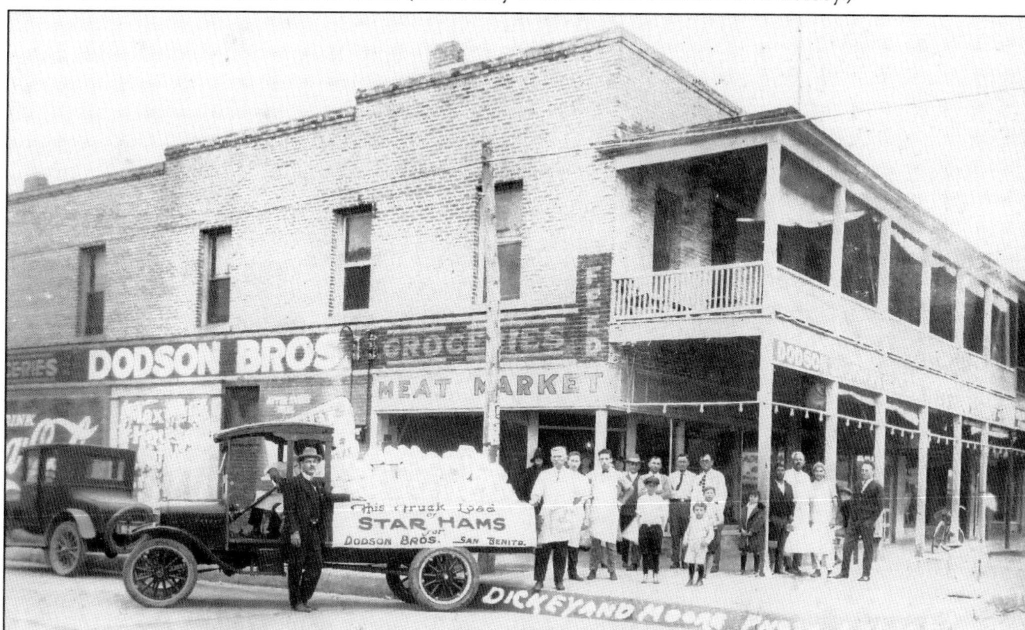

One of the busiest corners in early San Benito was the intersection at Robertson Street and Sam Houston Boulevard. The San Benito Bank and Trust stood on one corner, the San Benito Land and Water Company stood on another, and across from it was Dodson Brothers Groceries, owned by Asa E., Claude, and Jay Dodson. They had grown tired of farming in East Texas and came down to San Benito in 1910 to open a grocery store in the newly platted town. (Courtesy Maxine Dodson.)

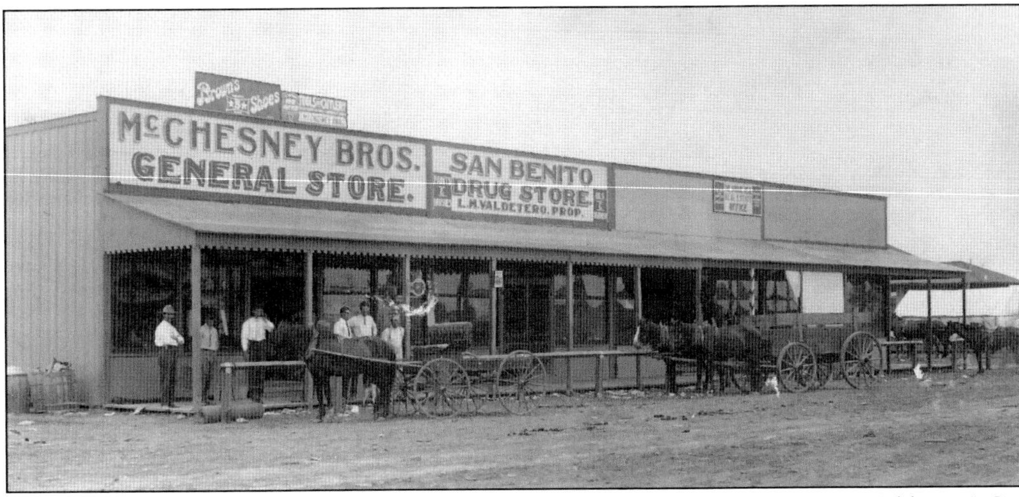

San Benito had several drugstores in 1910, but the oldest one was Lawrence M. Valdetero's San Benito Drug Store, 186 North Sam Houston Boulevard, located next to the McChesney Brothers General Store. Valdetero, an Italian American, was boycotted by the local KKK, who disliked the idea that a "foreigner" owned a business on the town's main street. (Courtesy Ernie Agar.)

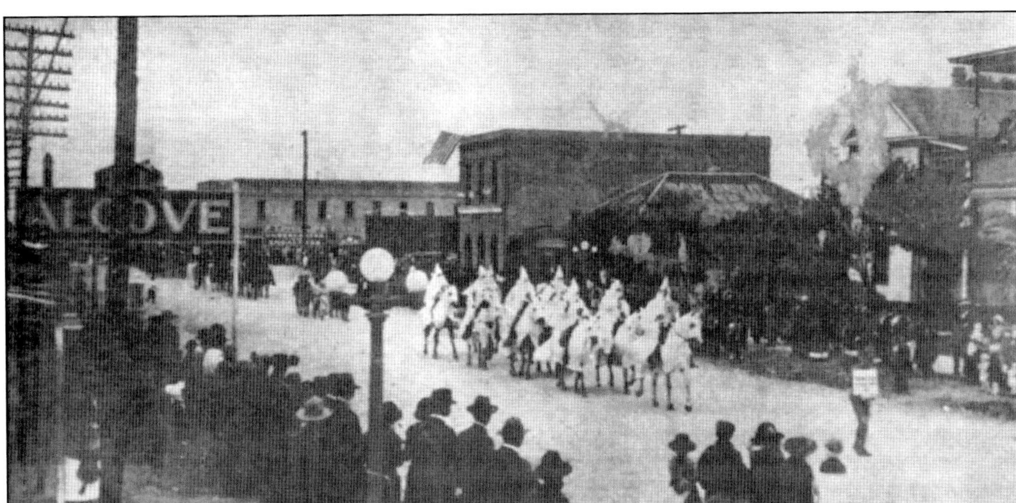

The KKK only marched once in San Benito, protesting the presence of Jews, Catholics, blacks, and new immigrants, but the group paraded several times in Harlingen. Longtime resident and recent World War I veteran Col. Sam Robertson had married a German woman, Adele, and he was anti-KKK. Making his opposition to the Klan his primary platform when he ran for Cameron County Sheriff in 1922, Robertson won the election and was elected again in 1926. Organized KKK activity stopped after he took office. (Courtesy Ernie Agar.)

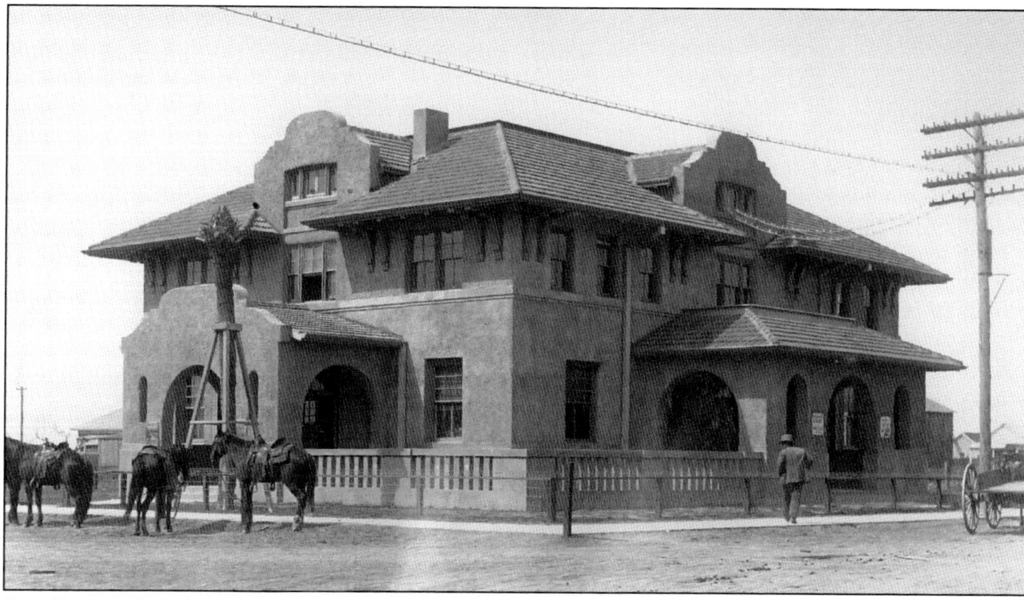

San Benito Land and Water Company built its mission style headquarters at 216 South Sam Houston Boulevard in 1910. Designed by the Austin architectural firm of Endress and Walsh, the structure cost $14,386.76 to build. The company moved into its new headquarters on July 15, 1910. The telephone company had an office on the second floor. Lupe Aguirre's brother, Tomas, ran the office, and Lupe would help after school. Nine phone lines ran into town at the time. (Courtesy San Benito Historical Society.)

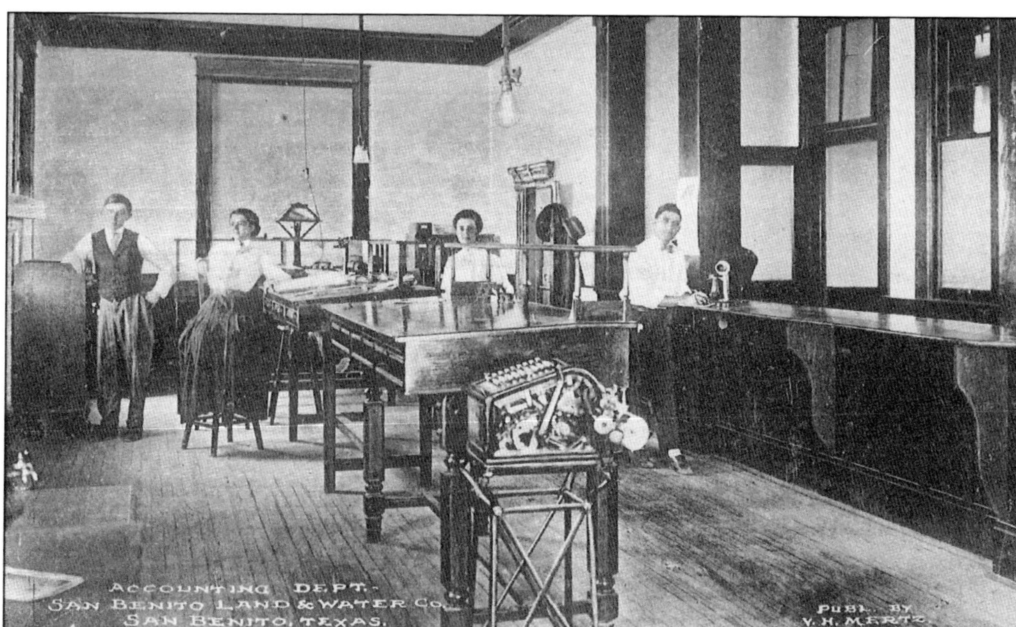

This interior photograph of the building on 216 South Sam Houston Boulevard shows the accounting department of the San Benito Land and Water Company. Notice the oversized adding machine and the early telephone at the window. (Courtesy Bob Tumberlinson.)

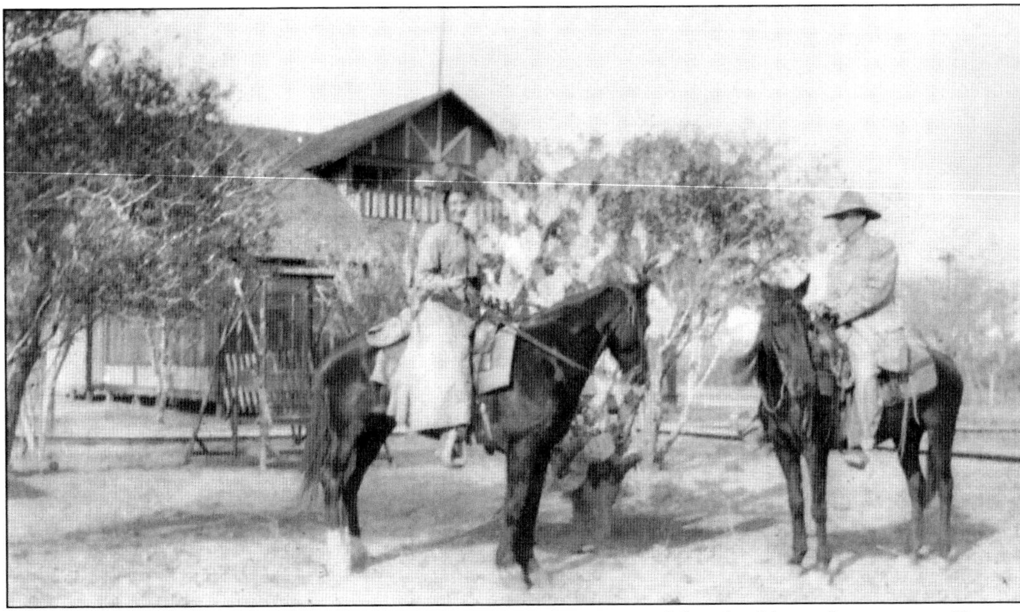

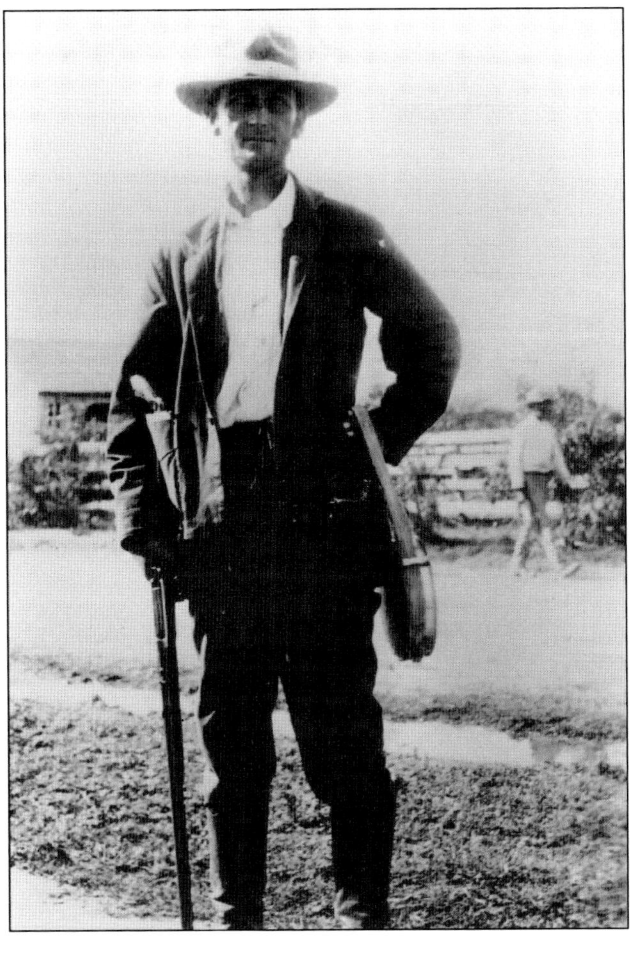

After building the sugar mill, Stanley Dodds and his crew were ambushed by bandits in 1915. Two men were killed, but Dodds was spared when a Mexican citizen pleaded for his life. It was this same man whom Dodds had carried to a hospital during the battle of Matamoros. Dodds testified about this before the Texas State Legislature. He was later a partner in Dodds and Wedegartner Construction Company, which helped build the jetties at South Padre Island. In this 1912 photograph, Rae and Stanley Dodds sit horseback in front of their new house at 749 North Reagan Street. (Courtesy Carolyn Gentry.)

From the 1910 beginning of the Mexican Revolution through 1920, banditry occurred on both sides of the river. During the troubles, Joe G. Ballenger carried a six shooter and a 30-30 saddle gun. His construction crews dug many of the canals for the irrigation project. (Courtesy Tommy Ballenger.)

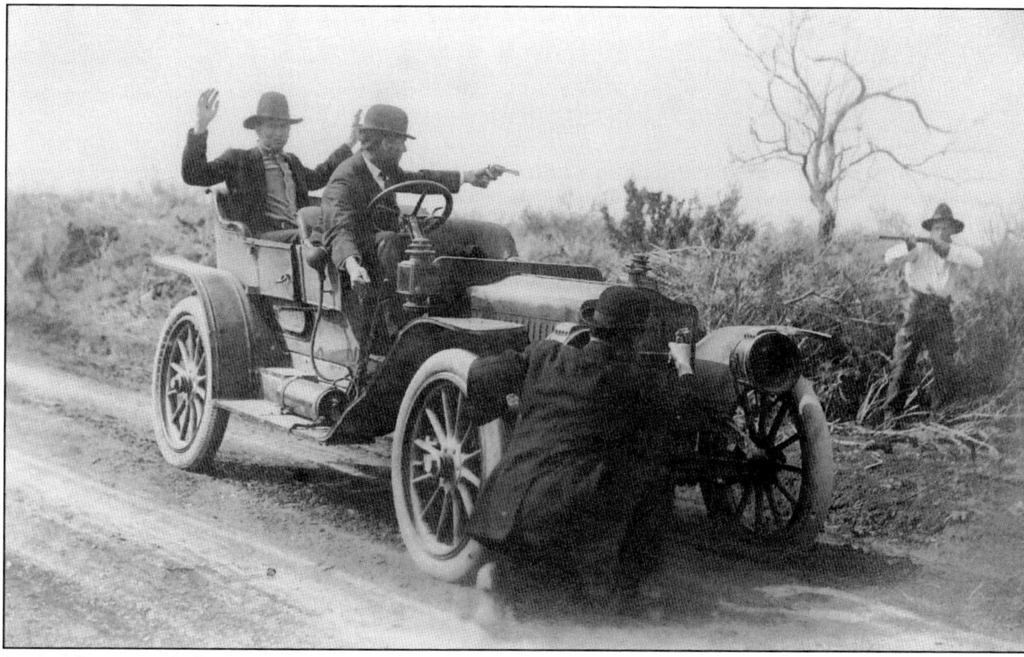

Probably a posed photograph to send back to the folks, this nonetheless testifies to the rampant fear of bandits found in early 1900s South Texas. Everyone, Hispanic and Anglo alike, took measures to stay safe. Women slept with guns under their pillows, and men patrolled neighborhoods at night. People were so nervous that at one point a mule was shot and killed when it was mistaken for a bandit. (Courtesy Tootie Madden.)

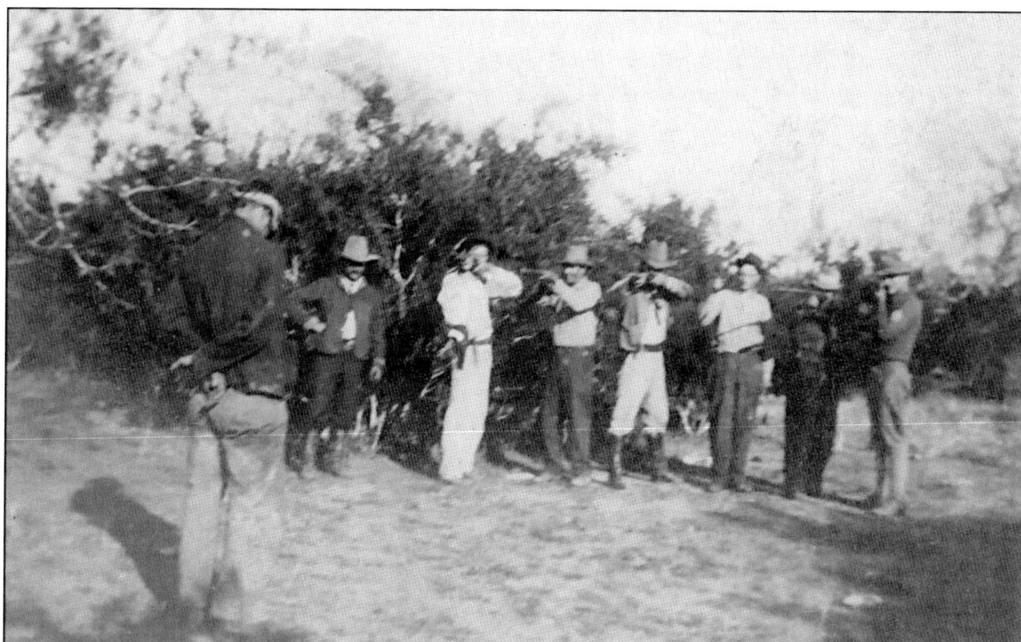

Hispanics suspected of being bandits were not often afforded proper legal proceedings. Many Texas Rangers, local sheriffs, and civilian vigilantes were said to shoot or lynch supposed bandits without a trial—and sometimes merely on sight. (Courtesy Tootie Madden.)

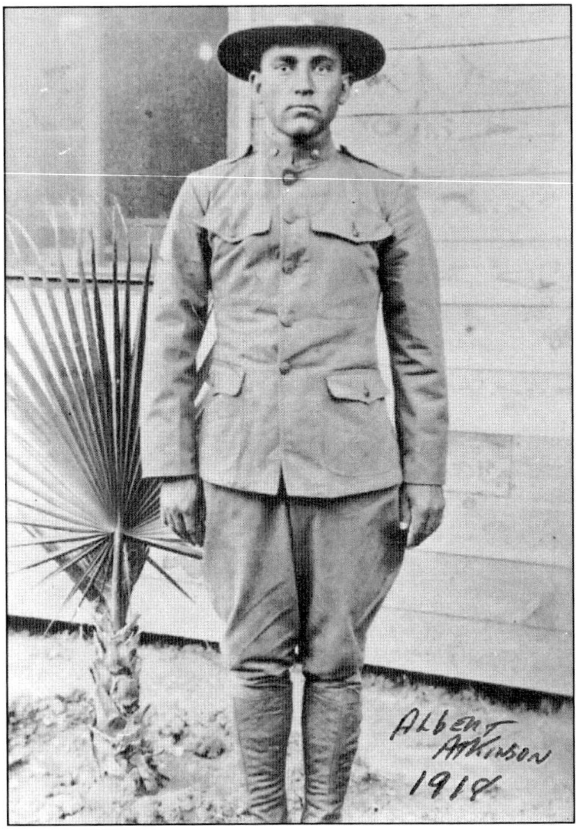

In 1836, George Atkinson, a merchant seaman from England, worked in Clarksville (Boca Chica) during the Civil War. When his first wife died, he married Dolores Aguilar, and they had three children, Edwardo, Tomas, and Victoria. During the 1867 hurricane, Dolores and two children died. George was able to save baby Tomas. Alberto, who served in World War I, was one of Tomas and Paulita's seven children. Alberto became a mechanic at the sugar mill helping convert the boilers into electric generators when it was sold to the Central Power and Light Company in the 1920s. (Courtesy Ernie Atkinson.)

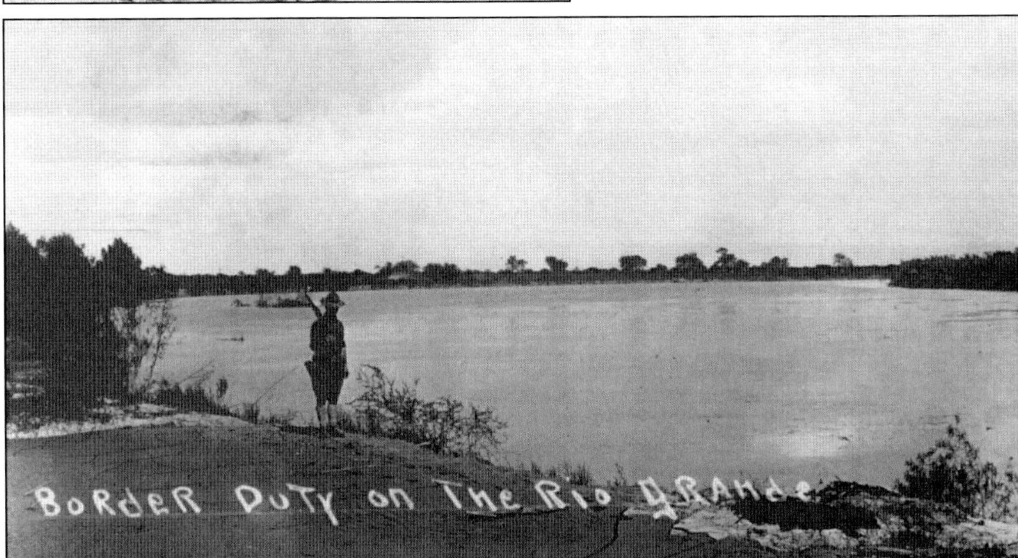

The nation's earliest border patrol was conducted by U.S. soldiers stationed here prior to World War I. This lone soldier could represent the first U.S. Border Patrol. While stationed in the Valley prior to World War One, many soldiers stood duty on the Rio Grande river during the "bandit days" of the Mexican Revolution. This man stands as a symbol representing the numerous U.S. soldiers who effectively made up the first border patrol. (Courtesy Carolyn Gentry.)

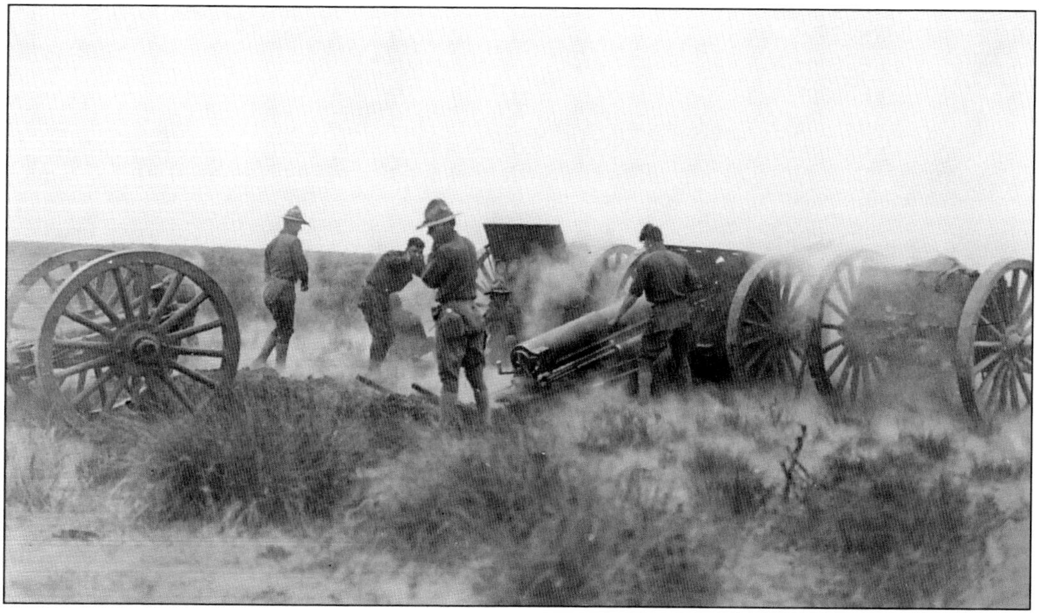

Prior to World War I, thousands of troops were stationed in the Valley, both to help quell border unrest caused by the Mexican Revolution and to practice maneuvers. Many times, bandits were found with German ammunition. It was believed that Germany, in its attempt to divert attention from the country's pre–World War I activities, paid Mexican nationals to start trouble and keep American soldiers occupied on the home front. In the photograph below, the original two-story Landrum Elementary School appears in the left background. Several U.S. Army companies were stationed in and around San Benito. Men camped all around the present site of Landrum Elementary and from South Reagan Street all the way to the 300 block of North Sam Houston Boulevard. They marched or rode horses in formation through town, and even volunteered at the high school, starting the first military training course for students at SBHS. (Courtesy San Benito Historical Society.)

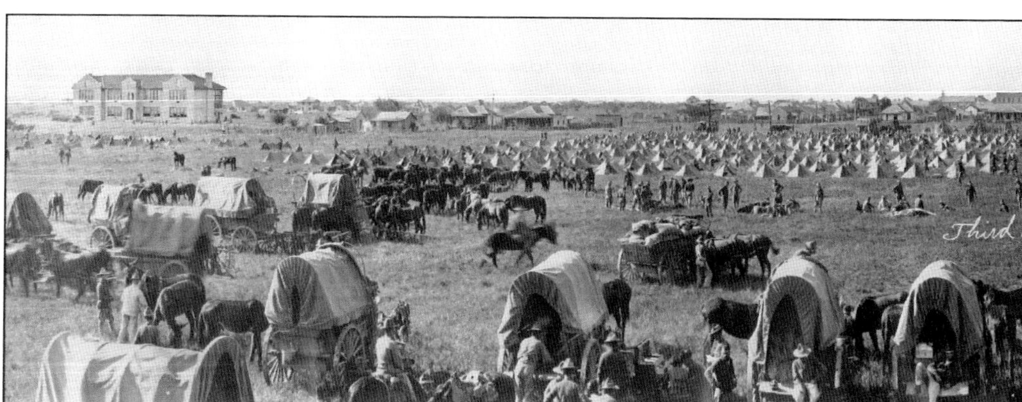

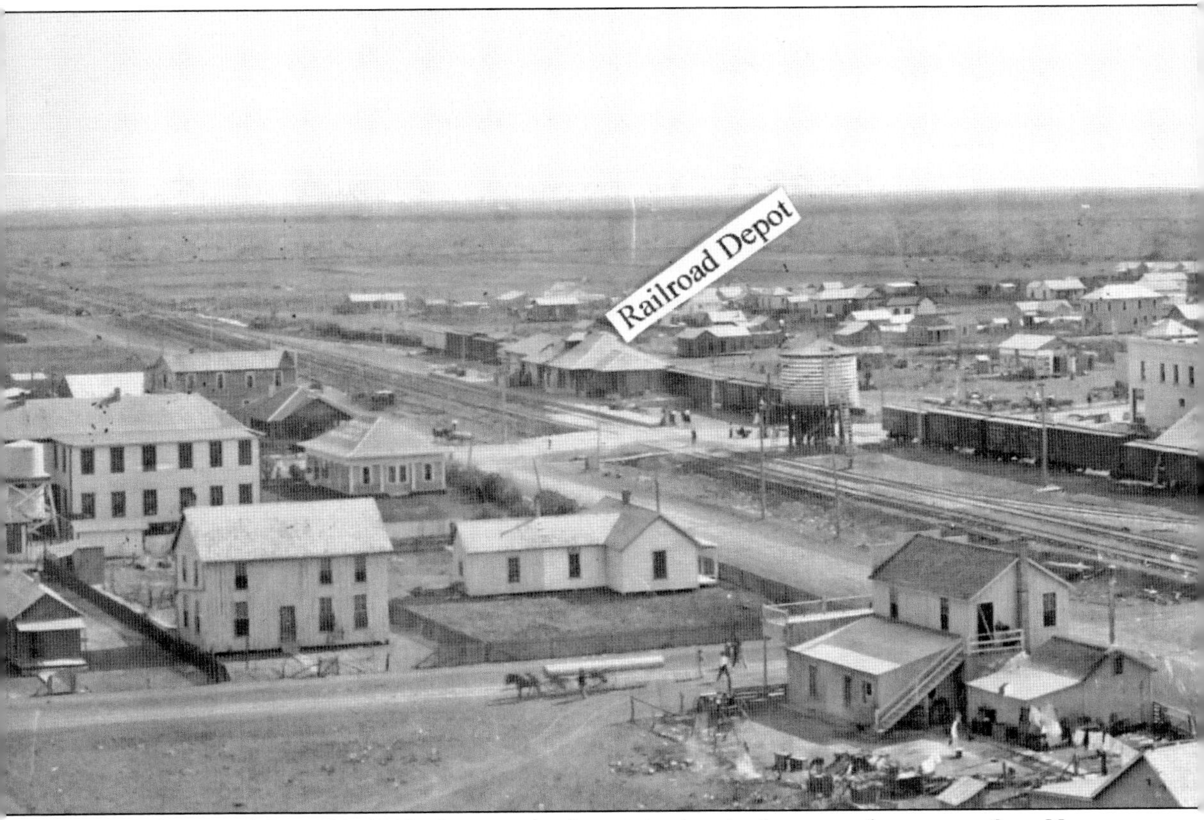

At the top of the 1908–1909 photograph, the original train depot can be seen on Sam Houston Boulevard, the main street. Following it, the San Benito Land and Water Company stands to the right, and across Robertson Street, the San Benito Bank and Trust building is being constructed. (Notice the scaffolding around it.) The buildings by the tracks are no longer here—that is East Rowson Street. At the corner of Rowson and Travis Streets, the side of Lopez Commissary,

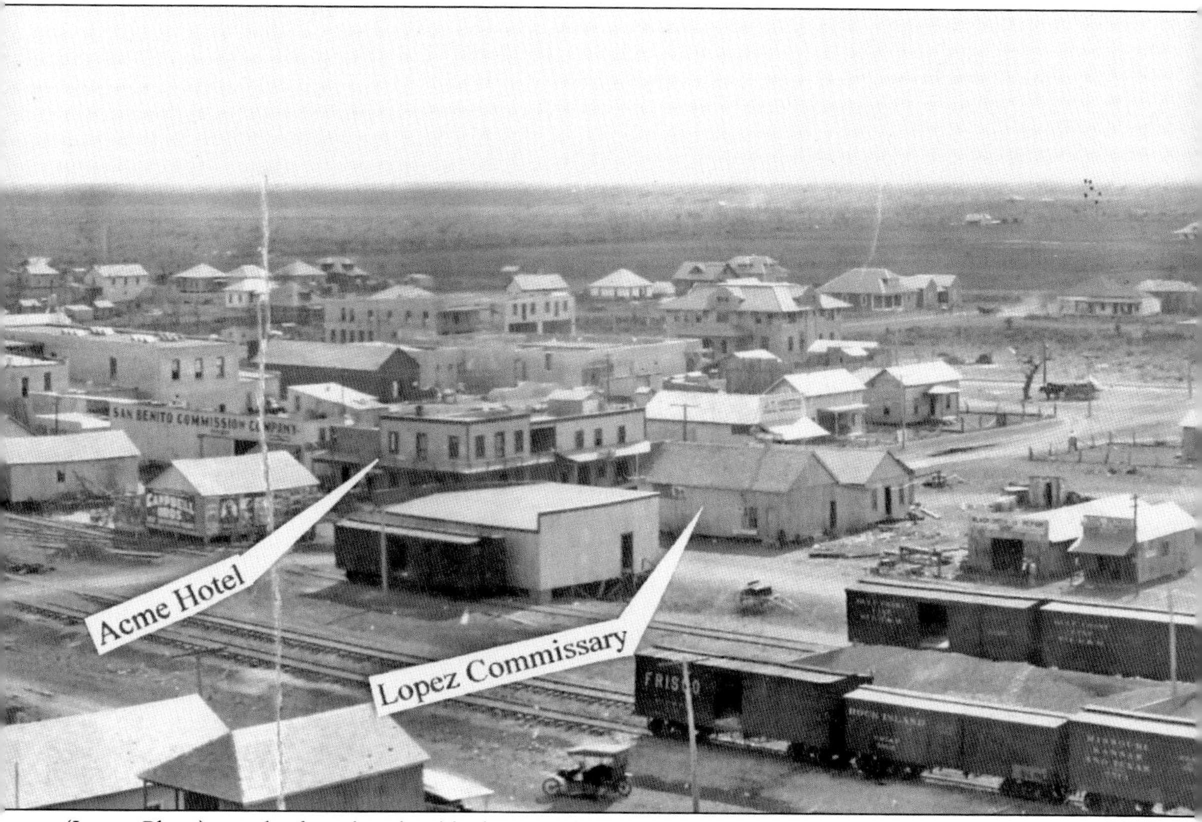

(Lopez Place), can be found with a blacksmith shop behind it. After the blacksmith shop closed, a two-story house was built on its site, and the Lopez family bought it. A lynching by the Texas Rangers had occurred there before they bought it. Across the street is the two-story Acme Hotel. Between the Acme Hotel and the San Benito Commission is the original U.S. Post Office, 181 West Rowson. (Courtesy San Benito Historical Society.)

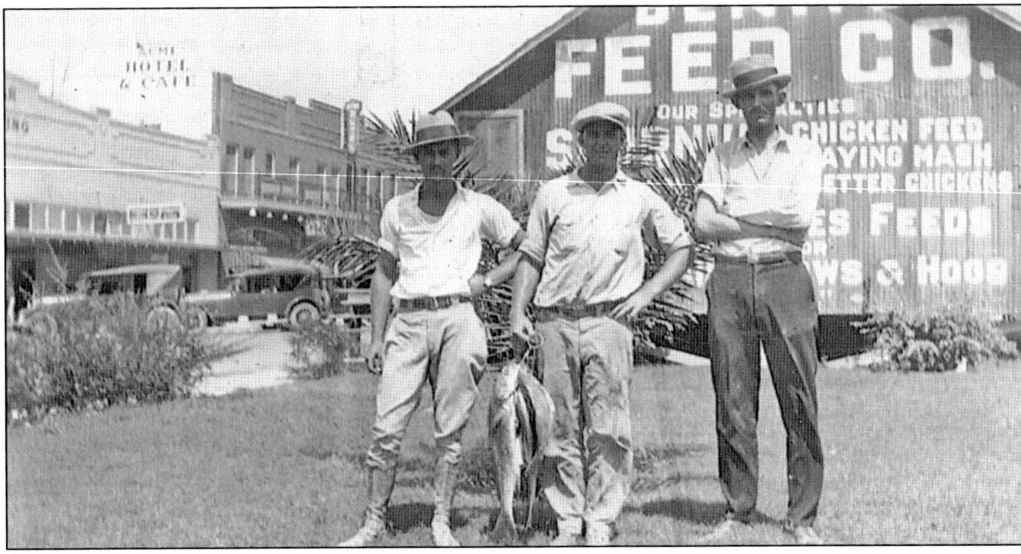

In the upper photograph, three men stand on the railroad right of way with West Rowson Street behind them, around 1927. The brick two-story Acme Hotel can be seen over the shoulder of William A. Saunders. The photograph below shows a local watering hole. When he platted the city, Sam Robertson limited the number of saloons that could be located between Robertson Street and the railroad. The L. O. and Company Saloon, shown in the photograph below, was built around 1906 at 100 South Travis. It was sold in 1912 to Santiago Lopez Sr., who left his paymaster job with American Mining in San Carlos, Mexico, during the Mexican Revolution to open and operate a commissary located in this building, which he did until 1936. During the Depression, his debtors forced him into bankruptcy. Relatives said that every morning they'd find sacks of vegetables and fruits left in repayment of debts. The place was rented to others who operated saloons, and in 1946, Santiago Lopez Sr. reopened it as Lopez Place. (Above photograph courtesy San Benito Historical Society; below photograph courtesy Tootie Madden.)

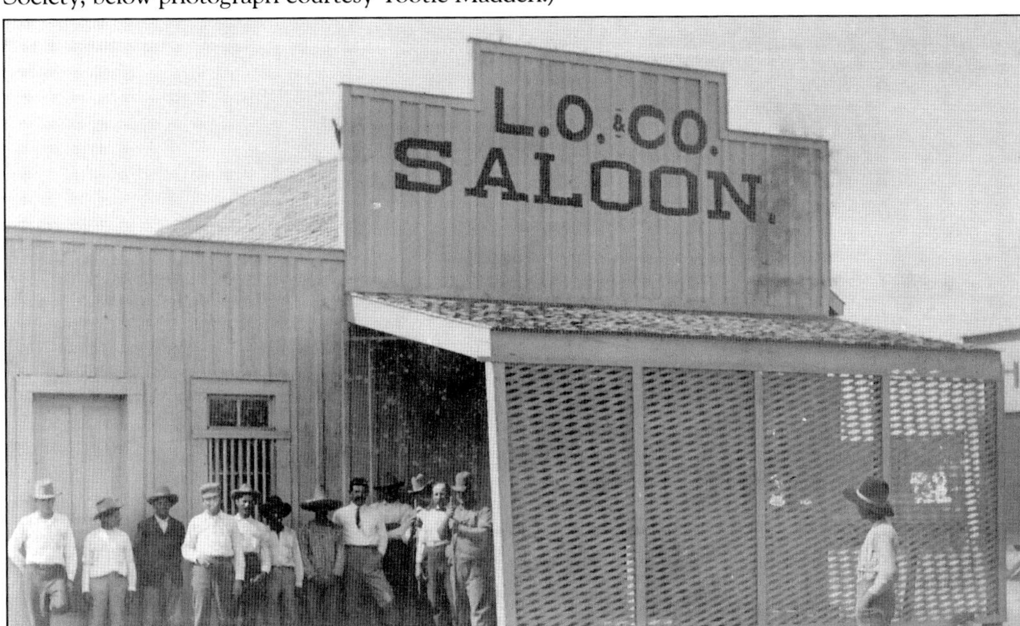

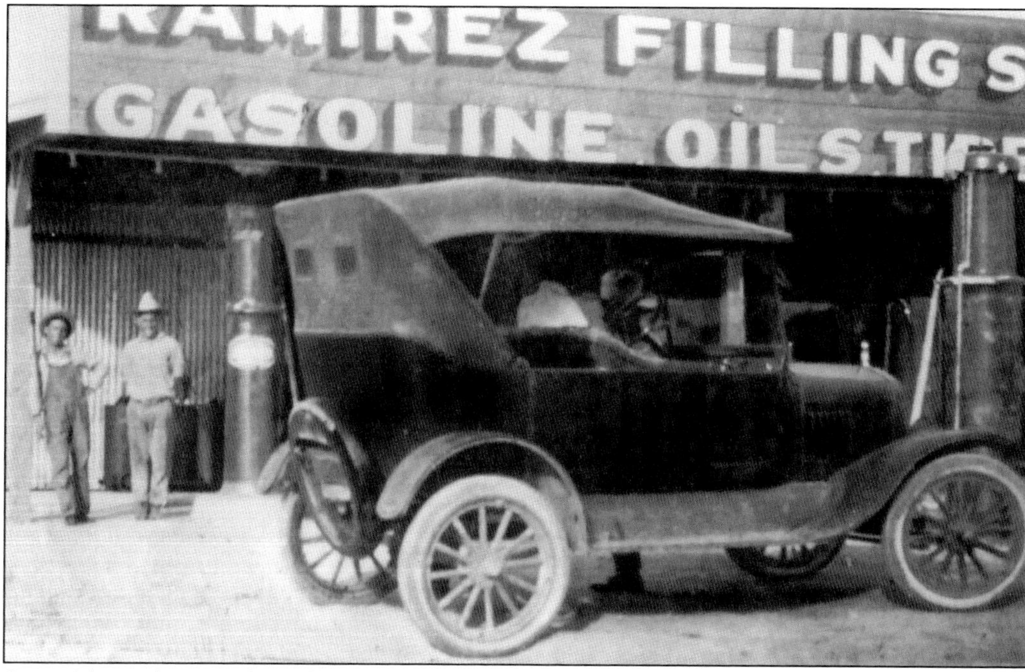

One of the earliest gasoline filling stations in town was built in 1915 at 796 West Robertson Street. Owner-operator Vidal V. Ramirez also owned a store at 500 Corral Street supplying farmers and laborers equipment and sundries, and extending credit until harvest time. In this photograph, a good customer, Dionicio G. Mancillas, has pulled in for service. (Courtesy Beto Ramirez.)

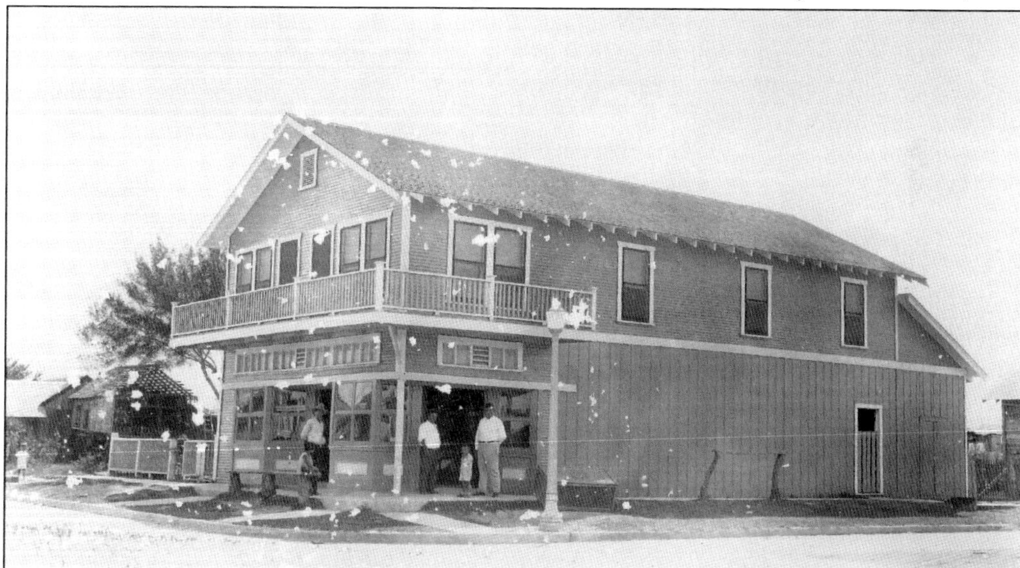

Dionicio Mancillas Sr. moved to San Benito 1907 from Paso Real on the Arroyo Colorado River and set up a general store at the corner of Julian and Carol Streets. He relocated to the corner of Diaz and Zaragoza Streets in 1922. The D. G. Mancillas General Store, in the oldest Hispanic neighborhood in town, operated through 1970. In this 1927 photograph, five-year-old Dionicio Jr. stands with his father (to his right) at the store front. Note the horse hitch to the side. (Courtesy Dionicio Mancillas Jr.)

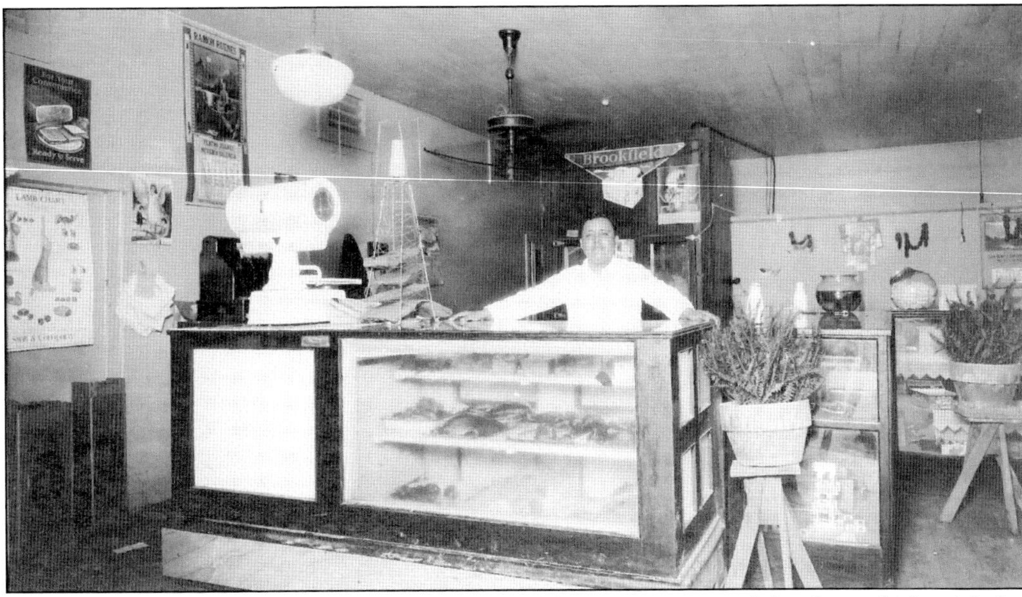

Francisco "Pancho" Villarreal and his wife, Maria del Carmen, operated the Central Meat Market at 795 West Robertson Street. Pancho's store provided everything from basic school supplies, candy, and canned goods, with a special focus on its meat market. The store operated for 40 years until Pancho's death in 1964. Pancho Villarreal's sister married Dionicio Mancillas Sr. who owned a general store in the area. He employed his brother-in-law Jesus Contreras and his three sons, Francisco, Heriberto, and Enrique Villarreal. (Courtesy Dolores Vega.)

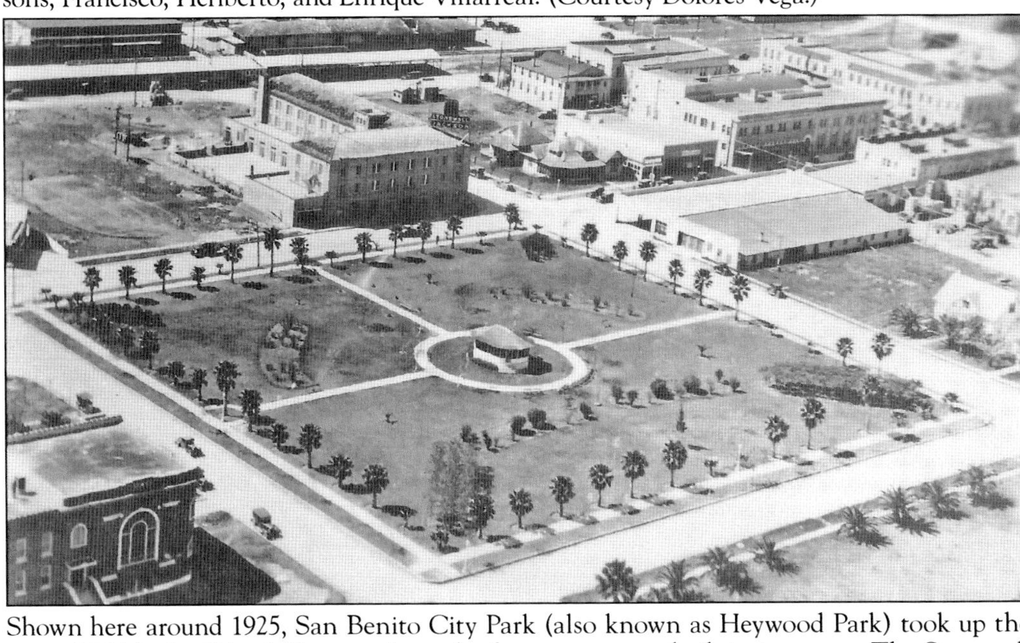

Shown here around 1925, San Benito City Park (also known as Heywood Park) took up the entire 200 block of North Reagan. A gazebo for concerts was built in its center. The Stonewall Jackson Hotel and original depot are visible at the top of the photograph. At the bottom is the First Baptist Church, located where the San Benito Consolidated Independent School District administration building is today. A public library later replaced the gazebo, and a community building was built on the right corner of the block. (Courtesy Tootie Madden.)

Three

How We Worked
Butcher, Baker, and Land-Deal Maker

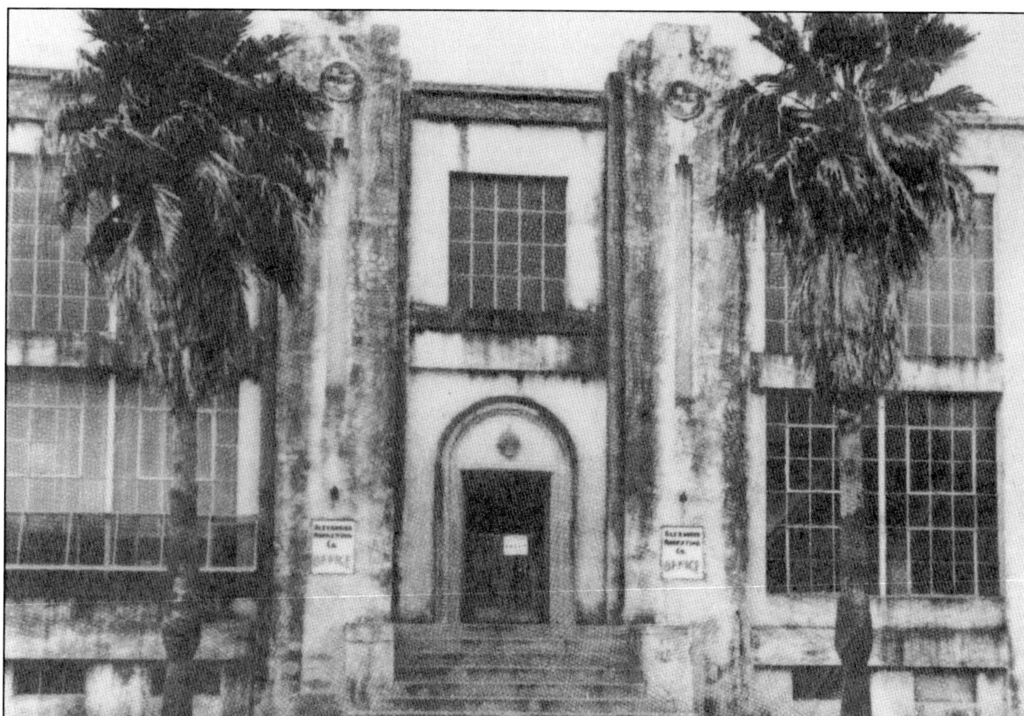

Once the railroad came in, packing sheds were built to process the now-fertile Valley's produce before shipping it out on the train. As evidenced by the citrus fruit in relief over the main entrance, the Alexander Marketing Company was part of the important fruit and vegetable industry that once thrived in San Benito. The building is located at the corner of West Stenger and Travis Streets with close proximity to the railroad tracks. At one time, it had its own ice production method to ice down the produce for shipment. (Courtesy Martin Salazar Jr.)

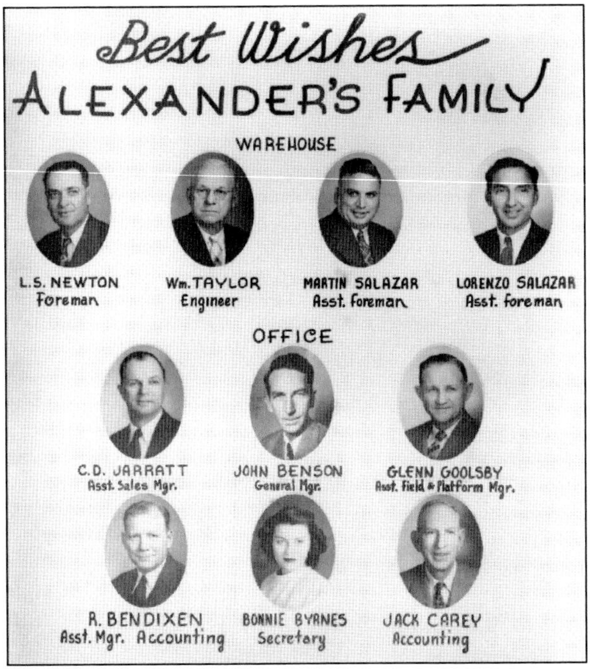

Broccoli, cauliflower, cabbage, carrots, onions, endive, escarole, celery, peas, green beans, and bell peppers were just a few of the vegetables processed at the Alexander Marketing Company, started in 1917. John Benson, who later owned the company, was the manager in 1947. Brothers Martin Salazar Sr. and Lorenzo Salazar were the assistant foremen, and their sons, Martin Salazar Jr. and Jose "Pepe" Salazar, started working there right after high school graduation and continued until their retirement. (Courtesy Martin Salazar Jr.)

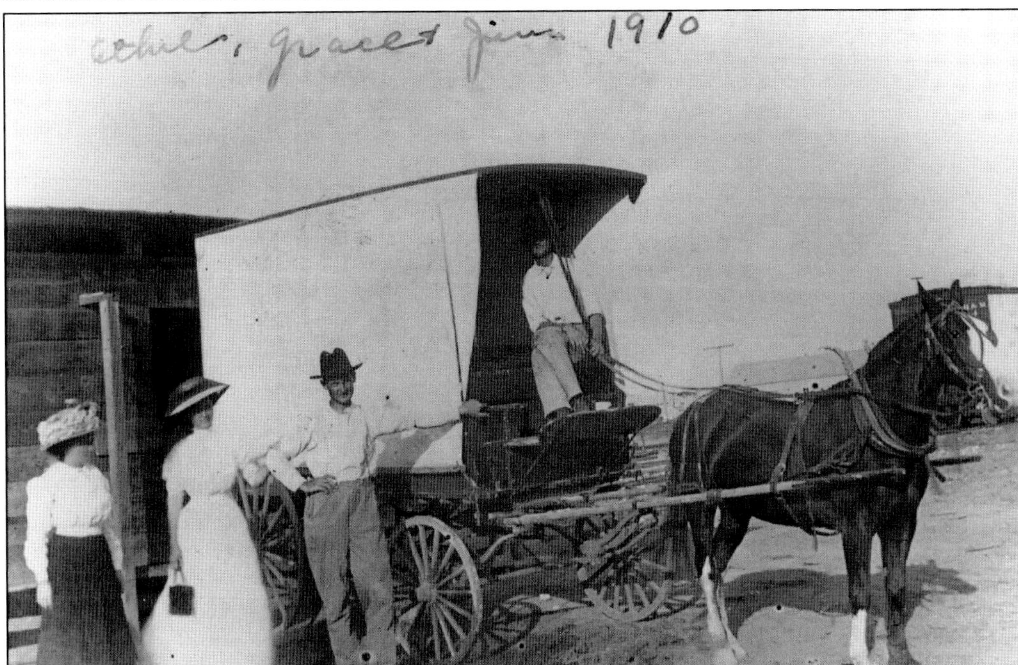

San Benito Ice and Cold Storage, begun as a community project in 1910 by Stanley Dodds and Sam Robertson, became the Rio Grande Valley Ice Company in 1914. The company installed the first pre-cooling unit in the Valley and one of the first in the country. By 1961, the plant supplied clear ice for the entire Valley. In this 1910 photograph, children Ethel (left), Grace, and Jim Ballenger stand with their father, Joe Ballenger, in front of one of the first ice wagons in town. (Courtesy Tommy Ballenger.)

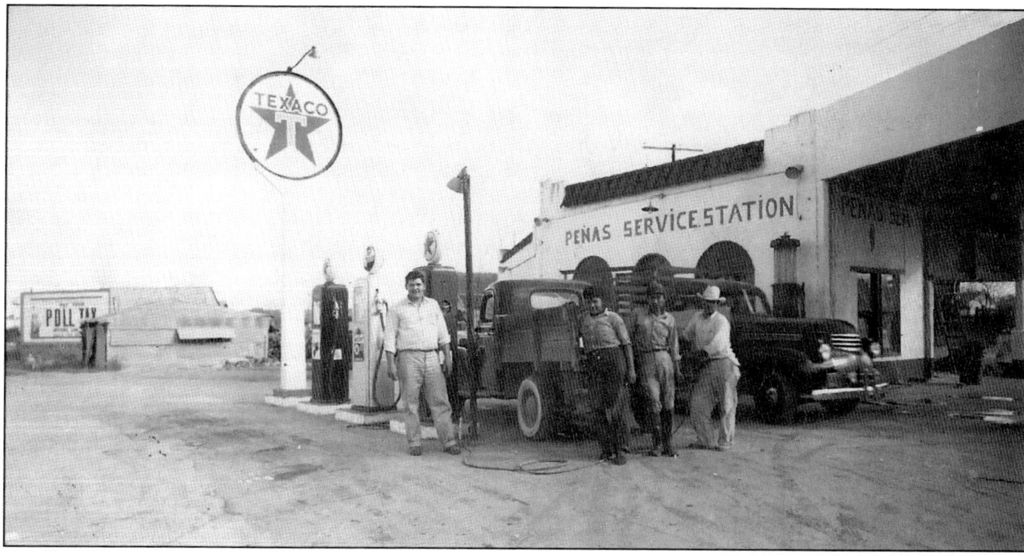

Peña's Texaco Service Station, originally owned by Manuel Peña, was established in the late 1930s near the Corral and Robertson Streets intersection and later moved to 989 Combes Street. Standing under the lamp post, Rodolfo Peña, Manuel's nephew, eventually took over ownership of the full-service station. The other men pictured are unidentified patrons and an unidentified employee. The large sign to the left of photograph reminded citizens to pay their poll tax. (Courtesy Lydia Peña.)

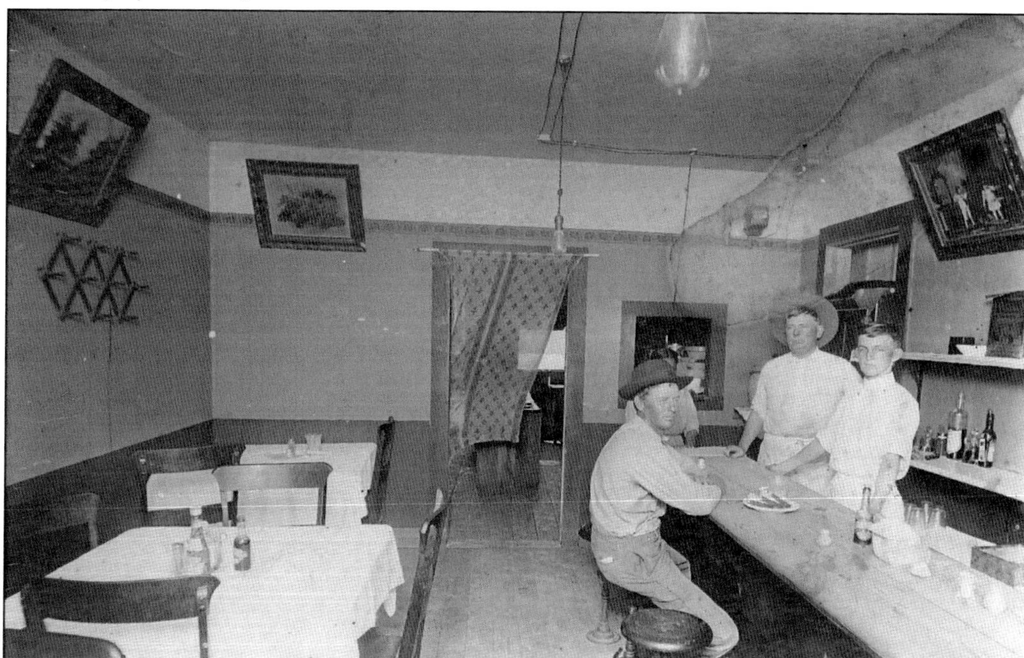

West Rowson Street was a busy place in 1915, and Collins Beanery was in the middle of it. Just out of high school, young Richard T. Collins, owner, stands to the right of the waiter behind the counter. Collins went on to enlist in the army in World War I, and after returning, entered the insurance business with his father, John Richard "J. R." Collins. Richard also served as city secretary during Scott Brown's mayoral term. (Courtesy Mary Catherine Lovett.)

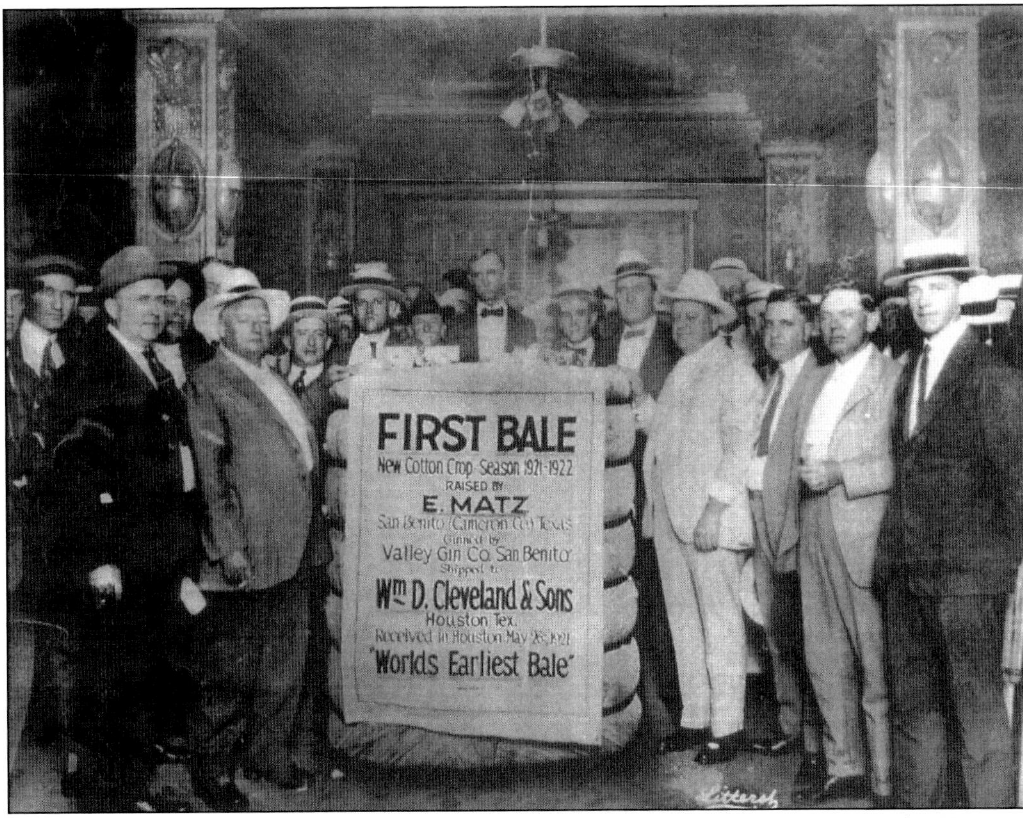

Standing to the immediate left of the first bale of the 1921–1922 cotton crop at the Houston Cotton Exchange is Ernst Matz, a sharecropper who grew cotton on Ben Hicks's land adjacent to the Rio Grande River, just south of town near today's Los Indios Free Trade Bridge. Matz's cotton was ginned in San Benito. This bale weighed 493 pounds and was delivered by train in May 1921 to Houston, where it was auctioned. (Courtesy James Matz.)

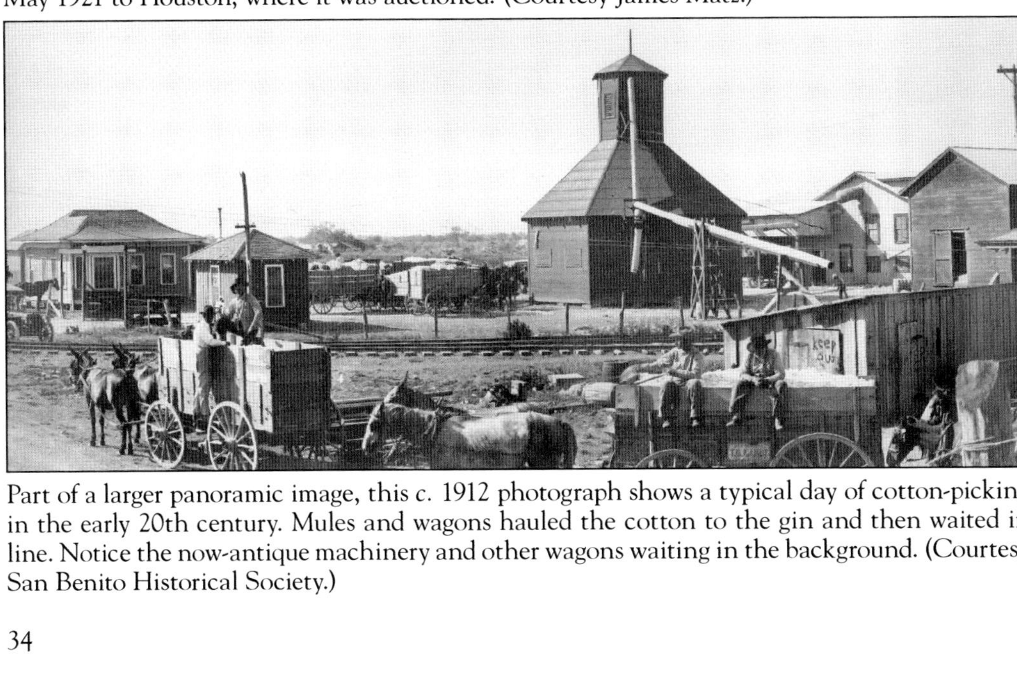

Part of a larger panoramic image, this c. 1912 photograph shows a typical day of cotton-picking in the early 20th century. Mules and wagons hauled the cotton to the gin and then waited in line. Notice the now-antique machinery and other wagons waiting in the background. (Courtesy San Benito Historical Society.)

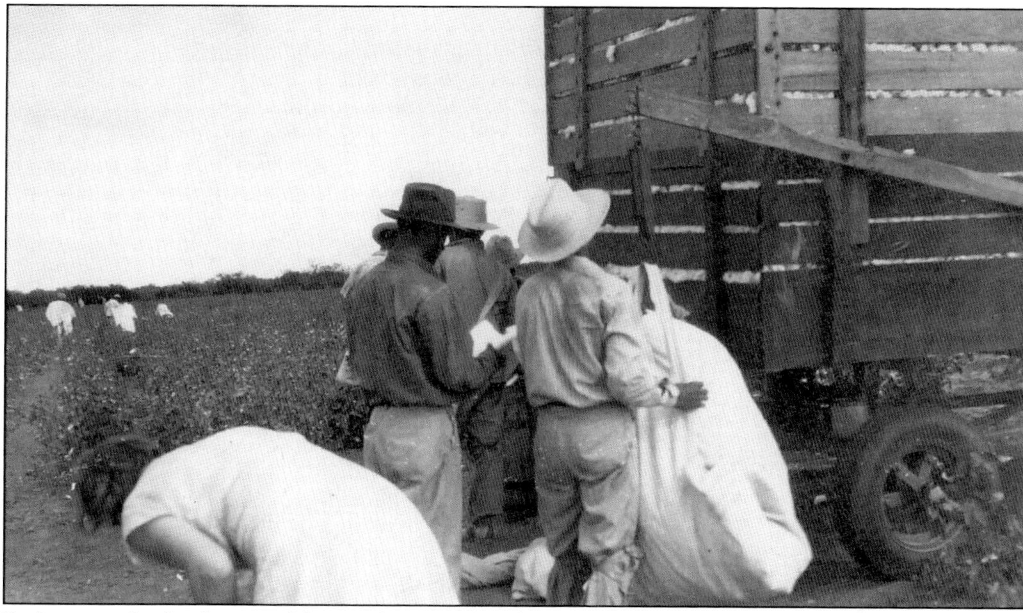

Pickers in the background bring their 12-foot-long cotton sacks to be weighed at George W. Gamble Farms on Gamble Road. Many field workers were part of the Bracero Program, named for the Spanish word meaning "arm." From 1942 to 1964, this program allowed laborers from Mexico to be temporarily contracted for work in the United States. Employers were required to provide housing, food, medical care, and a minimum wage. (Courtesy Suzanne Gilbert.)

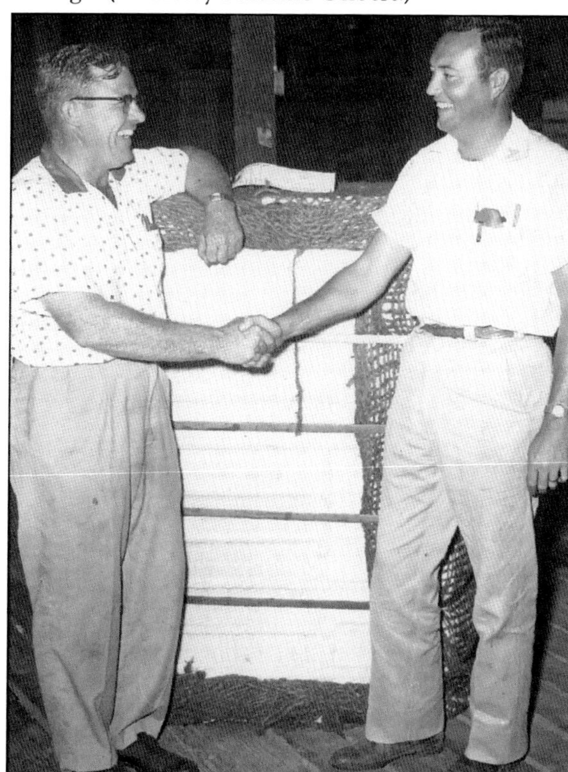

Bales of cotton weighed an average of 500 pounds and were wrapped in jute at cotton gins. It took 1,200–1,500 pounds of pre-ginned cotton to create a 500-pound bale after trash and cotton seed were extracted in the ginning process. The finished cotton bale was taken to the Harlingen Cotton Compress, which would reduce their size by roughly half before they were shipped out. Woolam Gin, started by Vernon Woolam, was located in the La Palma neighborhood. In this photograph, Vernon's son, gin manager Pete Woolam (left), and cotton farmer Adolph Thomae Jr. share a friendly handshake. (Courtesy San Benito Historical Society.)

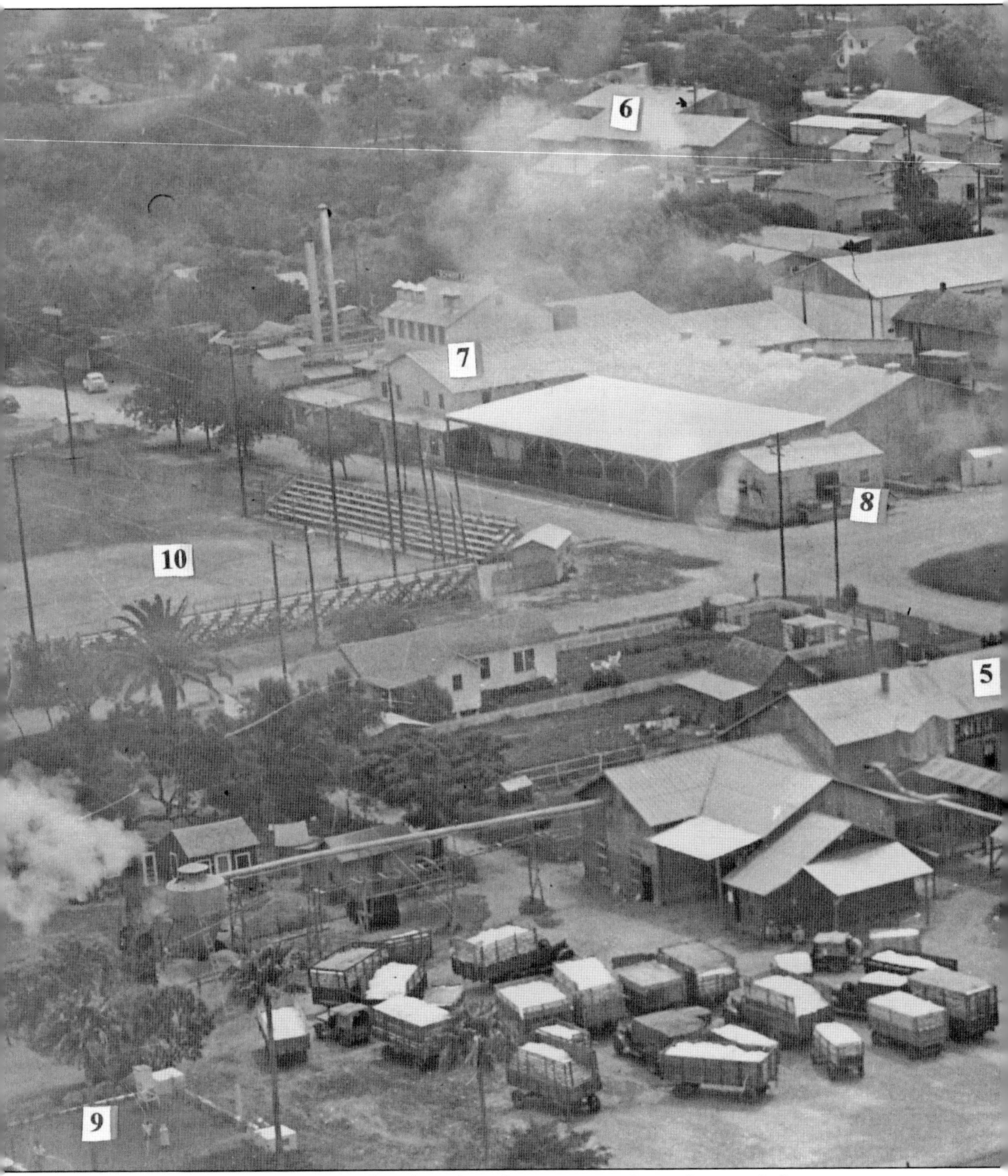

The corner of town by the railroad track and resaca was where the town's first cotton gin was built. A whole agricultural industry grew adjacent to the tracks and thrived well into the last quarter of the 20th century. Located at the bottom of this c. 1940s photograph along the railroad track, the following companies are identified: No. 1 is Crawford Produce; No. 2 is Charles Bando's Resaca Gin; No. 3 is the Black and McGinley Gin; No. 4 is San Benito Coop Gin (today the

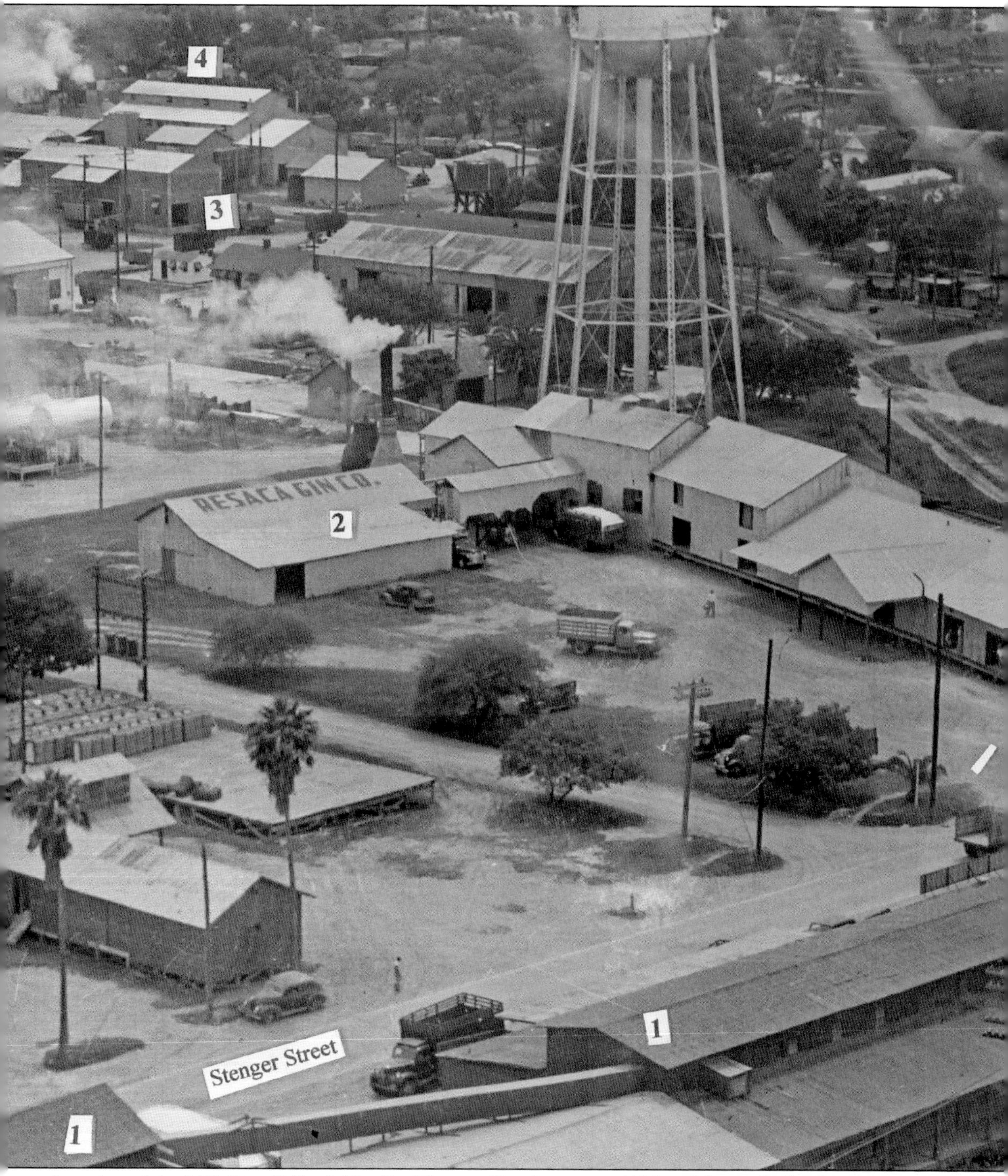

location of the U.S. Post Office); No. 5 is Electric Gin, begun in 1936 and formerly the San Benito Gin (from 1923 to 1936); No. 6 is the Craig Gin; No. 7 is Bill Hervey's Cannery (formerly the Schmidt Cannery); No. 8 is Harold Hollon's Magnolia Oil Company, which later morphed into Mobil Oil; No. 9 is the San Benito Water Filtration plant; and No. 10 is the Kiwanis Baseball Park. (Courtesy Bob Duncan.)

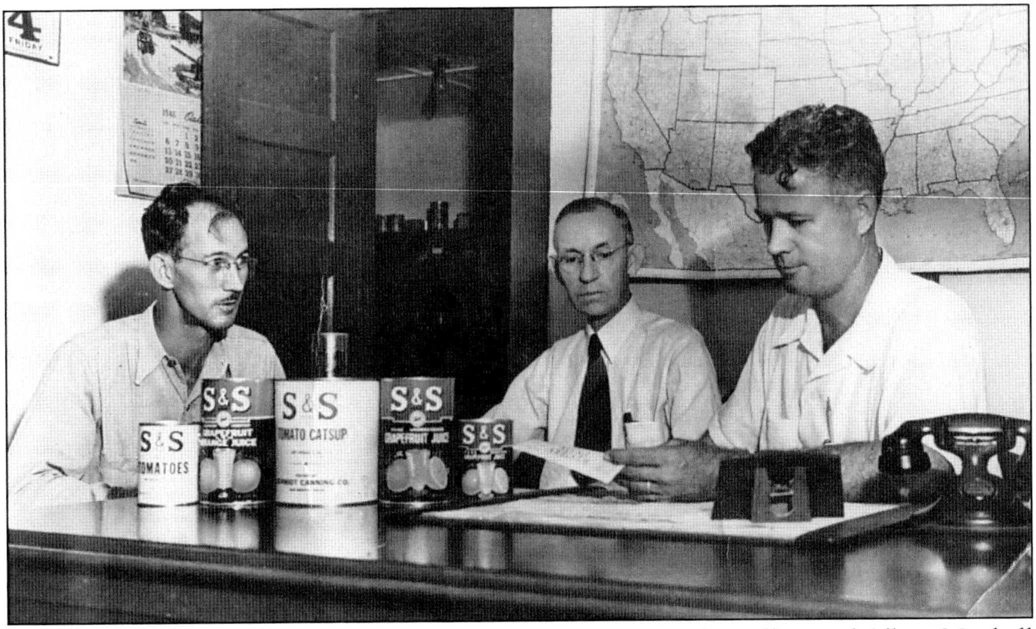

The Schmidt family sold their cannery about 1941 to Robert "Bob" Collins and Albert Mitchell "Bill" Hervey. In this photograph, Robert Collins, Mr. Schmidt, and Bill Hervey discuss the sale. Collins and Hervey operated the cannery, which was located in the vicinity of the gins, until about 1958. Tomatoes, green beans, and other produce from area farms were canned and marketed throughout the Midwest. (Courtesy Mike Hervey.)

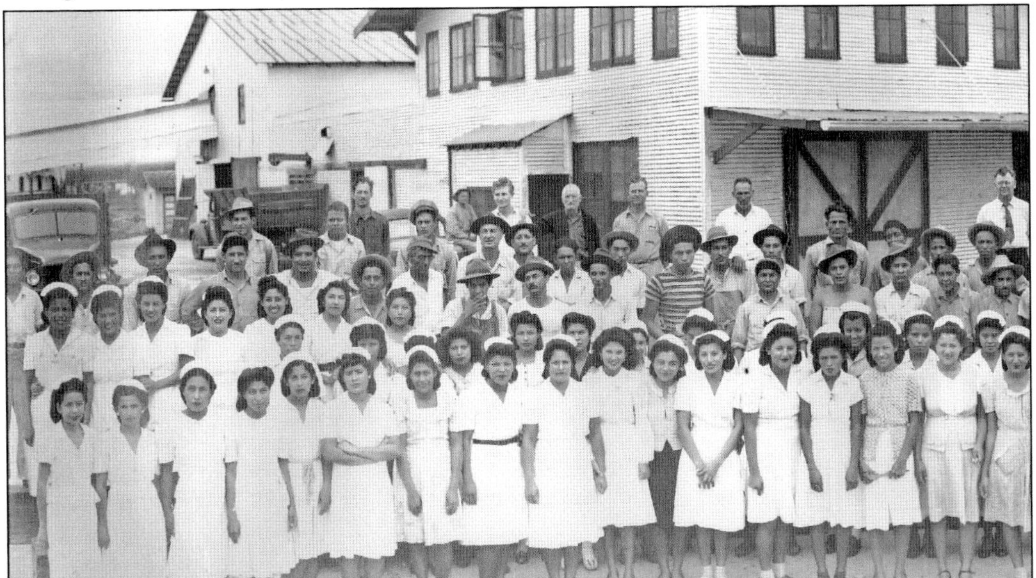
From the women who worked the line to the men who hauled the crates, over 100 of the employees of Schmidt Canning Company, stood outside the cannery one day in 1947 and had their photograph taken. In the first row, ninth from the left, is Francisca O. Gallegos. Unfortunately, the panoramic photograph was so large that only this side could be shown, but her husband, Guadalupe Gallegos, who also worked at the cannery, was on the opposite side of the picture. (Courtesy Francisca "Panchita" Gallegos.)

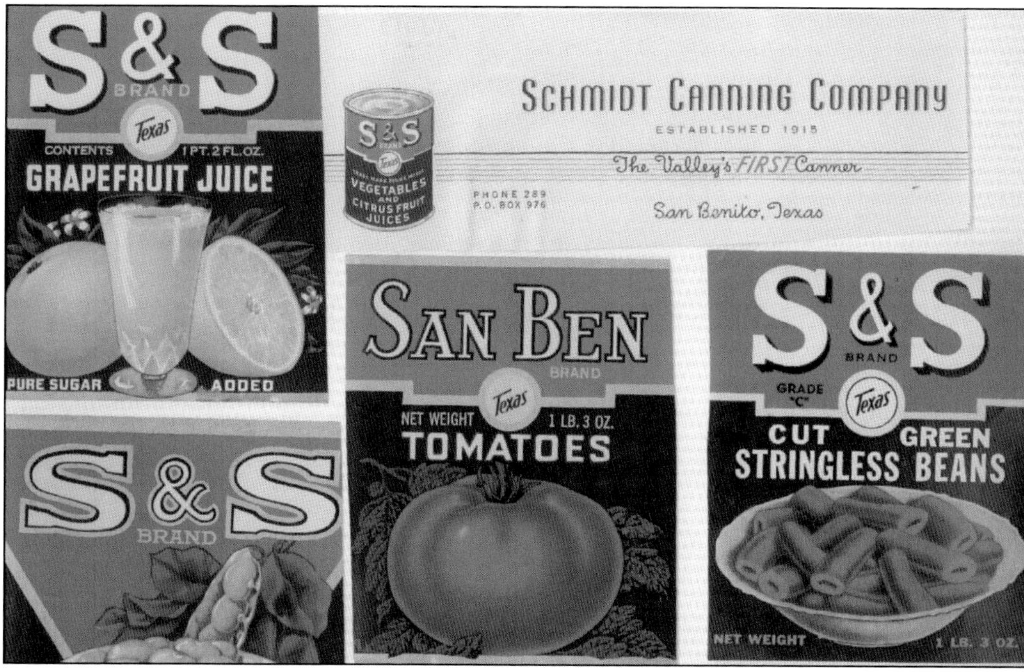

This letterhead trumpets the arrival of the first cannery in the Valley in 1915—quite a proud accomplishment for San Benito. Other brands such as S and S, San Ben, T.V. Woolam, Alexander's, and U-Lika-Me were some of the colorful labels placed on canned vegetables. Albert M. "Bill" Hervey was a president of Schmidt Canning Company. In 1946 he was elected president of the Texas Canners Association and served two terms. (Courtesy Mike Hervey.)

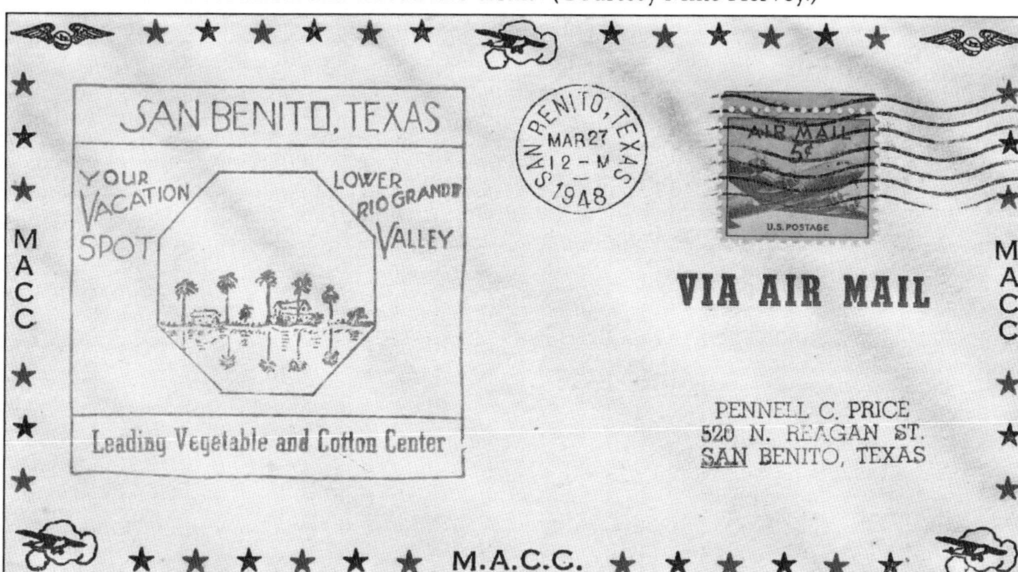

San Benito's marketing and tourism spread all over the world with free advertising on envelopes mailed in San Benito. One business that didn't need advertising was La Especial Bakery on Robertson Street. By 1944, the Enrique Ornelas family had begun baking *pan dulce* (sweet bread) in the oldest brick oven in the Valley for the residents of San Benito. The family's bakery still operates today, now run by second- and third-generation bakers. (Courtesy San Benito Historical Society.)

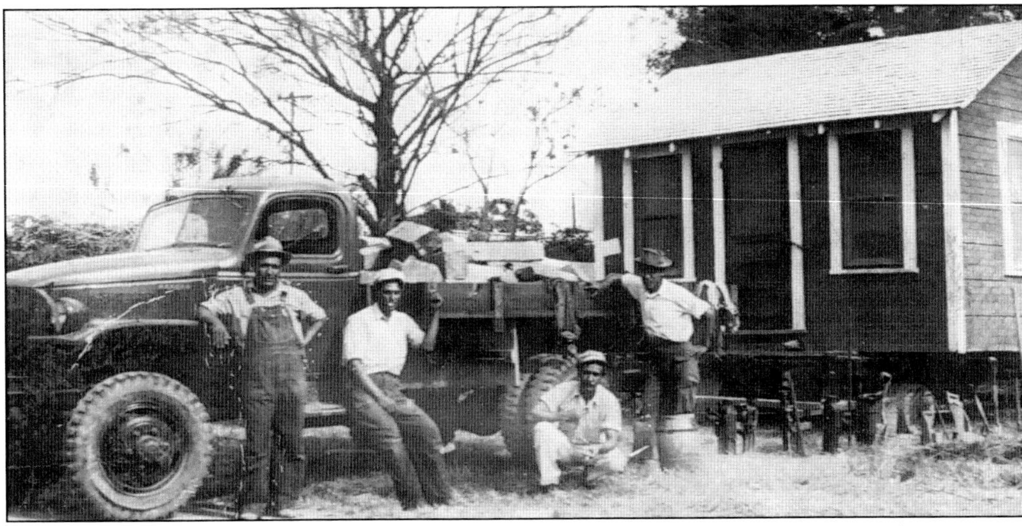

Crispín and Damiana Avila, who arrived from San Luis Potosi, Mexico, in 1908, were sharecroppers who also had a business moving small houses. During a move, the Avilas used the same mules they used to plow fields to pull the house. In the mid-1950s, their son Pedro quit farming and became a full-time house mover, moving two-story houses up to 50 miles. In this photograph, from left to right, Pedro L. Avila moves a small house with a 1945 army truck, assisted by Lupe Villegas, Salvador De Leon, and Emilio Avila. (Courtesy Rey Avila.)

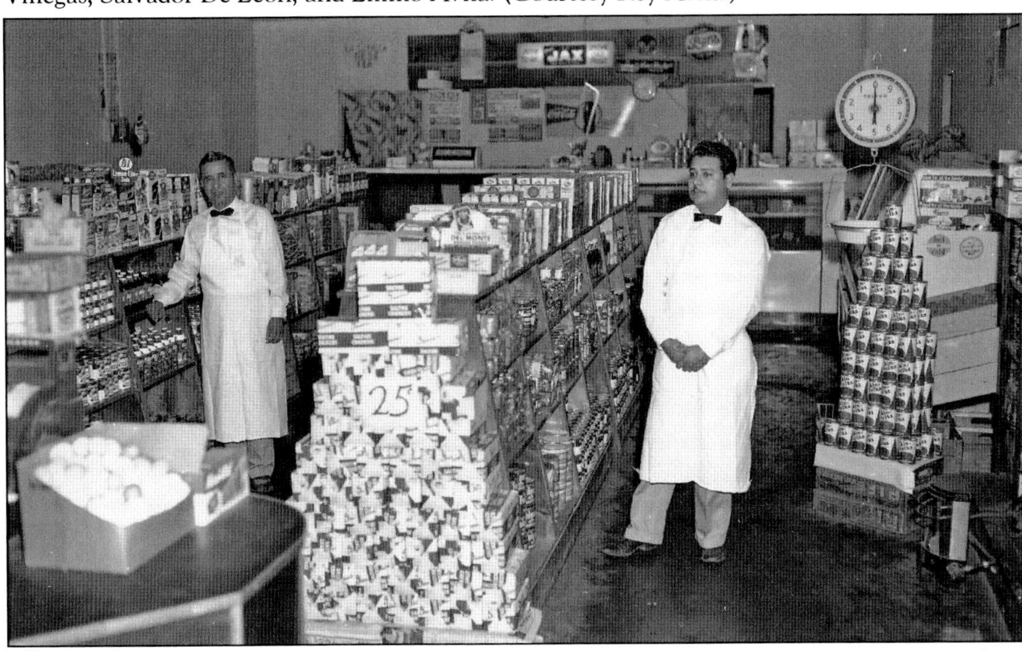

The Salome Martinez Grocery and Meat Market at 490 Hidalgo Street opened in 1940 and was soon known for its concern for its patrons. Salome and Librada generously enabled customers to charge groceries during hard times, and this created goodwill that helped make the couple well-respected community leaders. Their son-in-law Jose Angel "Kelo" Torres ran the meat market, and their son Salome Jr. "Chale" and his family continue the tradition in grocery and catering services today. In this photograph, Salome Sr. and Kelo Torres stand ready for business before store opening at the start of another busy day. (Courtesy Blanca Petrovics.)

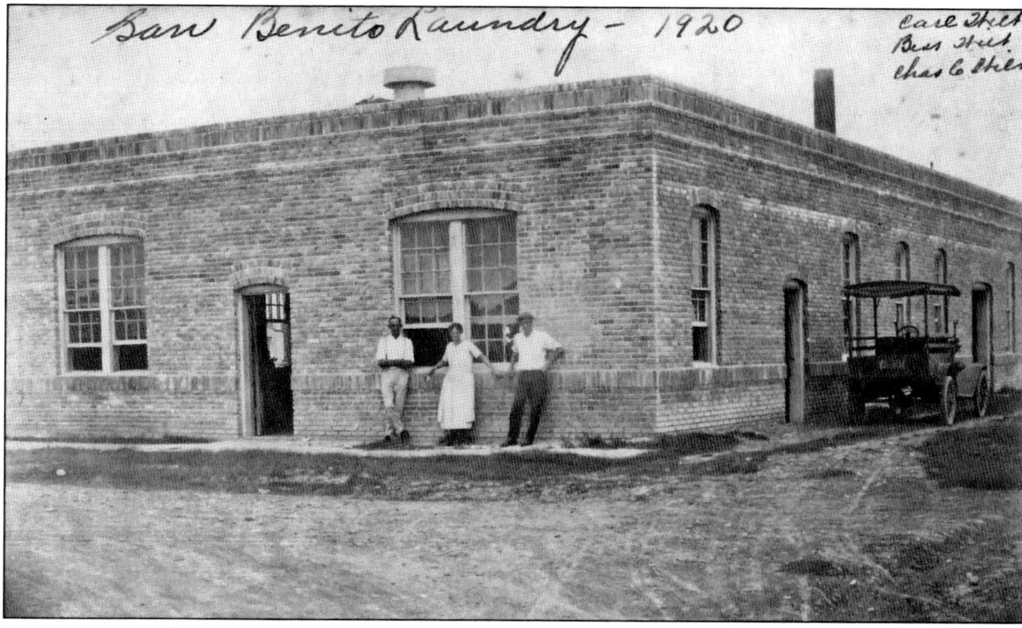

In 1916, the soldiers camped around San Benito lacked laundry facilities. Those camped on South Reagan across from the Carl C. Wilts home convinced Bess Wilts to allow her washwoman to do their laundry. Word got around, and the following Monday, she found her back porch piled high with dirty clothes. In 1919, Wilts opened the Steam Laundry with modern equipment on the same block as her home. Her husband and son joined her in the business. (Courtesy Jacqueline Chapman Hanshaw.)

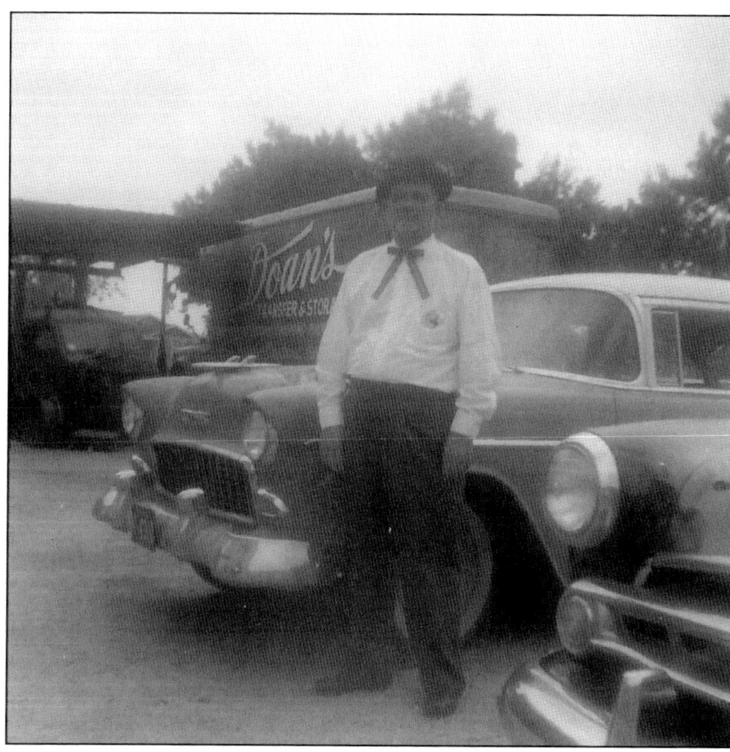

Allen Doan moved with his parents to San Benito in 1926 where he met his future wife, Amelia Cavazos Treviño, whose family lived on their Cavazos Spanish land grant north of town. Allen (pictured right), his father, and his brothers operated a trucking, moving, and storage company and also picked up mail from the trains for the post office. After they were married, Allen and Amelia Doan lived at 491 South Crockett. They had one son, Bobby, and daughters Jeanette, Betty, Mina, and Diantha. (Courtesy Jeanette Doan Horton.)

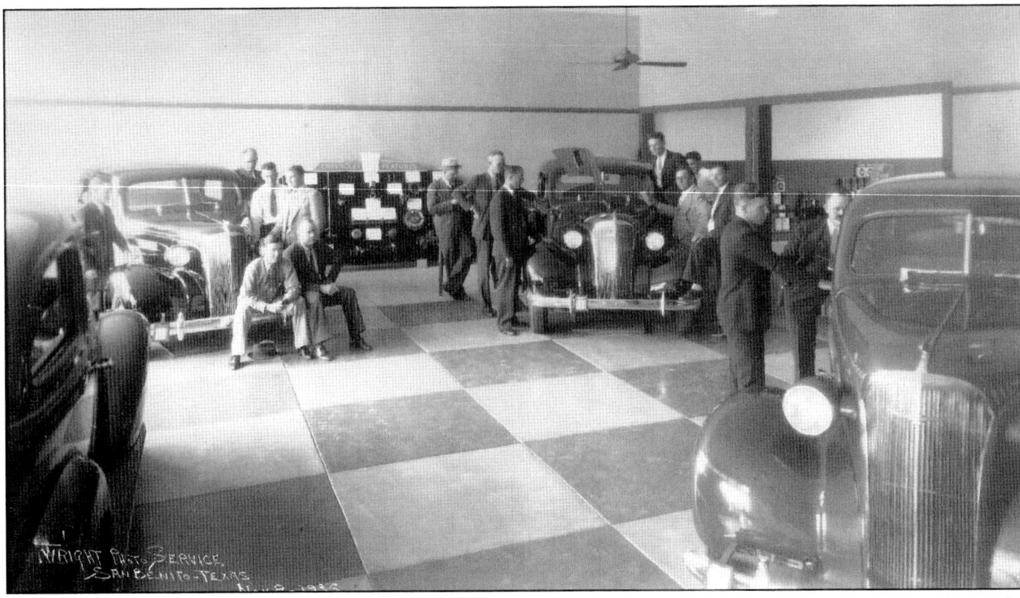

Here on November 8, 1936, salesmen in the Welch Motor Company showroom introduce the 1937 Chevrolet to their customers. Dealers were assigned areas, and Welch secured the territory bounded by the Arroyo on the north, the county line on the west, and the river and halfway to Brownsville on the south. (Courtesy Dick Welch.)

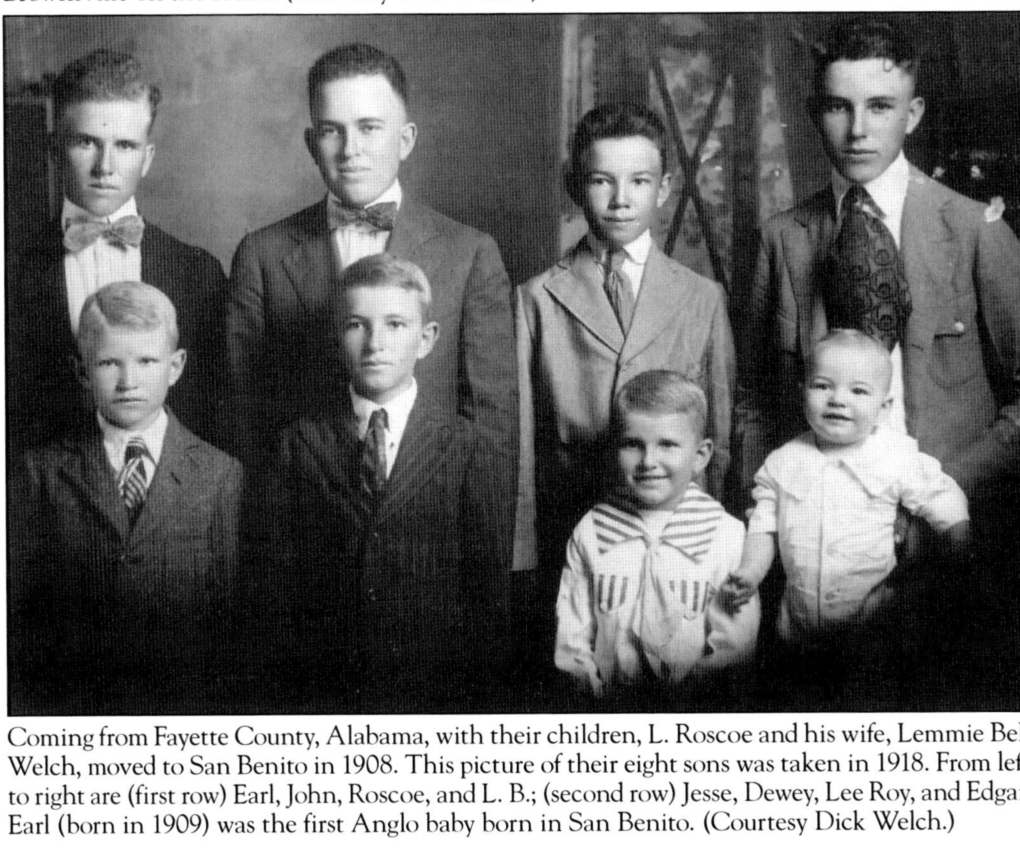

Coming from Fayette County, Alabama, with their children, L. Roscoe and his wife, Lemmie Bell Welch, moved to San Benito in 1908. This picture of their eight sons was taken in 1918. From left to right are (first row) Earl, John, Roscoe, and L. B.; (second row) Jesse, Dewey, Lee Roy, and Edgar. Earl (born in 1909) was the first Anglo baby born in San Benito. (Courtesy Dick Welch.)

Sitting around the family dinner table, Leon Tolliver "Tol" Boswell Sr., Arline Penn Boswell, L. T. Boswell Jr., Sam Penn Boswell Sr., and Elizabeth Penn Enos enjoy dinner at the Tol Boswell Sr., home at 750 North Reagan. Tol Sr. served on the school board and owned the Ford dealership, which sons Tol Jr. and Sam continued. (Courtesy Tootie Madden.)

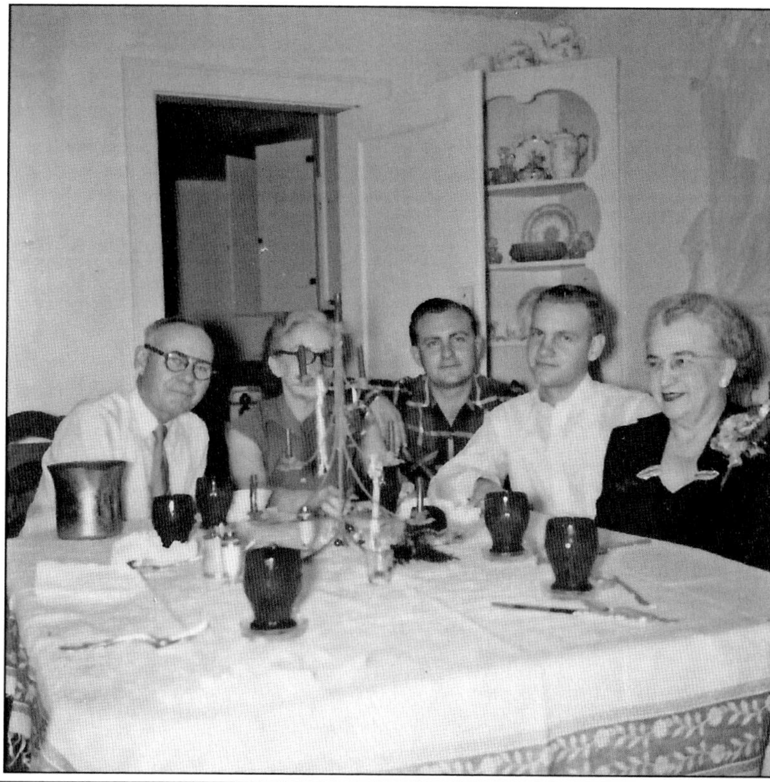

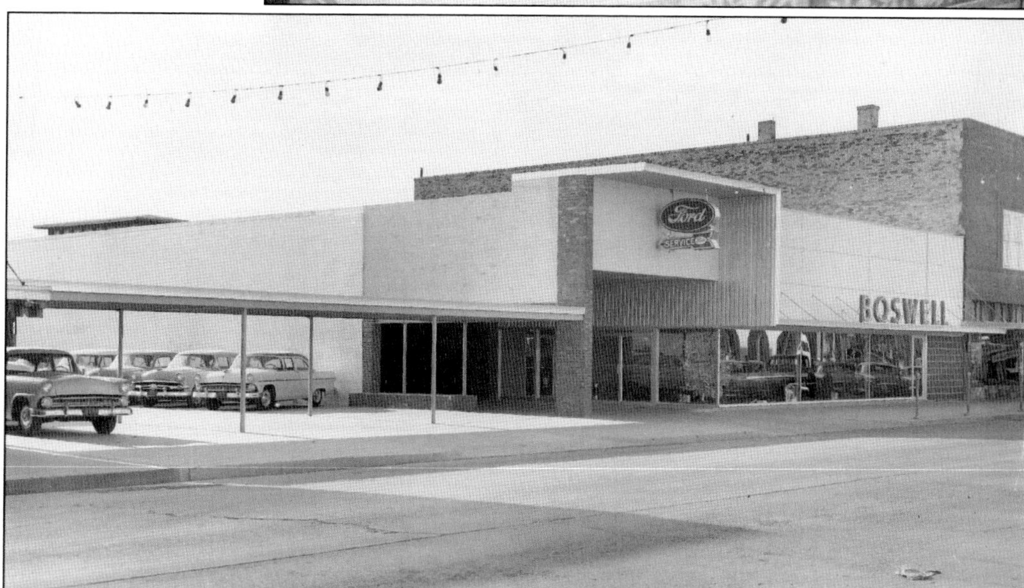

L. T. Boswell bought the Ford dealership in 1938. Under Boswell, the dealership sold new and used cars and operated a parts and service department. Located near the intersection of Robertson Street and North Sam Houston Boulevard, the dealership and the Masonic Lodge next door were sold and demolished in 1979 to make room for a bank's drive-through. Boswell's sons Tol and Sam became partners, building a new dealership at the intersection of Williams Road and Business 77. (Courtesy Tootie Madden.)

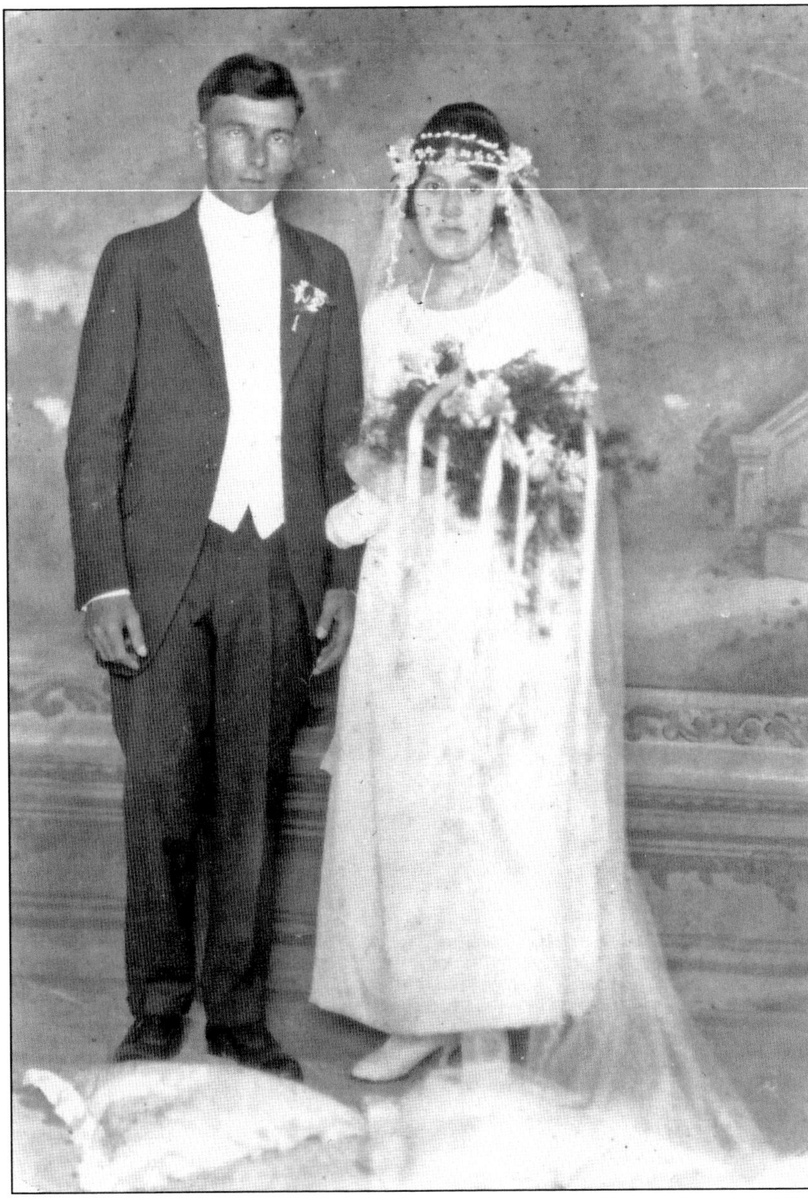

After the 1933 hurricane destroyed Alfredo A. and Anastacia Prezas Garcia's filling station, Alfredo began work patrolling downtown businesses. In 1932, he started work as the city's first tax collector, giving him the opportunity to advise Hispanics in danger of losing property how to fulfill their obligations. During this time, city employees were paid in scrip, a system introduced by Mayor Louis Whitte. Helping his neighbors learn to sign their names and vote was important to Alfredo, leading him to become involved in local and national politics, such as campaigning for the re-election of U.S. congressman Milton H. West. Politics must have been in Garcia's blood, as his uncle, Nestor Alcala was the first Hispanic county commissioner. Until his passing in 1971, Alfredo A. Garcia served the city as its first Hispanic city clerk and later, its first Hispanic municipal court judge. After his death, the court was dedicated in his honor. The Garcias had seven children: daughters Yolanda, Idalia, Norma, and Emilia, and sons Alfredo Jr., Arnoldo, and Arturo. (Courtesy Mila Salinas.)

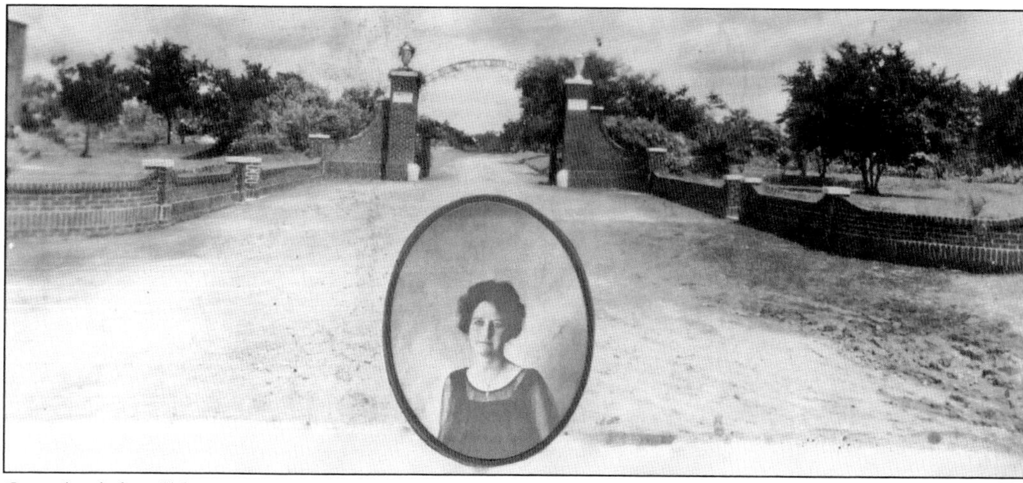

On a high knoll between San Benito and Rio Hondo, Fred N. Booth established his Mont Meta perpetual care burial park in 1926. Driveways were laid out in accordance with the slope of the land, which was most unusual because of the large amount of wild olive and ebony trees. Booth held a contest to determine the name of his new park, but he disliked all the names suggested and named the park for his wife, Margaret Chadwick Jackson Booth, whose nickname was "Meta" (pronounced "Meeta"). (Courtesy Fred Booth.)

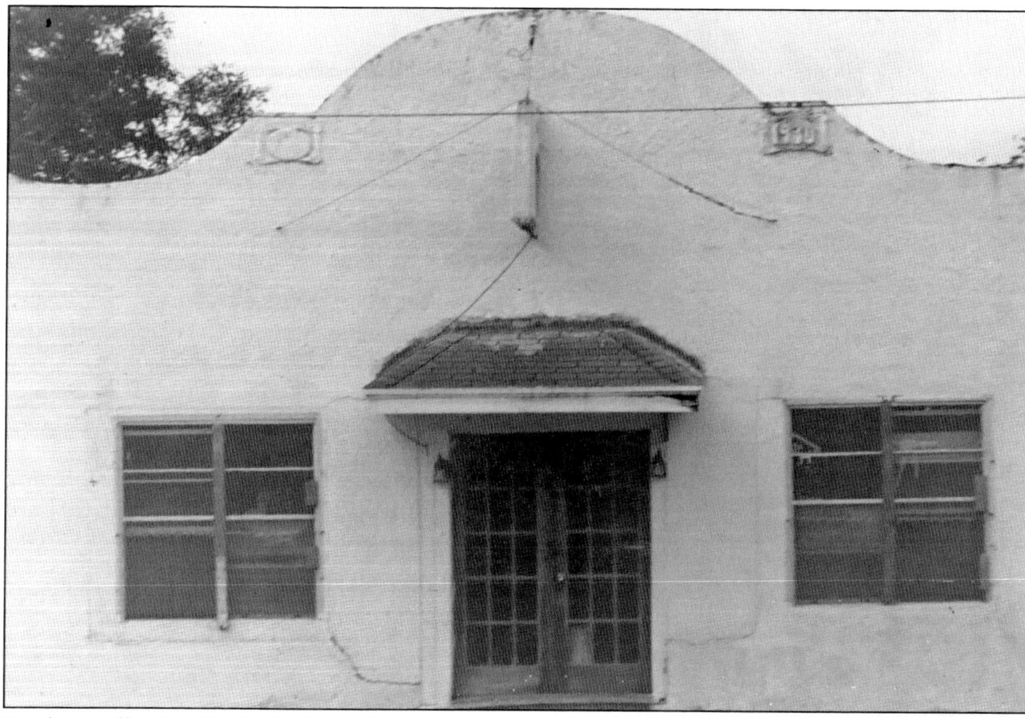

Traditionally, families held funeral visitations with the deceased in their homes. Leonardo and Angelita Perez ran their mortuary business from their home on Diana Street until 1940, when Leonardo bought this stucco-fronted building (which already had the 1930 relief at the top, to the right of the center arch) and moved it to 1180 Combes Street. The couple had five daughters: Lydia, Angelita, Irene, Elva, and Oralia. Leonardo operated the only Hispanic-owned funeral home in town until his death in 1960. (Courtesy Lydia Peña.)

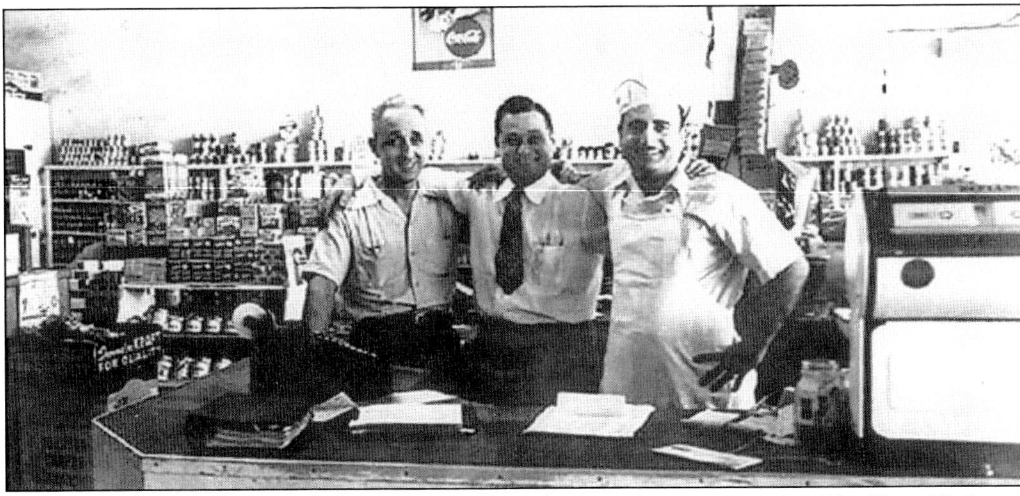

A&K Grocery Store, located on the 200 block, Robertson Street, was owned by Tony Kashouty and Jack Ayoub Sr. When they came home from the war, George, Jack Jr., and Dave followed family tradition, opening Ayoub Brothers' Grocery in the same building as their father's store. Eventually, Jack Jr. bought out his brothers and then formed a partnership with Tony Kashouty. They renamed the store A&K Grocery. In this photograph, an unidentified salesman stands between the two owners, Tony Kashouty (left) and Jack Ayoub Jr. (Courtesy Jack Emil Ayoub.)

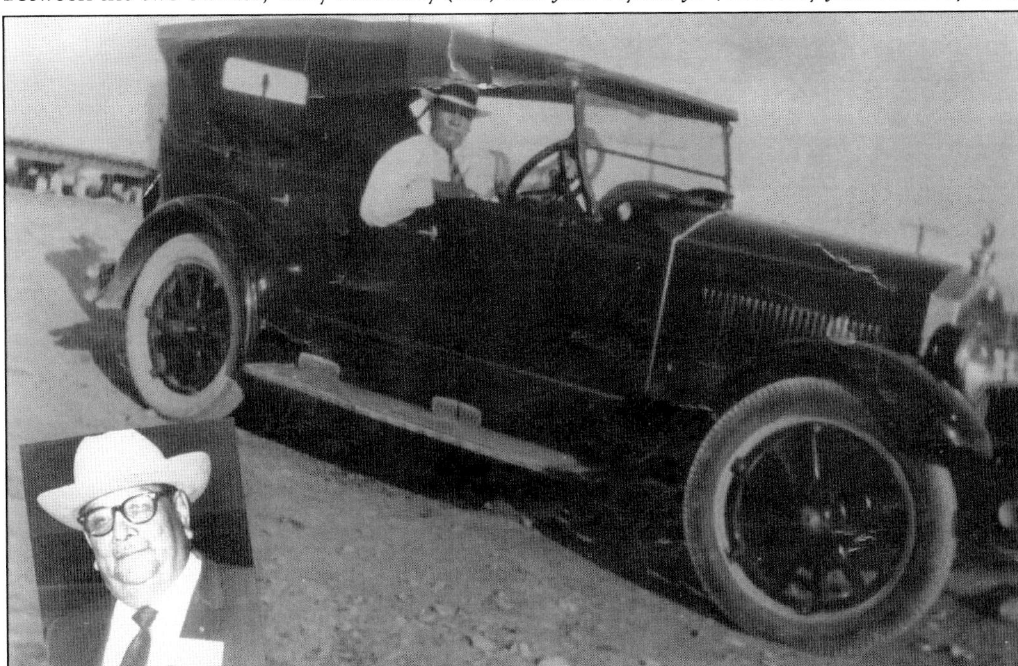

An early entrepreneur, Fernando Sanchez and his wife, Maria Eva, began La Villita dance hall, which was well-known throughout the Valley. Fernando named a soft drink after his wife, "Eva's Best Drink." He was also a supplier of salt, harvested at Sal del Rey Lake. His other companies included a transfer company, an ice creamery, a tile manufacturing firm, a contracting outfit, an ice blower service, and the San Benito Music Company. Fernando's only formal education was at Escuela Guadalupe Catholic School on Corral Street. (Courtesy Rey Avila.)

Pedro Lara Sr. learned the baking craft from his father, Anacleto, who fled Monterey, Mexico, during the revolution and settled in Rio Hondo, Texas, where he established a bakery. Pedro also worked at a bakery on the 200 block of Sam Houston Boulevard, and later at Holsom Bread in Harlingen. He married Consuelo Davila of San Benito in 1936, and a few years later, started Lara's Bakery on Morelos Street between Corral and Sombra Streets. Lara's Bakery operated from 1941 to 1955 and produced delicious pastries, especially for the mid-afternoon coffee break called a *merienda*. The Laras had two sons, Pedro Jr. and Marco Antonio Lara. (Courtesy Pedro Lara Jr.)

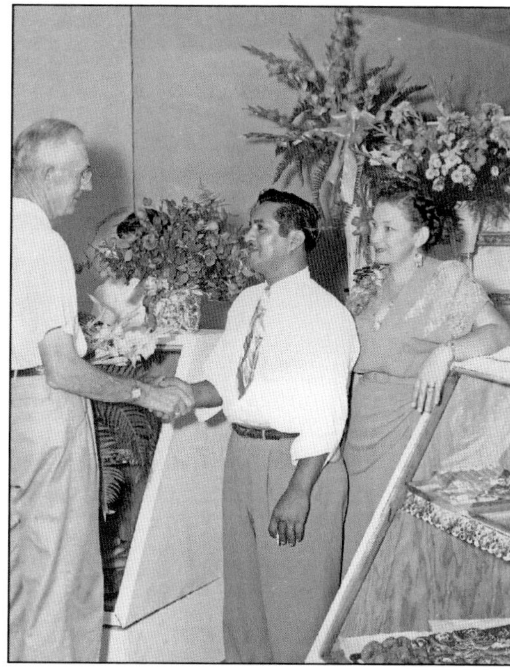

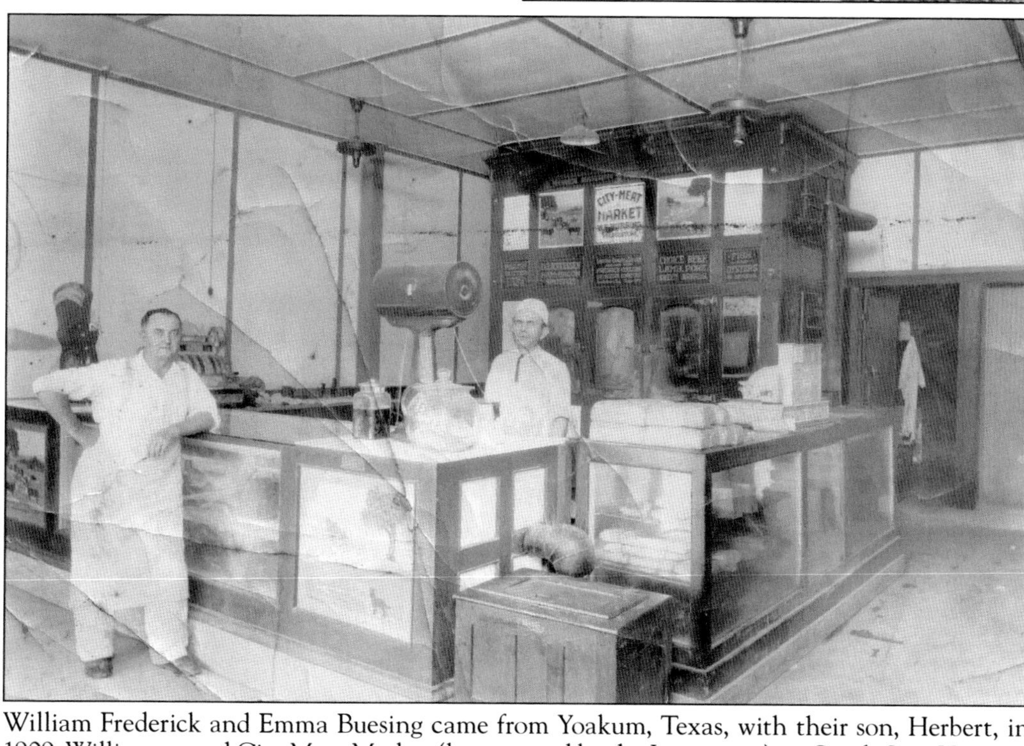

William Frederick and Emma Buesing came from Yoakum, Texas, with their son, Herbert, in 1909. William owned City Meat Market (later owned by the Lancasters) on South Sam Houston Boulevard and, later, on Rowson Street. The center panel on the locker behind the meat counter reads, "City Meat Market, W. F. Buesing, Proprietor." These 14-carat gold-leaf-on-black-glass panels were salvaged and hang today in the home of granddaughter Jacqueline "Jack" Buesing Boswell. (Courtesy Tootie Madden.)

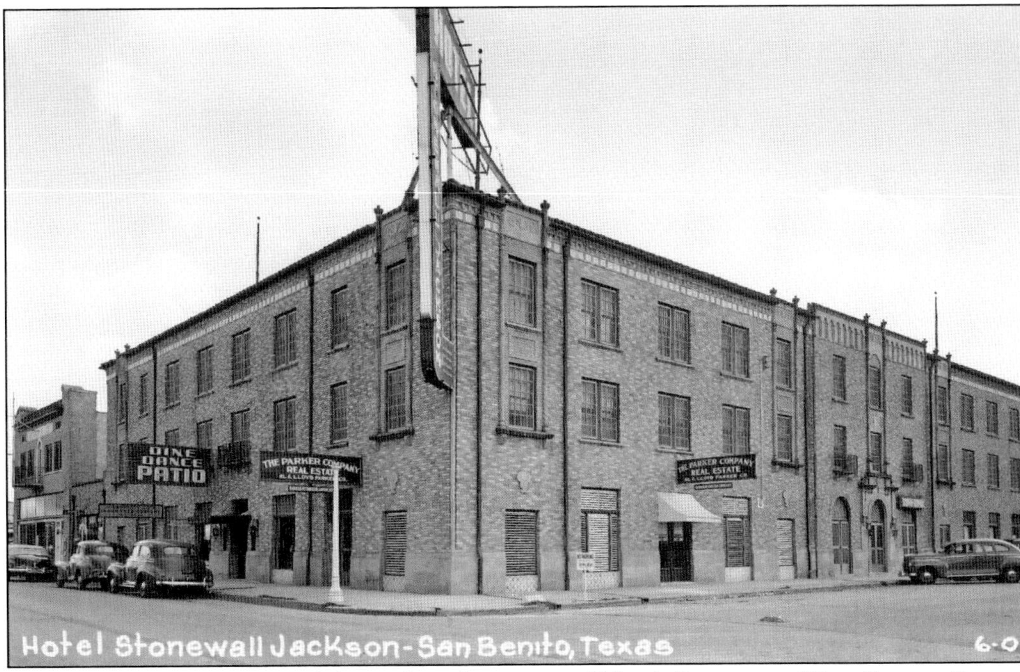

The Stonewall Jackson Hotel, located on the corner of North Reagan and East Stenger Streets, began with a 1925 community effort to provide a more modern hotel for visitors to San Benito and a more modern event facility for local residents. San Antonio architect Harvey P. Smith designed the structure, which cost $225,000 to complete, including the land, the building, and its furnishings. Through the years, many wedding receptions, parties, dances, and meetings were held in the hotel's beautiful patio and dining room. (Courtesy San Benito Historical Society.)

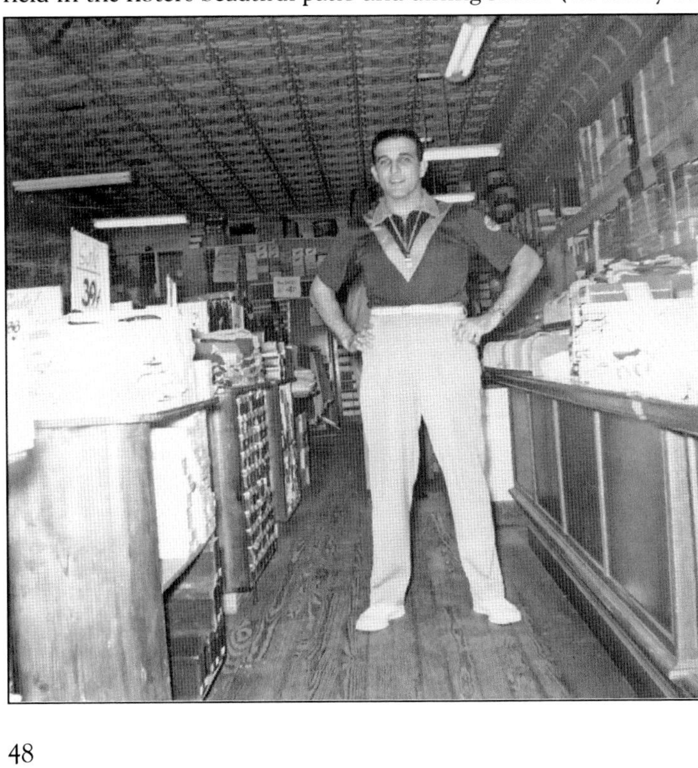

Dressed in his basketball official's uniform ready to referee a game, George Ogdee takes a stand in his men's wear store at 172 South Sam Houston Boulevard. His father opened Ogdee's Store in 1934, and George rented it from his father from 1947 until he inherited the store upon his father's death. He sold the business to Val Garcia in 1972. Notice the tin ceiling. (Courtesy George Ogdee.)

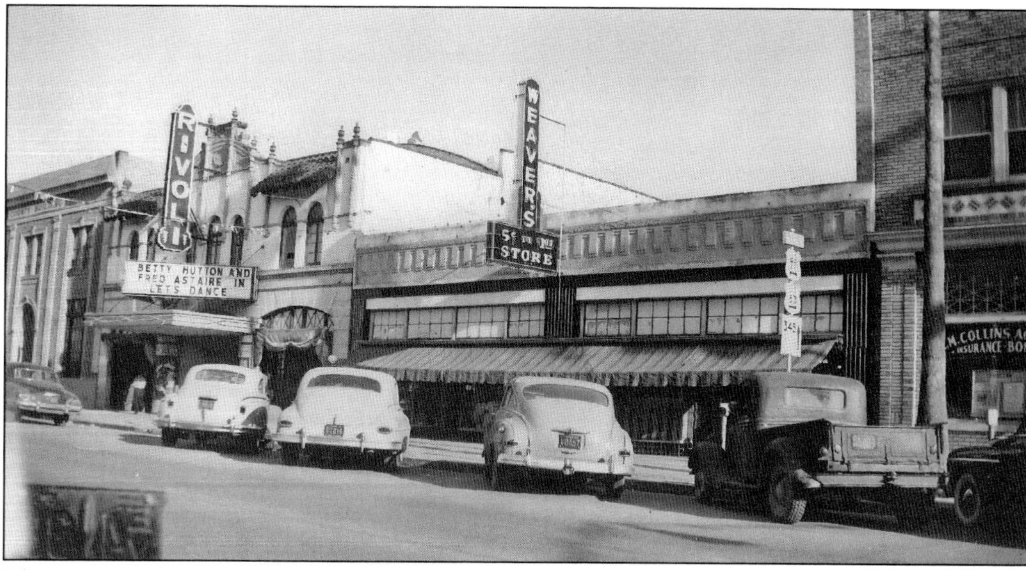

This *c.* 1951 photograph shows two of San Benito residents' favorite places to go in the middle of the 20th century: the Rivoli Theater and Weaver's Five and Dime store. Notice the beautiful architecture of the Rivoli's facade. At the Rivoli, for 10¢, a moviegoer could watch a double feature plus cartoons. On Saturday nights, patrons played bingo during intermission. Note how the small transom windows above Weaver's large front windows mimic the rectangular design across the top of the building. (Courtesy San Benito Historical Society.)

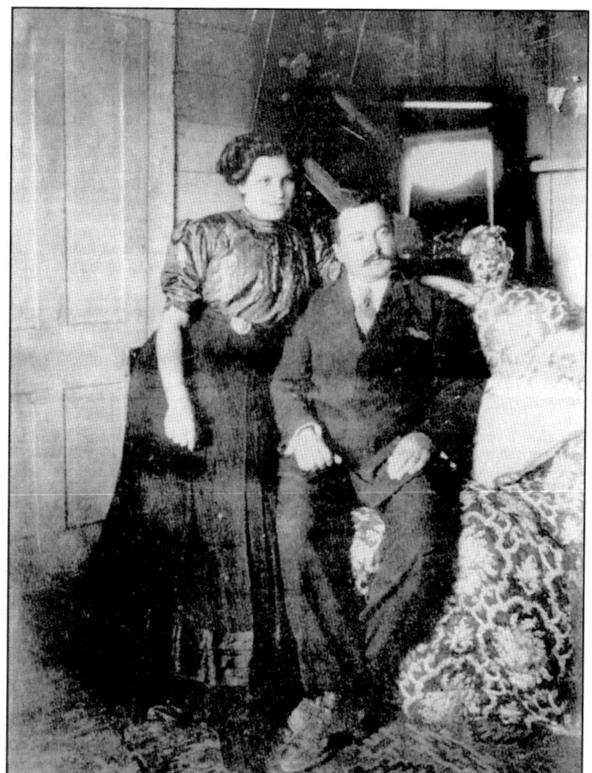

Ramon Ruenes and wife Ester Ramirez Ruenes owned the Juarez Drive-In, the Ruenes Theater on Robertson Street, the Juarez Indoor Theater, Port Isabel's Roxy Theater, and Harlingen's Azteca Theater, along with many others. Ramon Ruenes arrived from Asturias, Spain, in 1902. He and Ester hosted many of the Mexican and Spanish stars whose movies played in their theaters, and they maintained these friendships throughout their lives. (Courtesy Linda Lara Mata.)

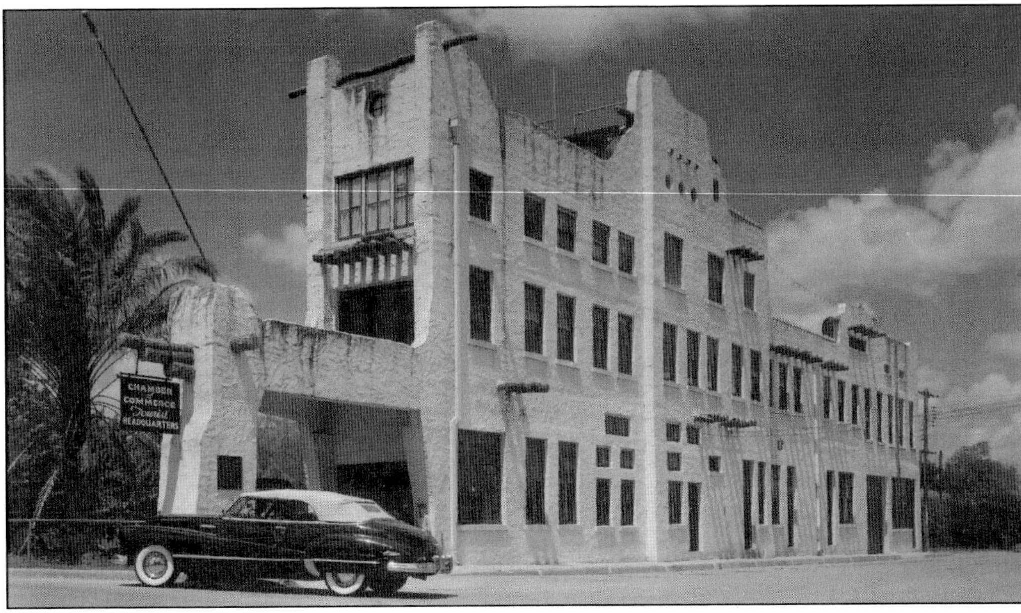

The Aztec Building, constructed by William B. Hinkley about 1925, once housed city offices prior to the chamber's occupancy. It served as one of two polling places, in the days when the railroad tracks divided the precincts. On the third floor, Markoleta Elstner (Epstein) ran a dance studio. The Bohemian Club held dances on the roof, and orchestras played under a huge shell. During World War II, the Aztec Building housed the USO club, and after the war, the Well Baby Clinic. Sobre Las Olas Mexican restaurant, pictured below, was located on the first floor of the Aztec Building and featured both an atrium and an aquarium. Its owners advertised it as "The Valley's Original Genuine Mexican Restaurant" and promised a meal "as good as it is different." Looking at the Aztec Building from across the resaca, passersby saw what resembled a huge ship on the water. (Courtesy Enriqueta L. Ramos.)

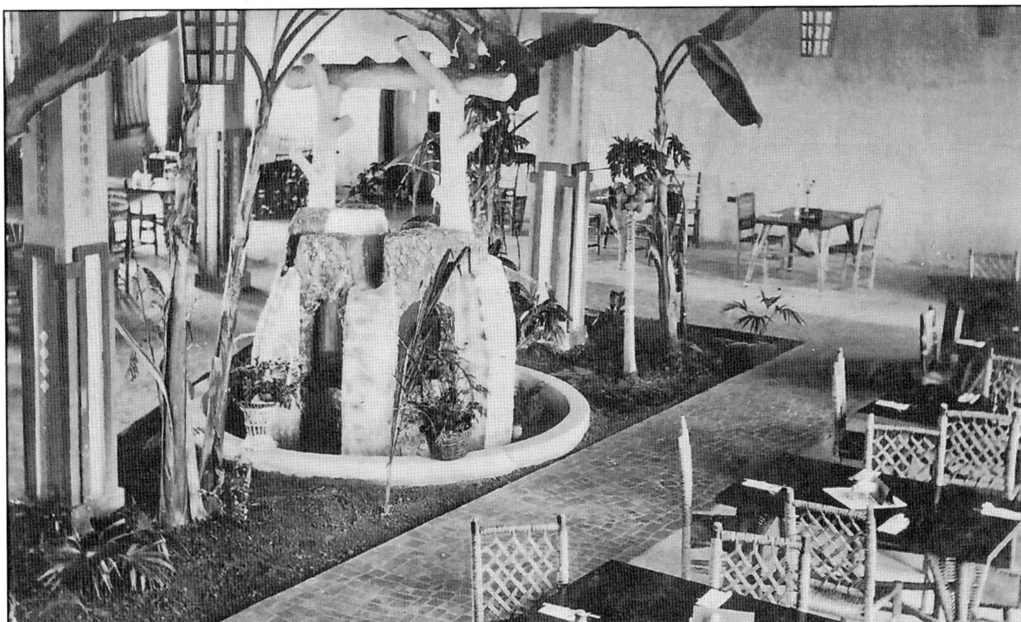

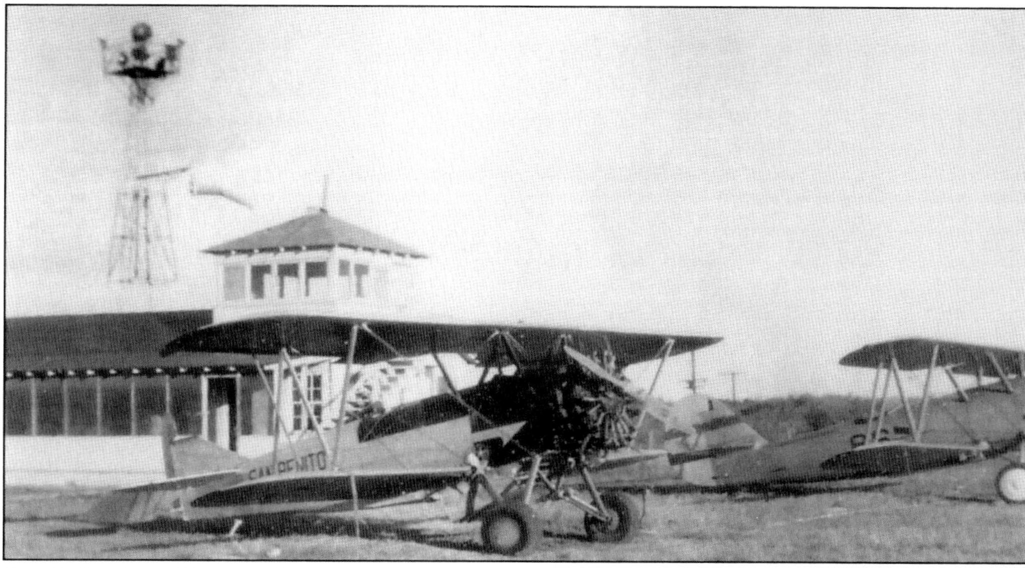

The dedication of the San Benito Airport was commemorated by a special postmark, dated November 11, 1930. The San Benito Airport progressed through several hands over the years: the city (which first purchased the land in 1930), the Civil Aeronautics Authorities, the Civil Air Patrol, the U.S. Navy, and finally privately owned flying services. In 1942, the Civil Air Patrol leased it for patrolling the coast and was cited as assisting the navy in eliminating the U-boat threat in the Gulf of Mexico. In 1943, the navy leased the airport and continued to patrol the coastal waters using a blimp manned by navy personnel. A concrete blimp mooring circle built there can still be seen on the property. In 1944, the city bought the administration building and erected the hanger. From 1944 to 2002, the airport served as a multifunction air facility. Following World War II, the airport was a busy transshipment point for the delivery of several aviation aircraft to Latin America. Under King Cruse and his brother John, Cruse Aviation operated San Benito Flying Service providing air-ambulance services to any point to and from the Valley. In 1951, Ken Medders Sr. purchased the existing buildings and leased the airport grounds for operating Sun Valley Air Services and Ken Medders Aircraft sales. The airport lease was returned to the city in 1978. (Courtesy Steve Cruse.)

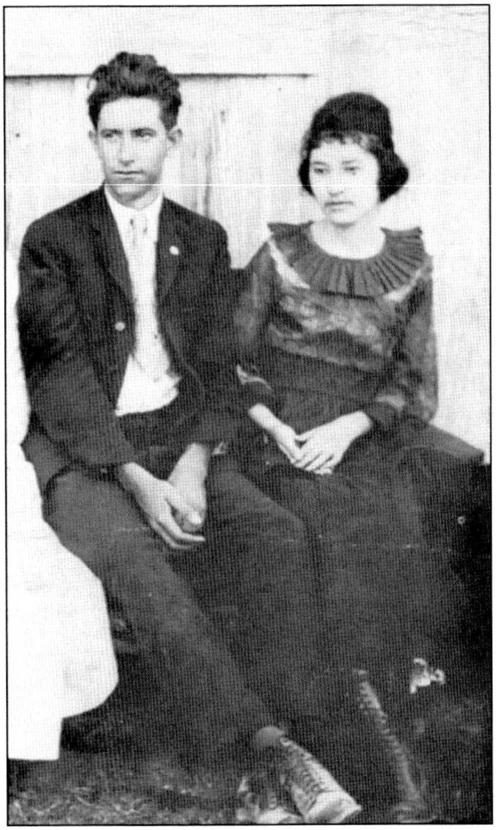

The broom factory at 600 South Austin Street was started by Miqueas and Rebecca Lopez in the 1920s. Born in Brownsville in 1898, Miqueas would travel in his 1924 pickup to Rio Grande City and buy broom supplies. His parents, Clemente and Severa Lopez, were founding members of the first Presbyterian congregation in town. Miqueas was a ruling elder at the Mexican Presbyterian Church and sold insurance after closing his broom business. Pictured here, in 1918, are Miqueas and his sister Alicia. (Courtesy Getsemani Presbyterian Church.)

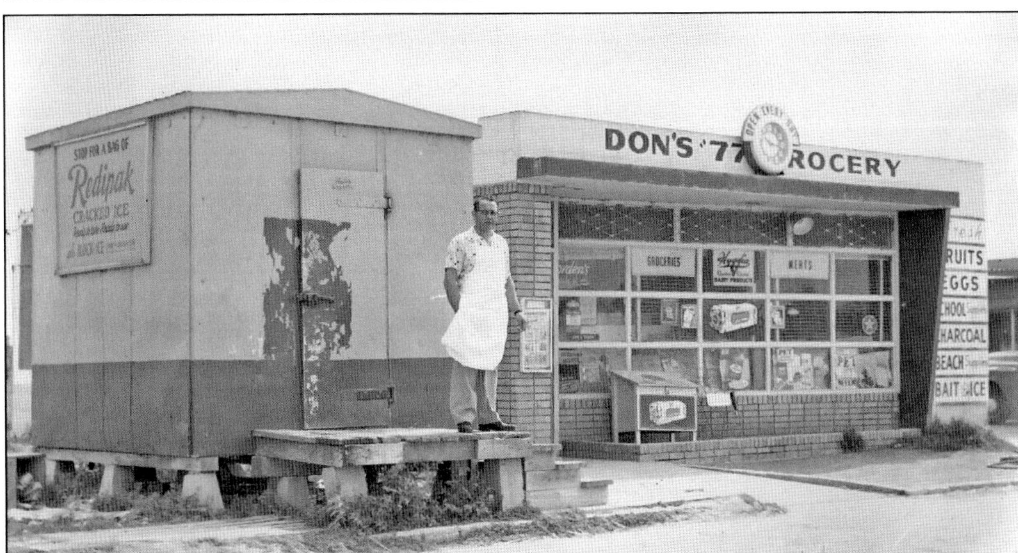

Don's 77 Grocery was built about the same time as Dolly Vinsant Memorial Hospital. Don Martin bought the grocery from Carl C. "C. C." Woods in 1950 and ran it for 15 years. The store was a landmark for many heading to South Padre Island since (before Wilson's supermarket moved to the highway) it was the only grocery store on that stretch of road where one could buy picnic supplies and ice. (Courtesy Don Martin.)

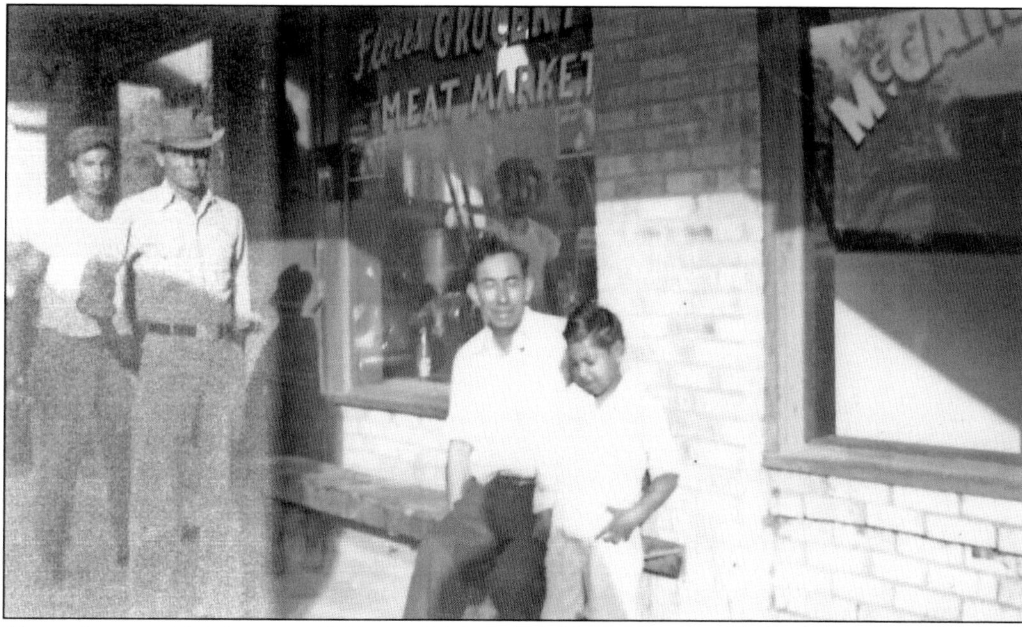

The only one of Melecio and Hilaria G. Flores' children who was born in San Benito was the youngest, Oscar, seen here with his father in front of the family's grocery store and meat market. (The three older children were born in Kingsville.) Customers were always giving Melecio antiques, possibly in barter. Later his son Hector donated these pieces to the museum in San Benito. (Courtesy Hector H. Flores.)

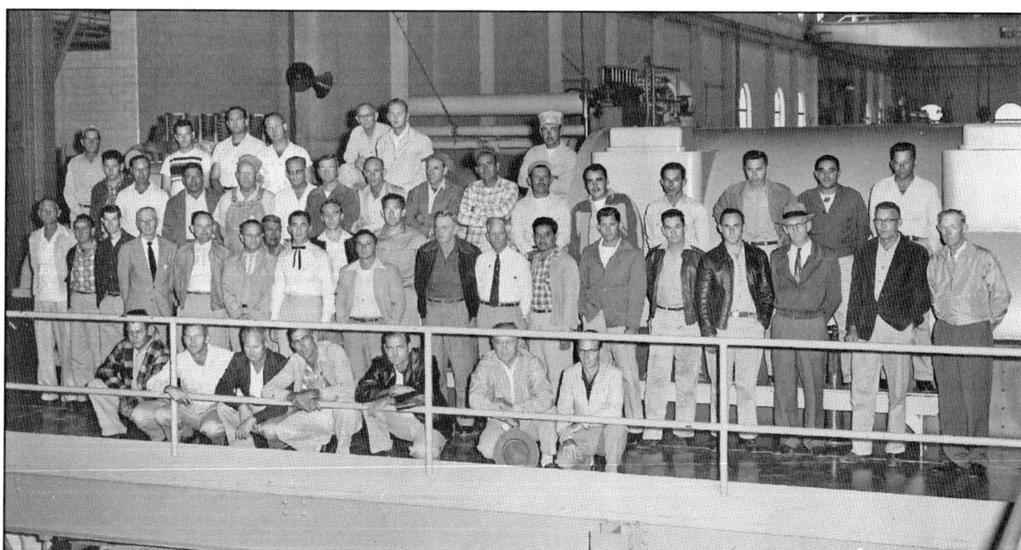

The sugar mill in San Benito was sold in the 1920s to Central Power and Light Company (CPL), and the wood-burning boilers were converted into natural gas power generators. One of the mechanics hired for the conversion was Alberto Atkinson, who continued working for CPL for 35 years. His son Ernie worked at the same plant for 15 years before his transfer to the Laredo plant, where he spent the next 26 years. In this 1951 photograph, Ernie is located second from right in the third row. Visible are the generators, and the very distinctive round windows of the sugar mill in the background. (Courtesy Ernie Atkinson.)

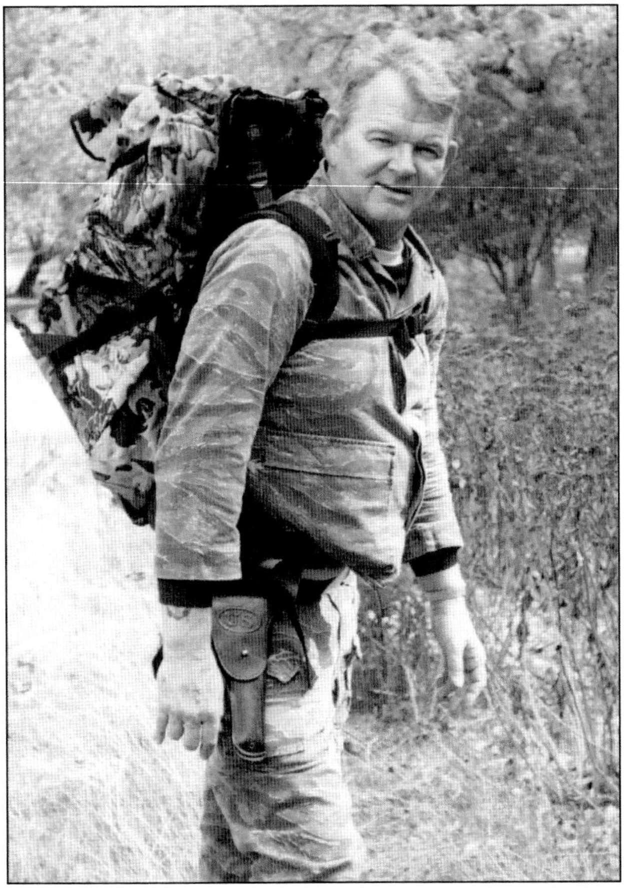

Author, illustrator, and San Benito native Charles M. Robinson III is a history expert and hunter. He has written more than 21 books that deal with the Old West, the Civil War, and the Conquest of Mexico. In 1993, he received the T. R. Fehrenbach Book Award. (Courtesy Charles M. Robinson, III.)

Originally started by two brothers, W. Scott and Alba Heywood, the San Benito Bank and Trust Company was chartered on December 17, 1908. The bank moved into this Spanish Colonial Revival building in 1911. During the bandit troubles of 1914, soldiers used the bank's balcony as a lookout post. In 1924, the San Benito Bank and Trust Company's deposits totaled $375,000; by 1956 they totaled $7.5 million. In 1962, the State Highway Department required the bank to remove the front of its building to allow for highway expansion. (Courtesy San Benito Historical Society.)

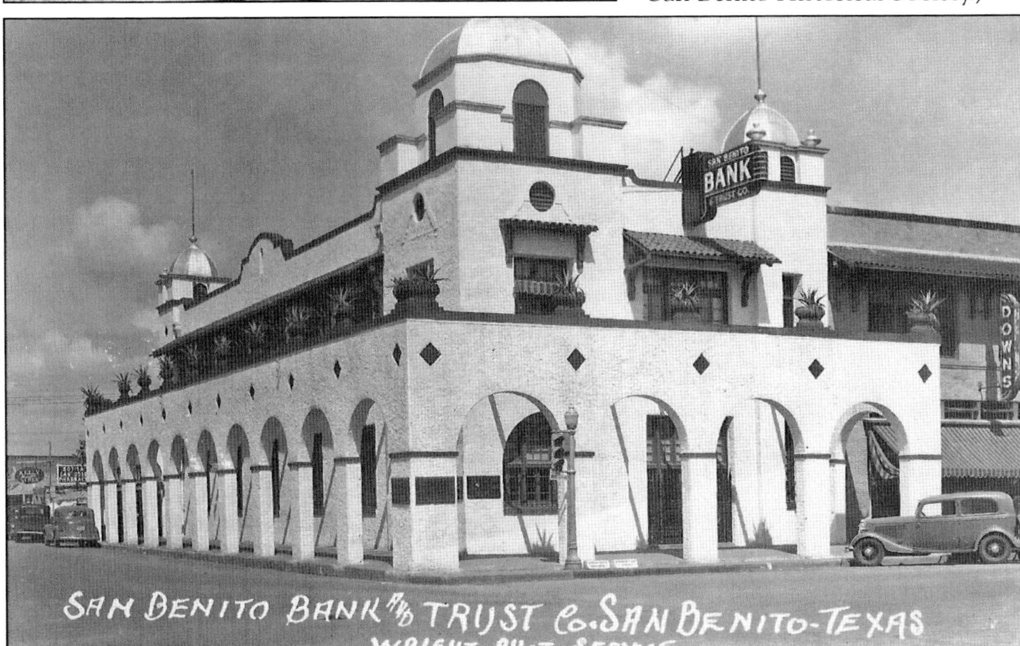

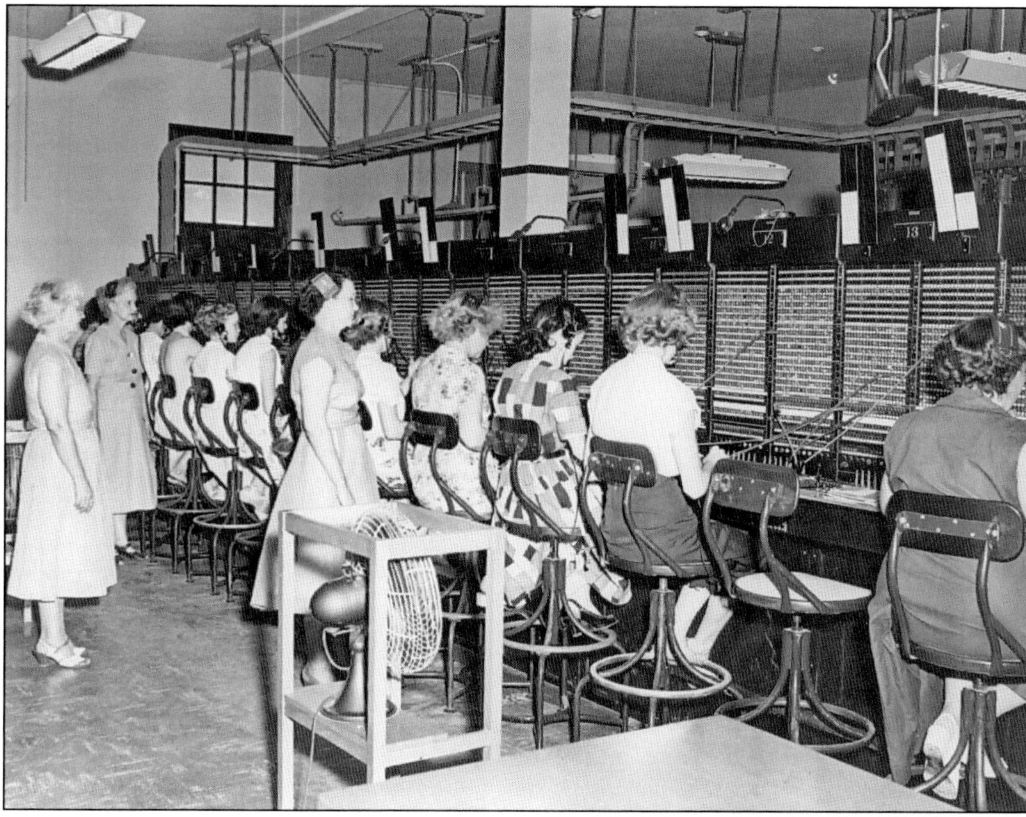

The telephone company originally operated on the second floor of the irrigation district building. Initially, just nine lines ran into town. At 291 North Reagan Street, 40 years later, thousands of phones meant many operators were needed to personally handle long-distance calls. Sue Corbello, seen here in the square print dress, worked as a telephone operator in the San Benito branch of Southwestern Bell Telephone. (Courtesy Sue Corbello Morgan.)

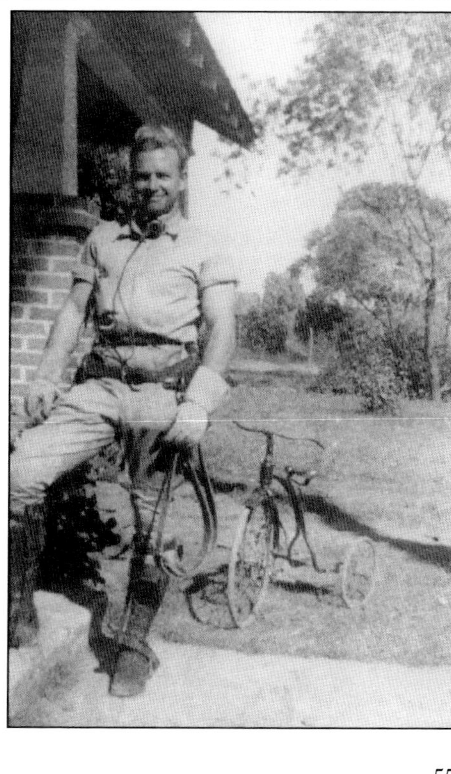

Telephone lineman Linard Gilbert works in 1945, heavily laden with a tool belt around his waist, headset around his neck, and telephone pole climbers attached to his calves. Linard and his wife, Mary Ann Gamble Gilbert (an operator), both worked for Bell Telephone Company for 42 years. (Courtesy Suzanne Gilbert.)

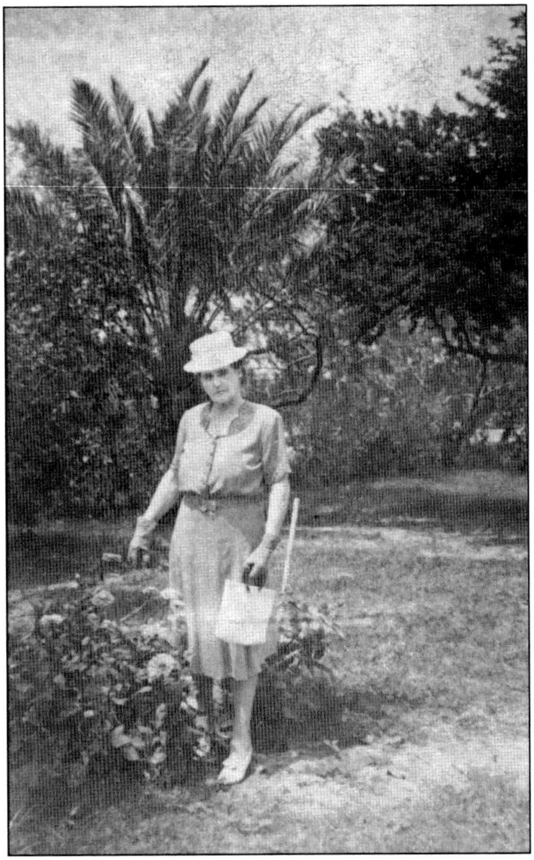

Well known for her gardening knowledge and beautiful plants, Ruth C. Riley Hughes turned her gardens into a professional nursery in the late 1940s. The Bouganvilla House, which operated until about 1970, sold all sorts of plants, shrubs, cut flowers, and potted plants. The nursery was located at what is now 1910 North Sam Houston Boulevard. Ruth was pleased to provide flowers every Sunday for the Baptist church worship services. (Courtesy Laurel Sarra.)

San Benito–born actor Ray Stewart (second from right) graduated from Texas Southmost College and the University of Texas and served two years in the army before moving to New York City to study at the famed Neighborhood Playhouse School of the Theatre. After more than 25 years of acting for film and television (including a recurring role on the Emmy-winning *Barney Miller*), Stewart retired to his native San Benito, where he remains active in local theater. Shown here in a publicity still from Mel Brooks's 1976 film *Silent Movie* are Marty Feldman, an unidentified extra, Bernadette Peters, Mel Brooks, Sid Ceasar, Ray Stewart, and Dom DeLuise. (Courtesy Ray Stewart.)

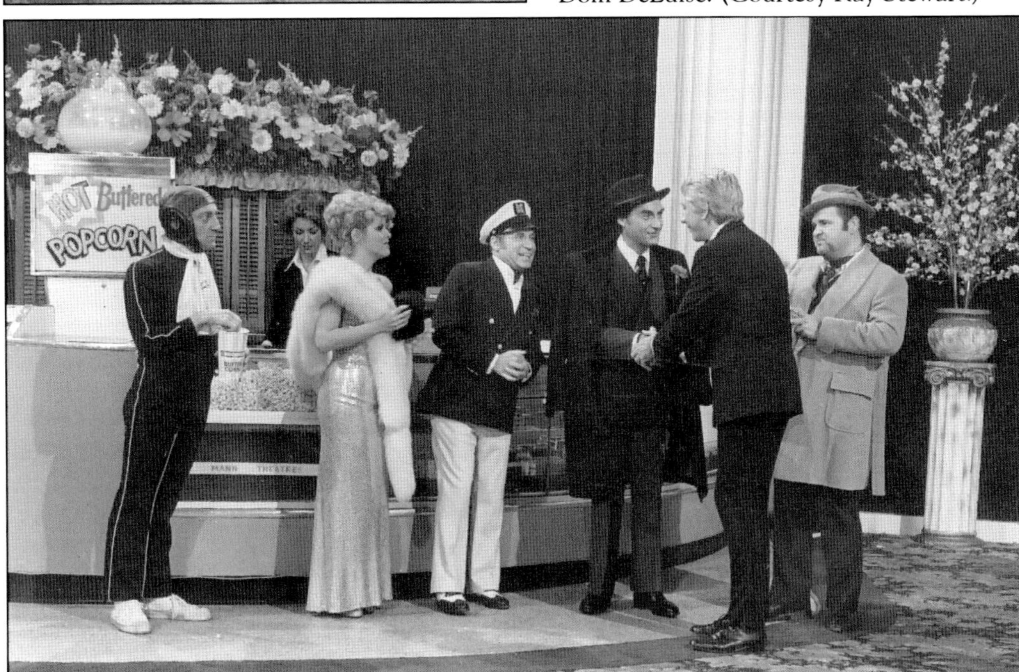

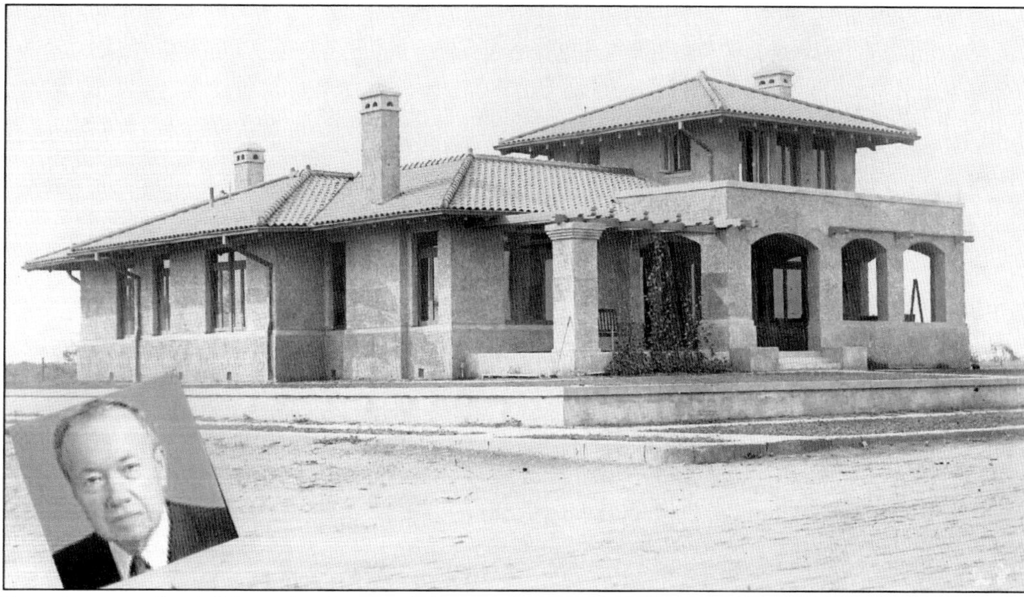

Born January 12, 1925, in the Sam Robertson House to a pioneer South Texas family, Theodore Reed "T. R." Fehrenbach is best known as the author of 18 nonfiction titles, mainly on historical subjects. His books have been printed in 10 languages. Most of them have been either book club selections or used as references in colleges and universities. "New people came, old people remained in a special border ambience perhaps found no where else in the world. I know; I was born there," said T.R. Fehrenbach in *A Shared Experience* by the Texas Historical Commission. (Courtesy San Benito Historical Society.)

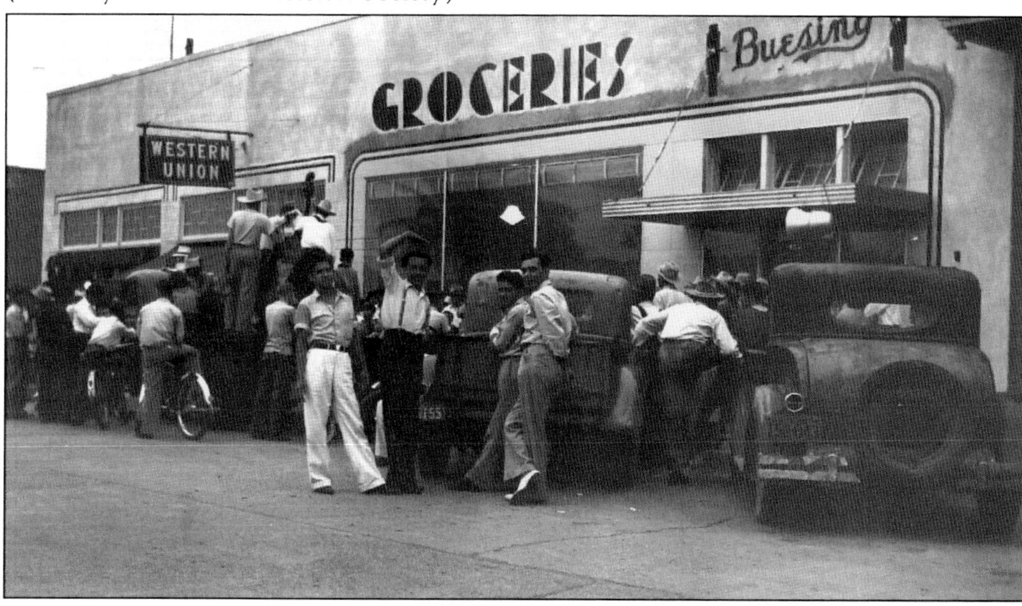

Located at 181 West Rowson, Buesing's New Delta Food Store held its grand opening on July 18, 1936, featuring live music. After 10 years at other locations, Herbert Buesing moved into a Rowson Street location which had formerly housed the post office. Buesing had faith in San Benito, and eventually he owned the entire quarter block, including the Acme Hotel. Subsequent grocery stores in this location included Stegall's and Joe and Oscar's. (Courtesy Tootie Madden.)

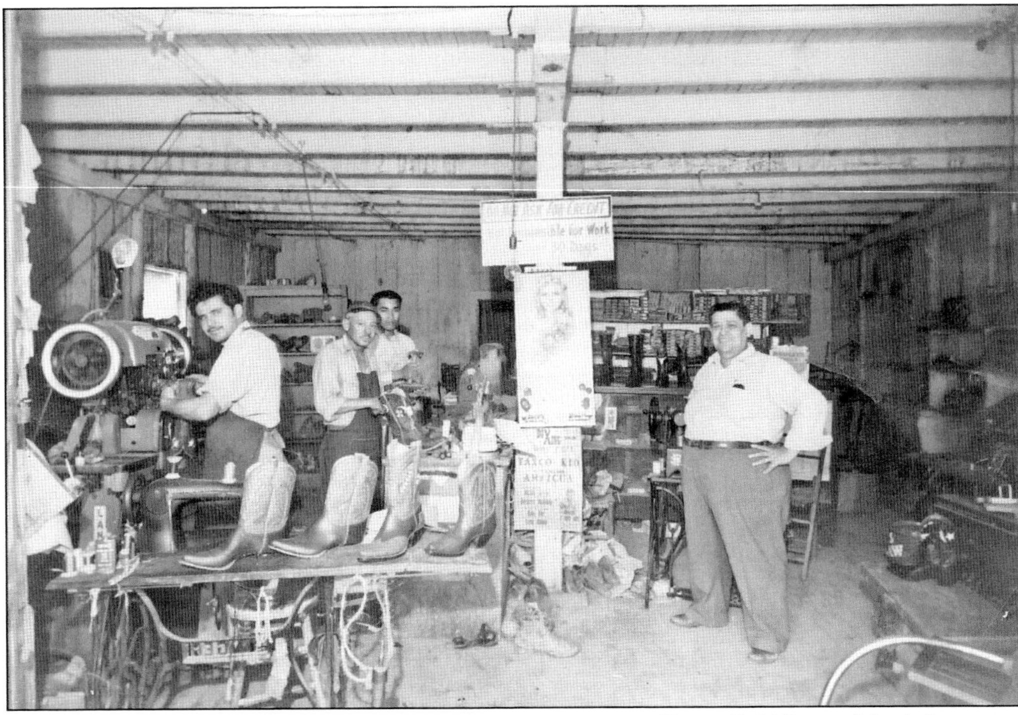

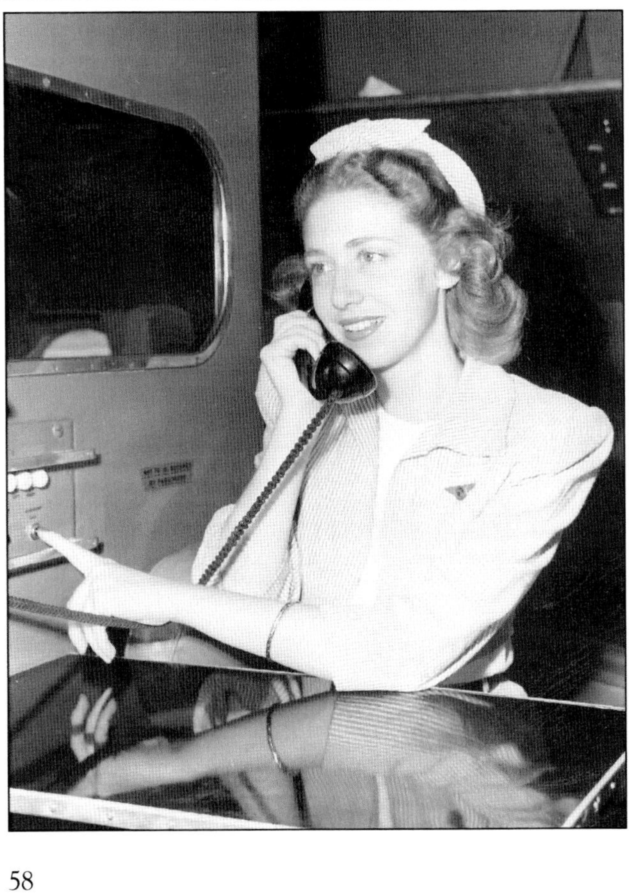

Eliseo S. Villarreal (right) repaired shoes and made custom boots for a living. La Moderna Boot and Shoe Shop, 344 West Robertson Street, was located one block east of the resaca. Eliseo and Maria Montalvo Villarreal ran the shop from 1937 until Eliseo's death in 1963, after which their son Eliseo Jr. dropped out of high school to help his mother run the business through 1966. In addition to their son Eliseo Jr, the Villarreals had two daughters, Mary Lou and Lisa. (Photograph Eliseo "Cheto" Villarreal.)

After she graduated from University of Texas, Austin, San Benito's Betty Bohner Cashin became an airline hostess for Braniff. She also trained both U.S. and South American hostesses and stewards, and was featured in Braniff public relations events and brochures. She later worked for 20 years for San Benito schools. (Photograph Betty Cashin.)

Tomas and Josefina Villarreal Cantu's La Colonial Grocery Store was at one time the largest wholesaler in San Benito, supplying goods to other businesses. The two-storied brick structure was located at the corner of Hidalgo and Morelos Streets. The second story was used for social events and as a meeting hall for fraternal organizations including Woodmen of the World. (Courtesy Simon Cantu.)

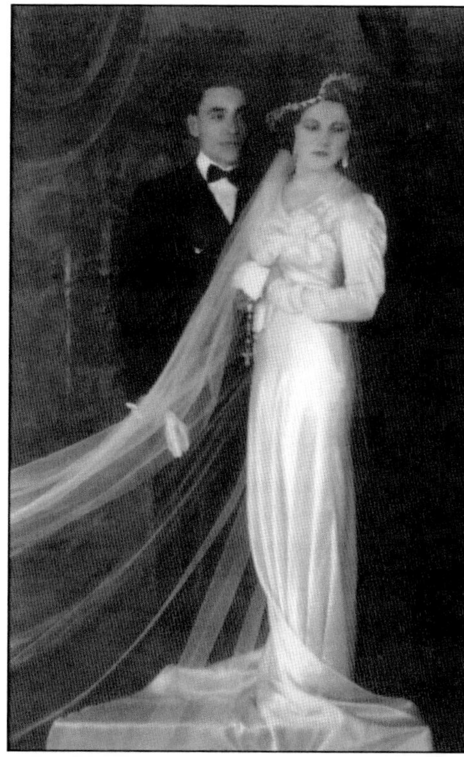

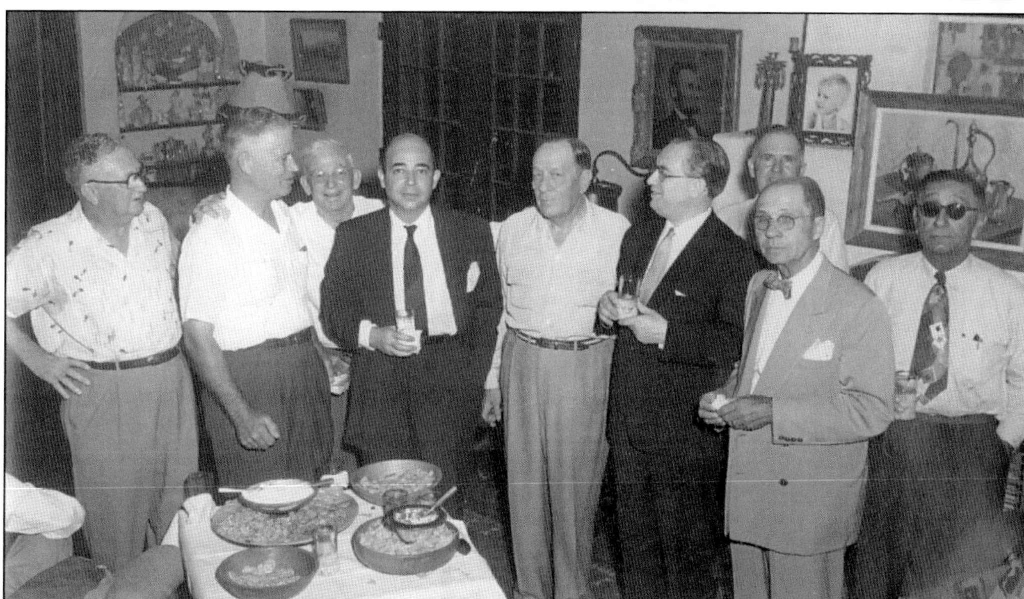

In this 1952 photograph, the movers and shakers instrumental in getting the Queen Isabella Causeway built between the mainland and South Padre Island celebrate at Stanley and Rae Dodds' home. They are, from left to right, Andy Bowie, Bill Hervey, Stanley Dodds, Spanish Embassy press representative Felipe Fernandez Armesto, John Jones, secretary to the Spanish ambassador Florencio Fiscowich de Fries, Jesse Welch, Walter W. Housewright, and Judge Joe E. Gerusa. (Courtesy Mike Hervey.)

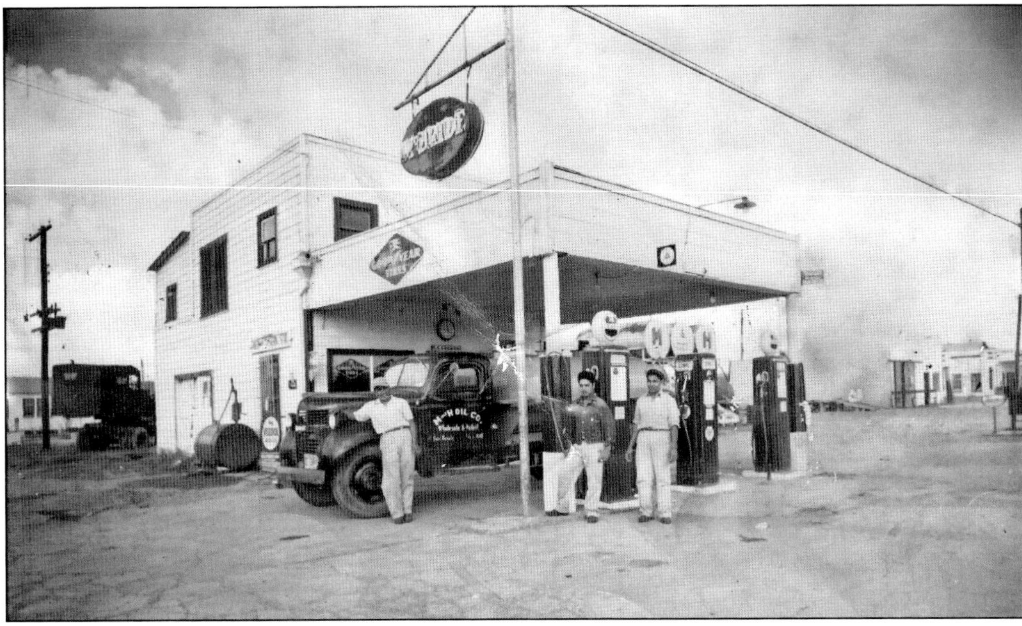

In 1960, after starting his gas station business at the corner of Combes and Virginia Streets, Bennie Guadiana (shown here leaning on the truck) moved his business to a new station he had built at the corner of Corral and Robertson Streets, on the former site of El Ranchero Pool Hall. The other men are Chicho Puentes (left) and Tomas Alvarez. Note the name "B. G. Guadiana" beneath the clock. (Courtesy David Esquivel.)

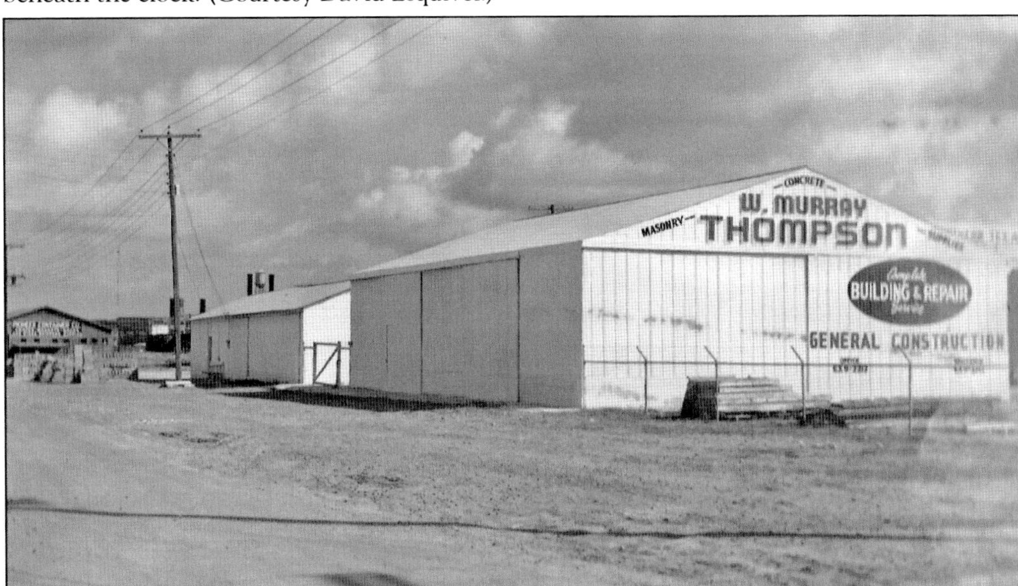

W. Murray Thompson Construction, located alongside the railroad tracks on La Palma Street, was established in 1946. Murray Thompson Sr., following in his father's footsteps, started by making concrete block, which led to foundation work and eventually to general contracting. Murray and Marian Thompson had four children: Billie Joe, Nancy, Murray Jr., and Nora. Today third generation contractor Murray Jr. continues this business, predominantly in commercial construction. (Photograph Murray Thompson.)

Four

How We Made Families
Love, Marriage, and Baby Carriage

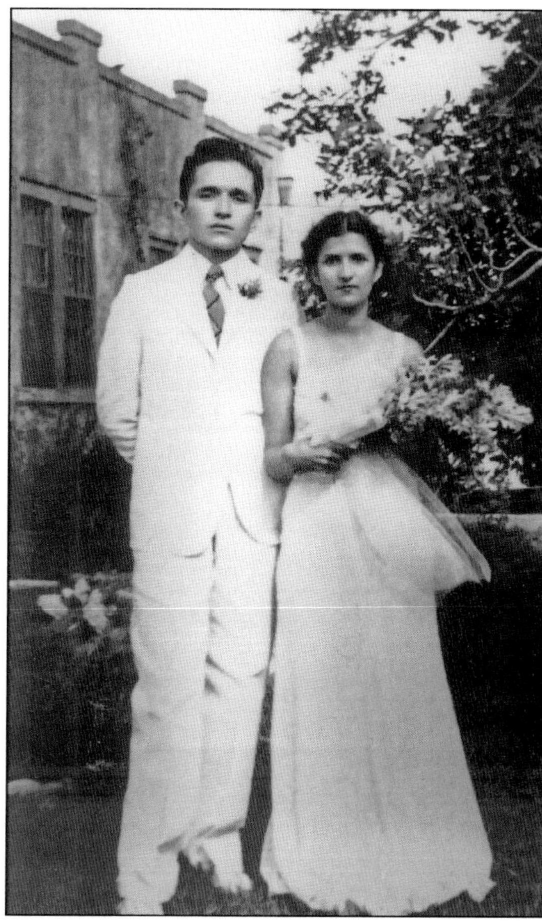

This 1935 photograph shows bridesmaid Herminia Esparza and her escort Rafael Cantu at the wedding of a friend; later, Esparza married her escort. The couple owned Cantu's Grocery at 227 South Austin Street. Rafael also worked at Whalen's Furniture from 1961 until his retirement in 1980. The Cantus raised five children: Rafael Jr., Ester, Berta, Carlos, and Dolores. (Courtesy Ralph Cantu.)

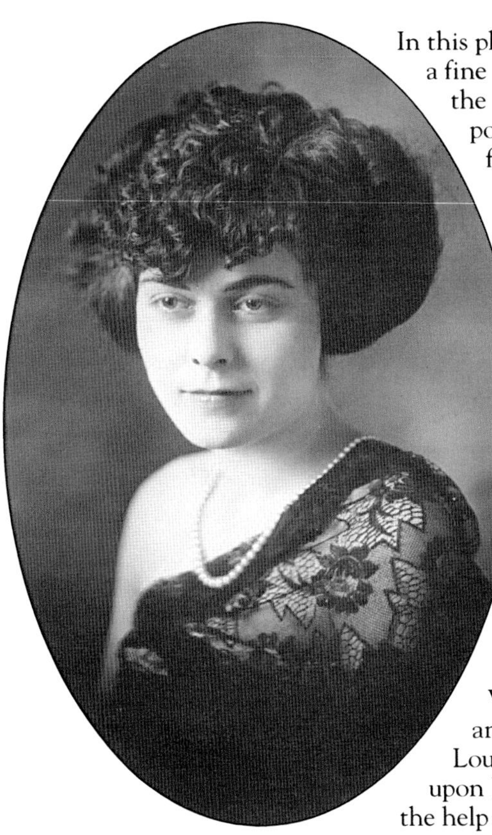

In this photograph, Eugenia Estelle Harvey provides a fine example of the hair and fashion styles in the early 1920s, before the bobbed look became popular. Eugenia Harvey was the youngest of five children born to John Younger and Bird Wood Harvey. While her brothers Harry and Cecil and sisters Lillian and Florene had no children, "Genie" and her husband, Herbert Buesing, had two daughters, "Jack" and Jean. (Courtesy Tootie Madden.)

The Thomas Vernon "T. V." Woolam family moved here from Stephenville, Texas, in 1910, and started the T. V. Woolam Gin and Produce Company on Stenger Street. In 1948 they moved the business to La Palma Street, on what today is the site of Bobby Morrow Stadium. From left to right, the Woolams are (first row) Yvonne, Ethel, Pete, and Eunice; (second row) Frankie Lee, Bud, and Louise. Pete ran the gin after his father died, and upon Pete's death, his sister Eunice managed it with the help of Pete's son, Tommy. (Courtesy Ethel Broman.)

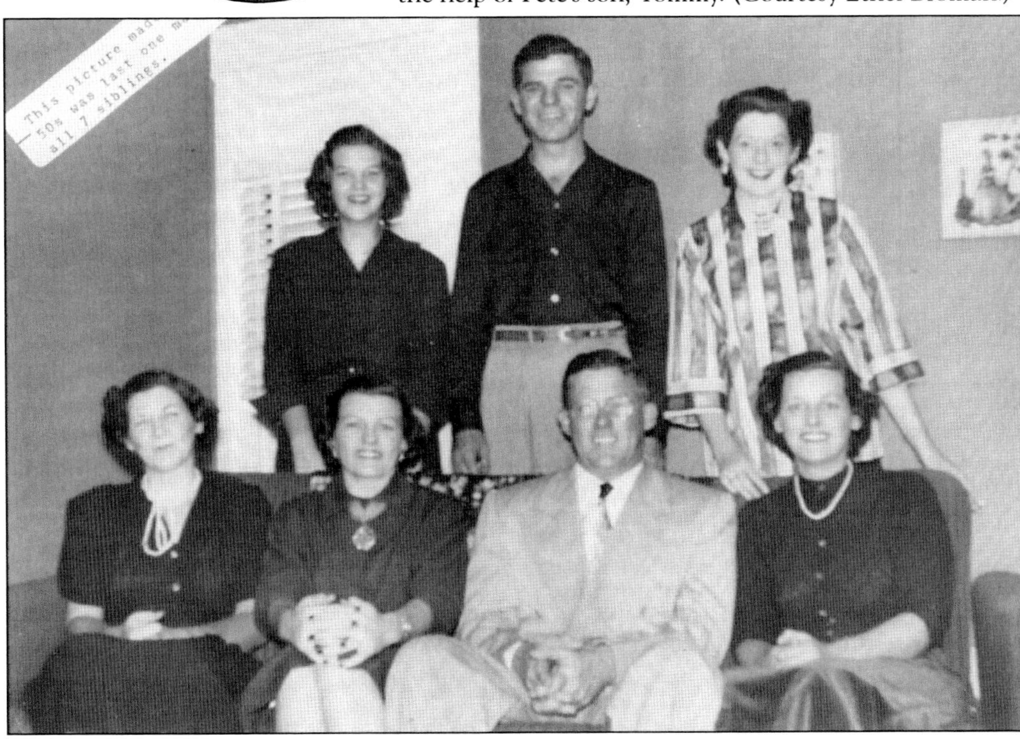

In 1919, these two unmarried young women, dressed in the high-buttoned boots, petticoats, and long-sleeved dresses of the time, were best friends. Luz Leal (left) became the stepmother of popular attorney Diego Leal. Teodora Davila married Enrique Moreno and was the mother of Celia, Enrique, and Mateo Moreno, and Estela Davila. In the photograph below, Celia Moreno poses for a photograph to send to her fiancé, Raul Longoria, then on active duty in World War II. Moreno stands in front of the public fountain, which is a well known city landmark, downtown. According to legend, Pancho Villa once led his horse to this fountain for a drink. In 1910, Indiana-born Quaker real estate developer Charles L. Jessup and his wife, Hannah, raised the money for a community fountain in San Benito. Made of cast iron, the fountain provided water for both humans and animals; a little bowl at the base provided drinks for dogs, the large trough was for horses, and between these was a tap for humans. Water was cut off to the fountain in the 1920s. (Courtesy Sandra Tumberlinson and Dolores Ramirez.)

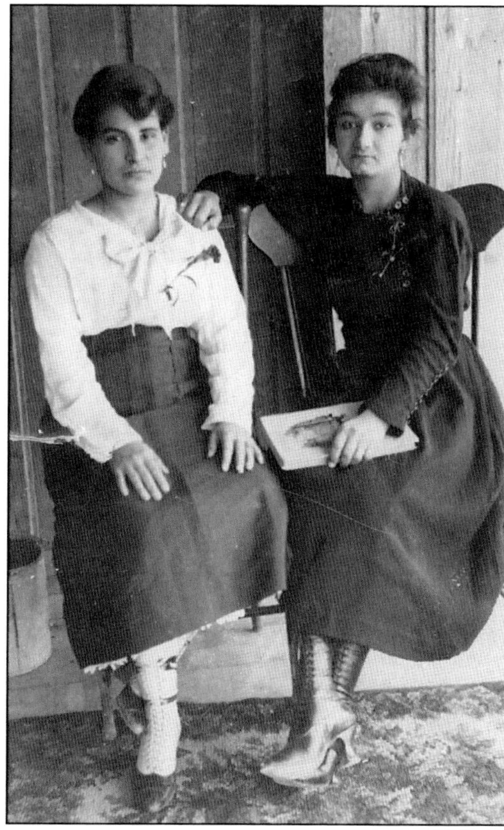

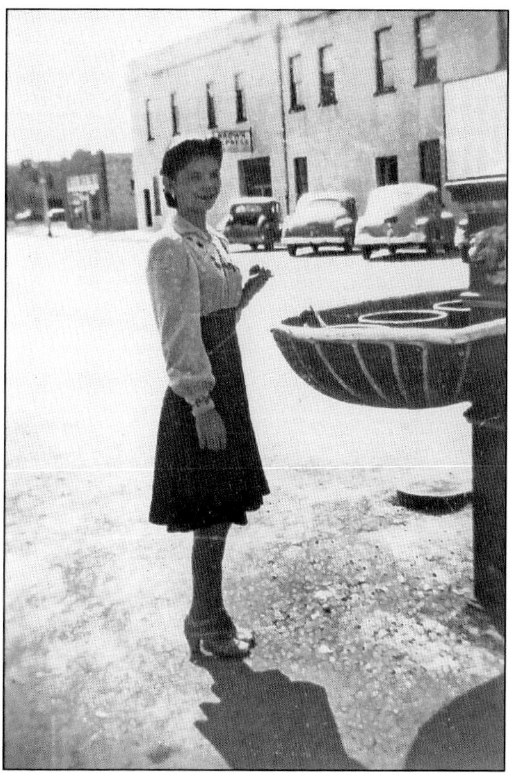

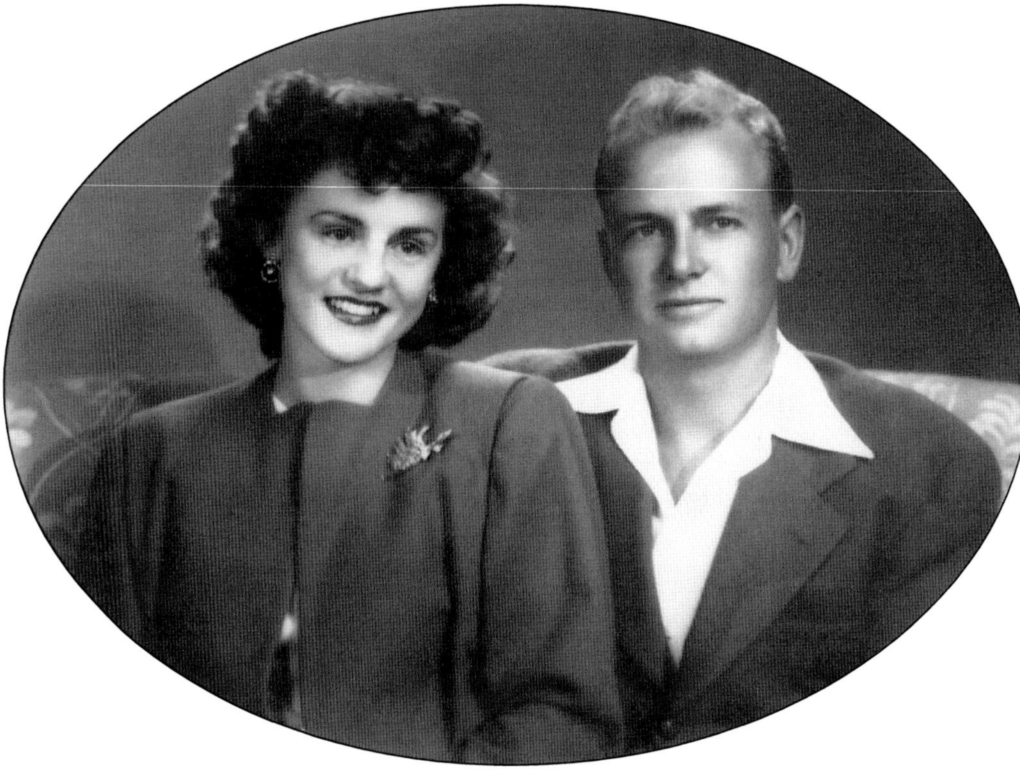

Mary Ann Gamble and Linard C. Gilbert are pictured here in 1945, shortly after announcing their engagement. Mary Ann's hairstyle is typical for the 1940s, and Linard wears his collar out, as men did then. Both Linard and Mary Ann worked for Bell Telephone and made their home at 860 North Travis Street. Their children were Monte and Suzanne. (Courtesy Suzanne Gilbert.)

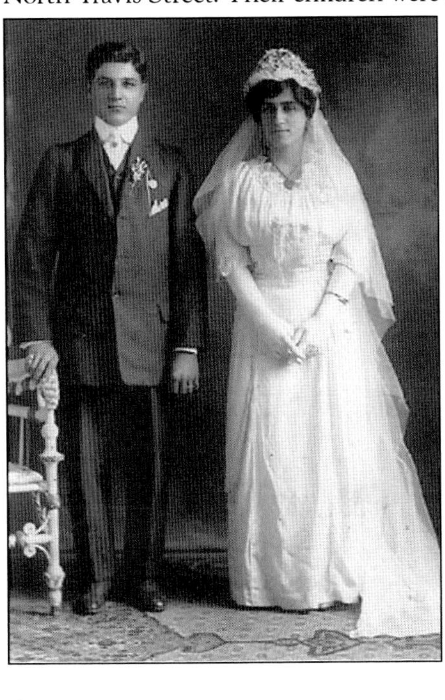

The wedding of Jack and Foutine Ayoub Ogdee, pictured here, was held in 1916. Born in 1896 in Tripoli, Lebanon, Jack Michael Ogdee worked with his father until he was 16. Two years later, he married Foutine Ayoub. Jack first visited the valley in 1917, and after World War I, they made their home here. The Ogdee's first child was Helen (named for her grandmother), then George (named for his grandfather), and Edward. (Courtesy Jack Emil Ayoub.)

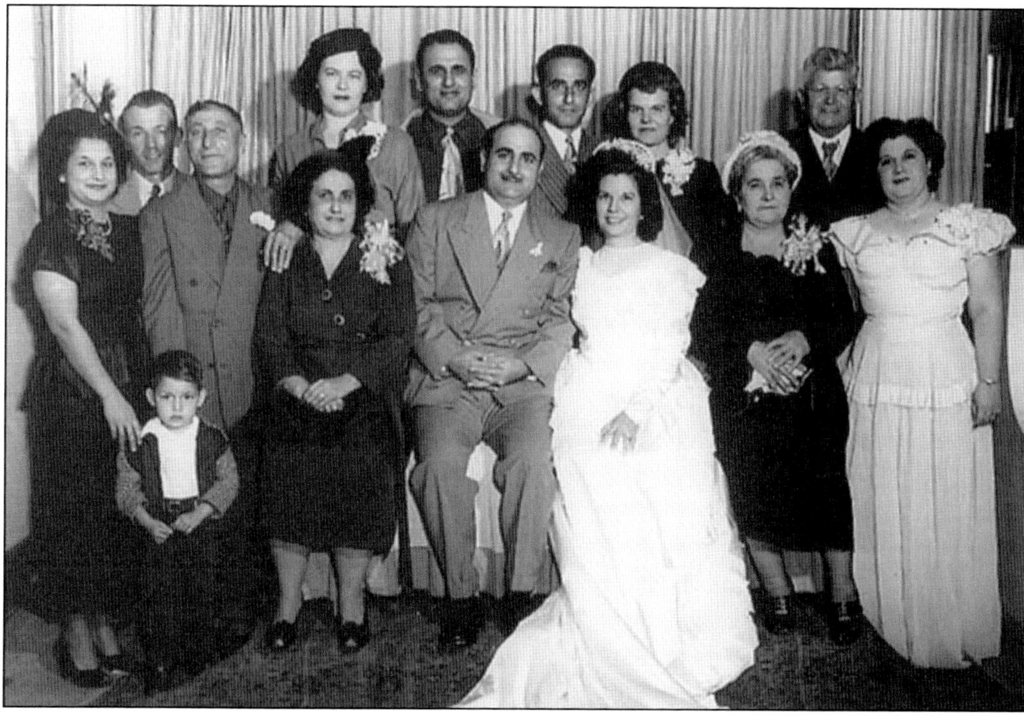

The marriage of Jack Ayoub and Virginia Zepeda united two prominent local families. Jack's family was of Lebanese ancestry; Virginia's mother, Maria Olivares, had descended from the recipient of a Spanish land grant. Shown here at the couple's 1950 wedding are, from left to right, (first row) Pauline Ayoub Fry, Wilson Fry, Ben Fry (son), Charlie and Mary Ayoub Moses, Jack and Virginia, Maria Zepeda, and her daughter Dora Zepeda; (second row) Alma and George Ayoub, Dave and Cleo Ayoub, and Damaso Zepeda. (Courtesy Jack Emil Ayoub.)

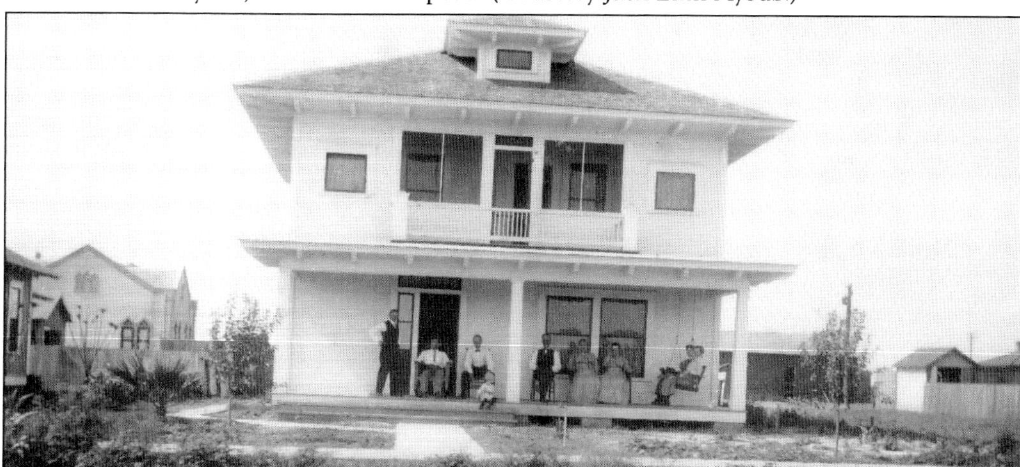

Albanus Clemens Purvis (1850–1919) came from Ohio to improve his health. He was the town's first Justice of the Peace, a realtor, and a farmer. His daughter, Kate, who married Scott Brown, became the town's first teacher in 1907. His daughter Emma married Henry E. Agar and was the town's first female postmaster in 1911. Albanus built this house at 441 North Reagan Street in 1911. The sleeping porch on the second story was used for hot South Texas nights. The house was awarded a Texas Historical Marker in 1974. (Courtesy Ernie Agar.)

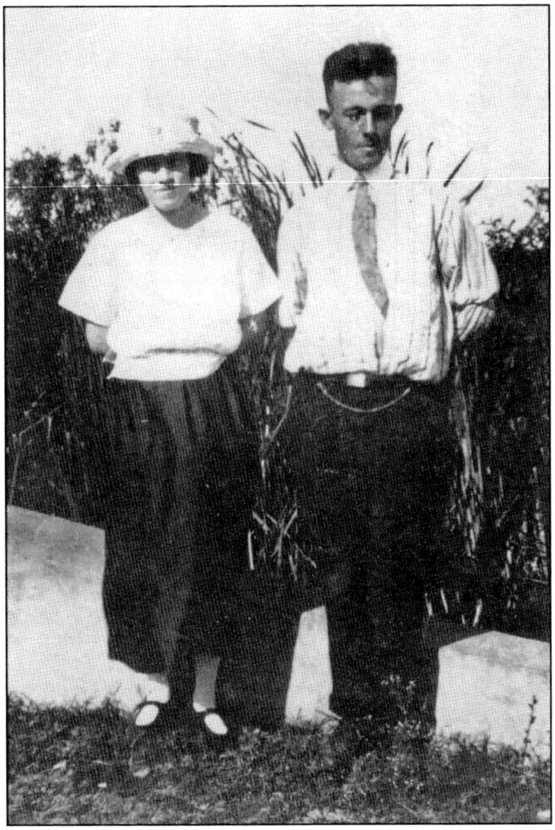

George W. Gamble and Grace McSpadden Gamble came from Burnet County in 1922 and became prominent area farmers. They had two daughters, Mary Ann and Virginia. George was vice-president of the San Benito Gin Association, a member of the Odd Fellows Club and Elks Lodge, chairman of the Cameron County Agricultural Association and the Community Farm Committee, and precinct chair for the Cameron County Democratic convention. Gamble Road, off Pennsylvania Avenue, was named after George and Grace. (Courtesy Suzanne Gilbert.)

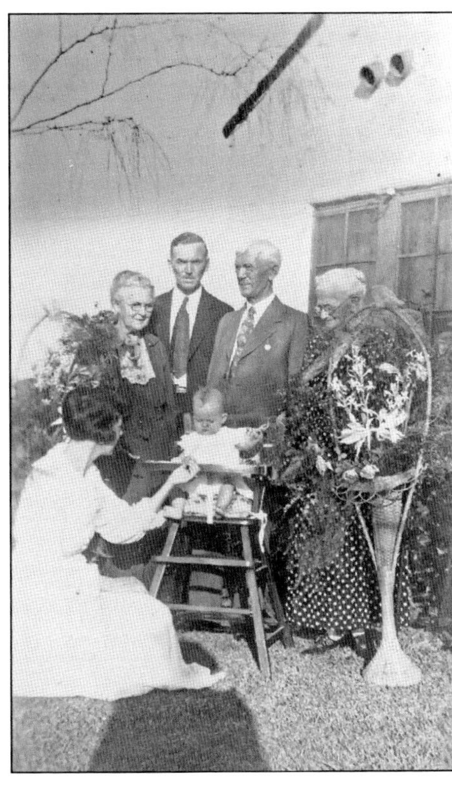

Emigrating from Scotland in 1904, John and Elizabeth Caldwell Bowie came to San Benito in 1915 with seven of their ten children: Jim, Dave, John, Bob, Alec, Andy, and Charlie. The Bowies were actively involved in many aspects of the town and the surrounding county. Shown here celebrating the christening of John and Elizabeth's granddaughter Patricia Lorraine Bowie are John and Elizabeth, with Patricia's parents Charlie and Leona Bowie. (Courtesy Pat Davis.)

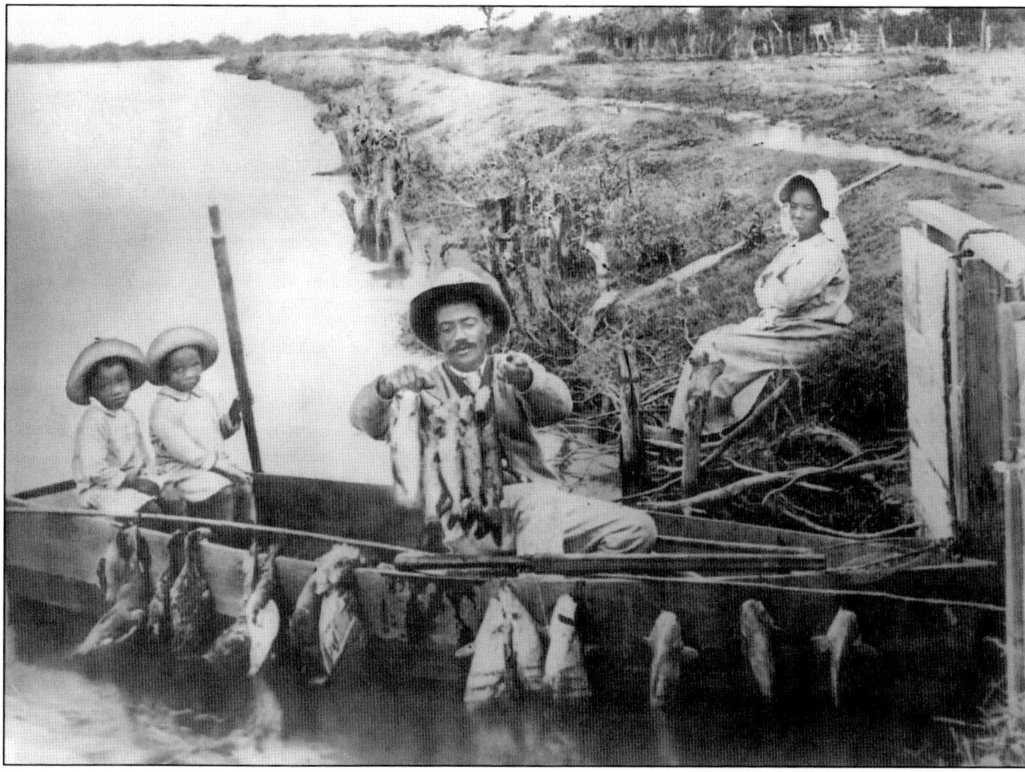

In 1908, Jean Marie "Joe" Callandret and wife Fannie arrived in San Benito from Louisiana. Jean was a farmer and owned a large amount of land in the El Jardin neighborhood where his granddaughters still live today. In an era when African American children couldn't attend school with whites, Fannie donated land to the school district so that local African American children could receive an education. The Callandrets had six children: Bertha, Grace, Arthur, Daniel, Ben, and John. Joe and his family often fished in the resaca as in this 1910 photograph. (Courtesy San Benito Historical Society.)

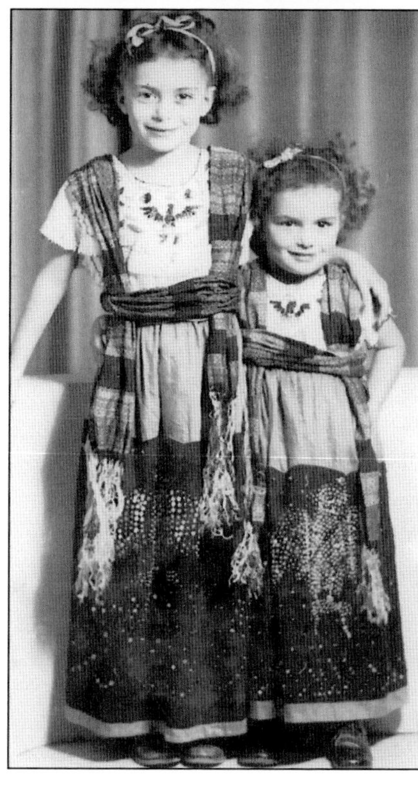

Jeanne and Betty Doan pose for the camera in the mid-1940s, all dolled-up in Mexican costumes for the Charro Days celebration. One-hundred-and-ten years ago, businessmen from Matamoros, Mexico, and Brownsville, Texas, got together to celebrate their businesses and friendship. Unfortunately, when the Texas Republic fought for independence from Mexico, the commemoration ended until 1937 when it was rekindled; it still continues today. (Courtesy Jeanette Doan Horton.)

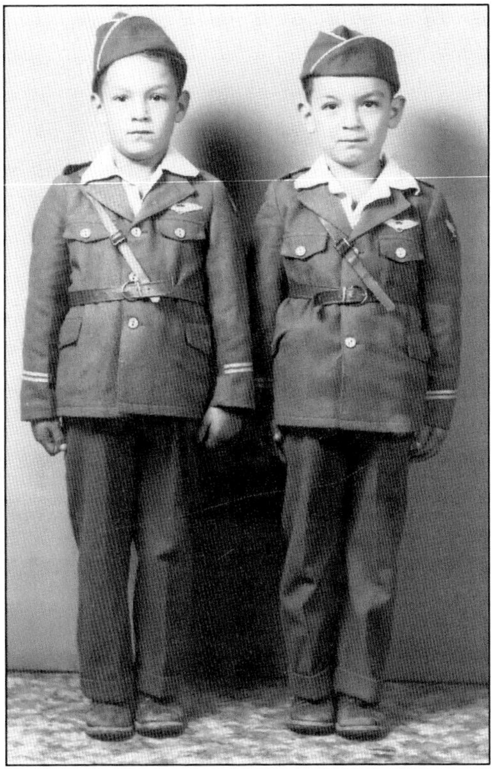

It was 1941 and Pedro Jr. and Marco Antonio Lara were not twins, but their parents, Pedro and Consuelo Davila Lara, frequently dressed them alike for holidays and celebrations, especially during World War II. The Laras owned a bakery, and every year, they'd take a picture of the boys holding a big cake between them. (Courtesy Sandra Tumberlinson.)

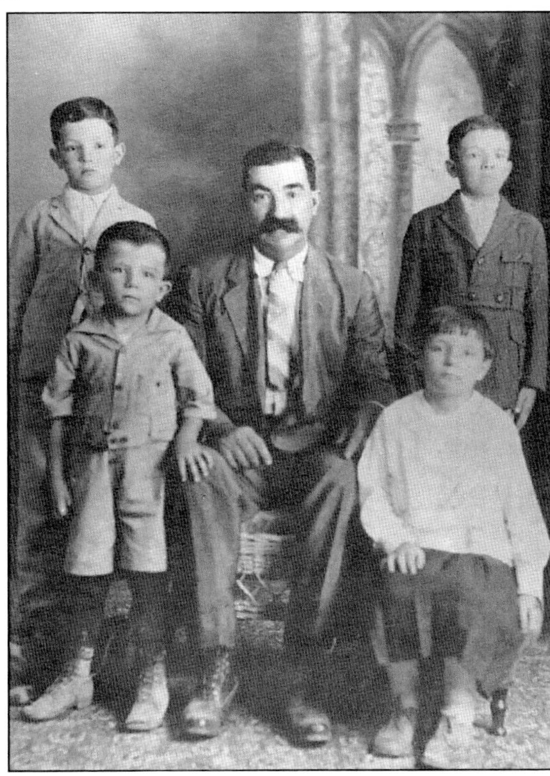

Carlos Zepeda's father, Pedro, was the first Zepeda to come to the United States in 1859, as a soldier with Mexican general Francisco Naranjo. With money made from his knowledge of curing meat, Pedro bought 1,000 acres of land on the San Pedro de Carricitos land grant. Carlos, born in 1882 at La Encantada, Texas, married Olivia Esparza, the daughter of Antonio and Hilaria Reyes Esparza. They had four children, and this picture shows the children with their father. Pictured are from left to right Edward, Gilberto, Carlos, Maria Luisa, and Pedro Zepeda. (Courtesy Clara W. Zepeda.)

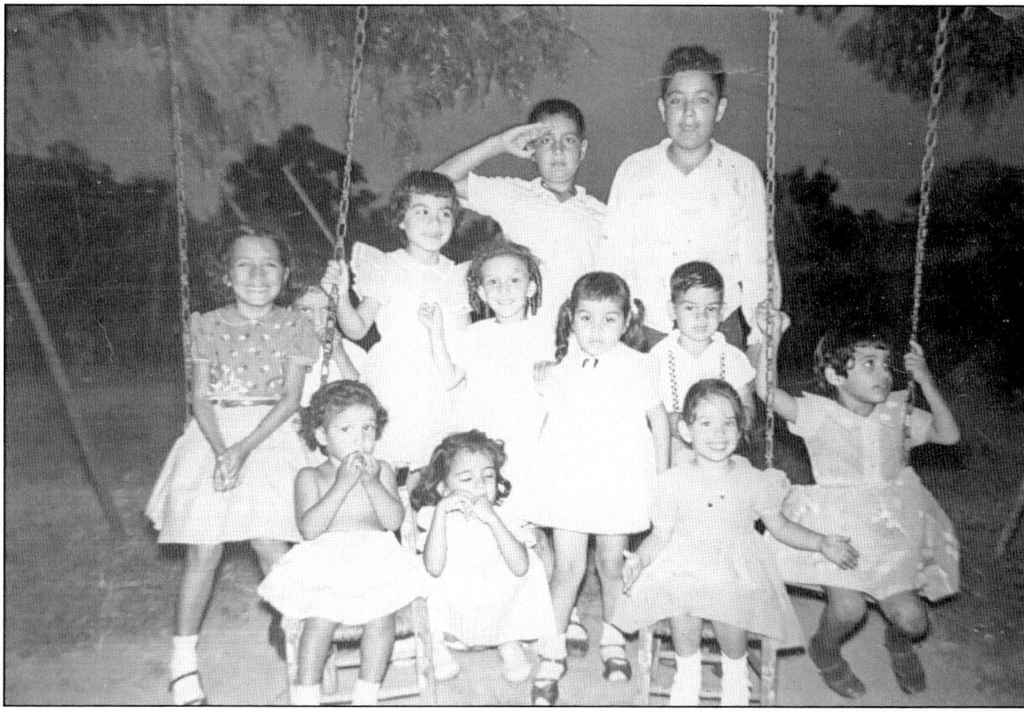

This 1956 children's party brought many families together. Seen here in the left swing is Norma Cantu. Hanky Moreno peeks over her shoulder. Sitting in the first row are Lily Moreno, Dalilah Moreno, and Sandra Longoria, and on the right swing is Anna Celina Ramirez. In the second row, holding the left swing is Oralia Ramirez, and standing to her right are Rita Moreno, Nora Belinda Ramirez, and Mateo Moreno. Saluting in the third row is Luis Cantu. To his right stands his older brother, Bobby Cantu. (Courtesy Sylvia Lee Moreno Garcia.)

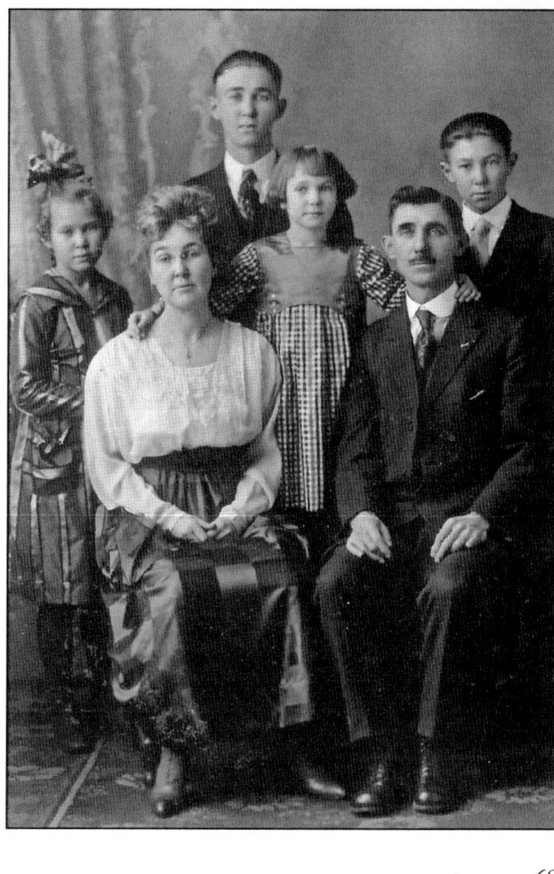

Dr. Merle Casey and wife Ella, with children Byrdine, Lyle, Norma, and James, came to town from Wisconsin about 1917. Their son, Dr. James D. Casey, married Fannie Housel, daughter of Frank and Janet Housel. He served as a physician in the navy during World War II, and afterwards, opened his offices above Collins Insurance. A few years later, he built the Casey Clinic on Business 77, adjacent to his home on North Shore Drive. The James Caseys had two daughters, Patricia and Connye. (Courtesy Connye Busa.)

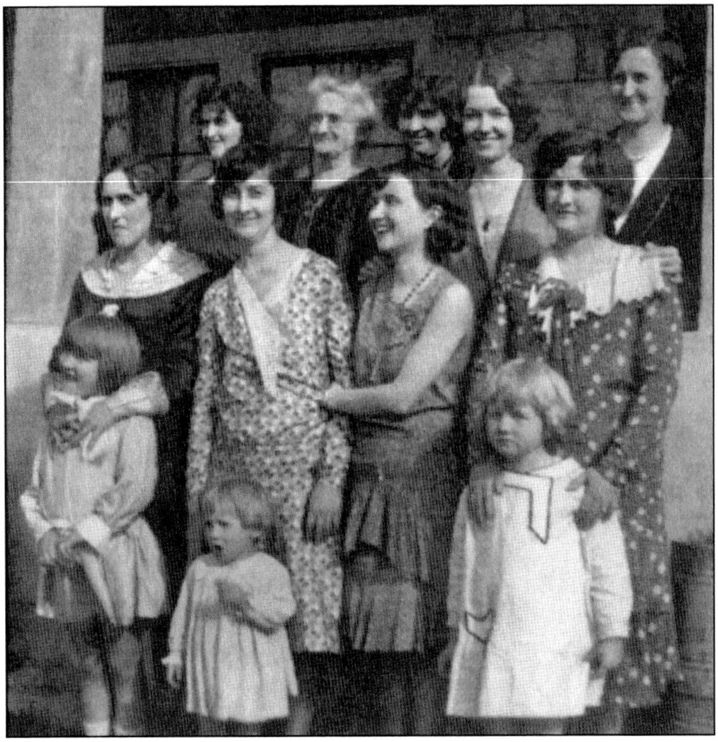

Members of the Prentiss family were well known for their ties to education. Vola was principal at North Ward and Cash and Downs Elementary Schools, and Alma was principal at Landrum Elementary School. This 1930 photograph was taken on the front porch of the family's stone farm house. From left to right, pictured here are (first row) D'Anne, Betty Lou, and Elaine Prentiss; (second row) Audrey Walk, Ethel Prentiss, Vola Prentiss, and Myrtle Finley; (third row) Erie Inman, Margaret Prentiss, Annie Prentiss, Marguerite Prentiss, and Alma Prentiss. (Courtesy Betty Lou Rogers.)

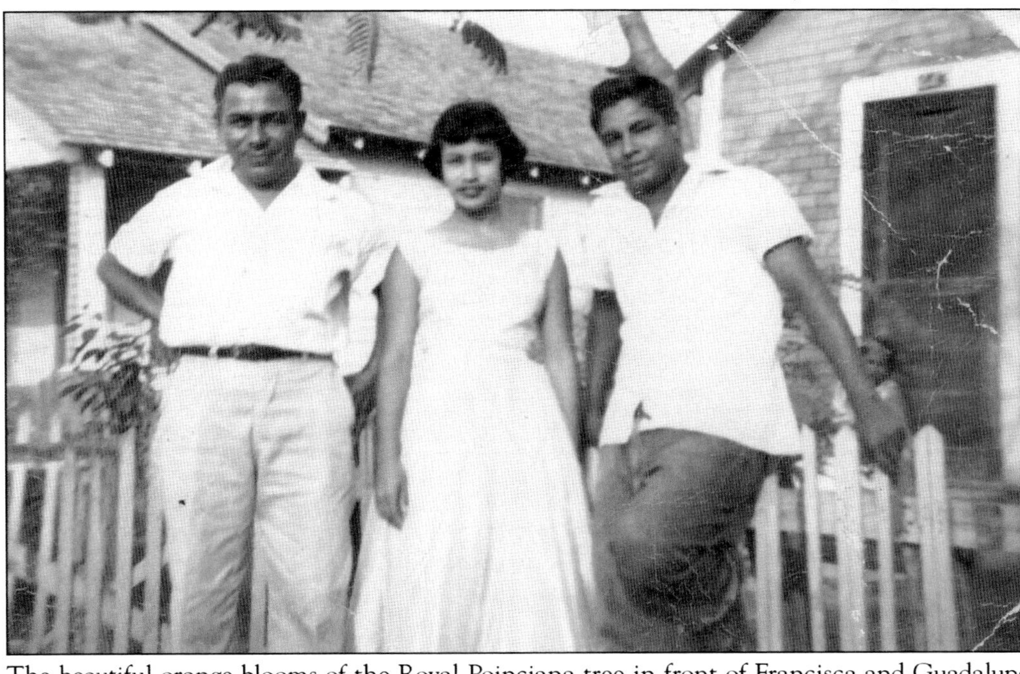

The beautiful orange blooms of the Royal Poinciana tree in front of Francisca and Guadalupe Gallegos's house at 443 Corral Street brought people from all parts of town to see it. In the 1950s, people said that it was the first Royal Poinciana tree in San Benito. In this photograph, leaves from the tree can be seen above the heads of, from left to right, Guadalupe, Mary, and Jesus Gallegos. (Courtesy Mary Tijerina.)

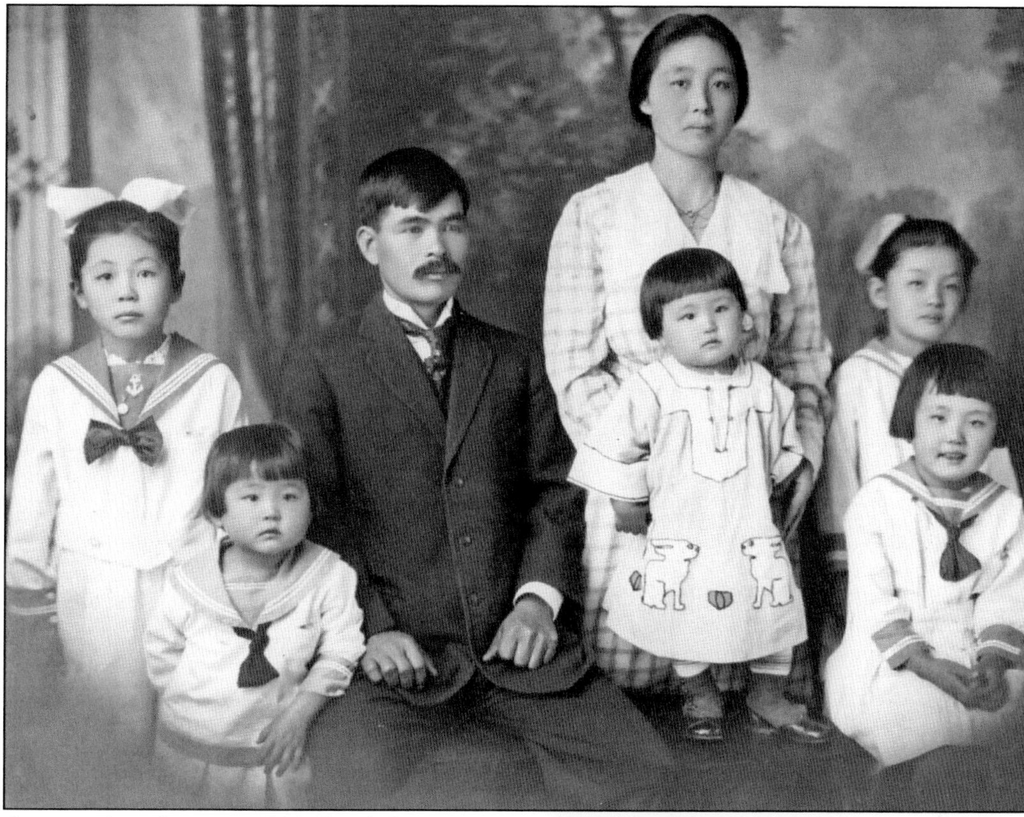

Arriving from Japan in 1908, Frank Sentaro and Kofumi Abe Otsuki farmed in California before moving to Terry, Texas, in 1920. The inadequate topsoil and the difficulty in getting their produce to the market pushed the Otsukis farther south to San Benito. It was here that the couple had hopes of farming and raising their seven children. Frank died in 1941, leaving his sons Frank and Carl to care for their mother and farm. Later, Carl attended Brownsville Junior College and then ran track at East Texas State University. (Courtesy Carl Otsuki.)

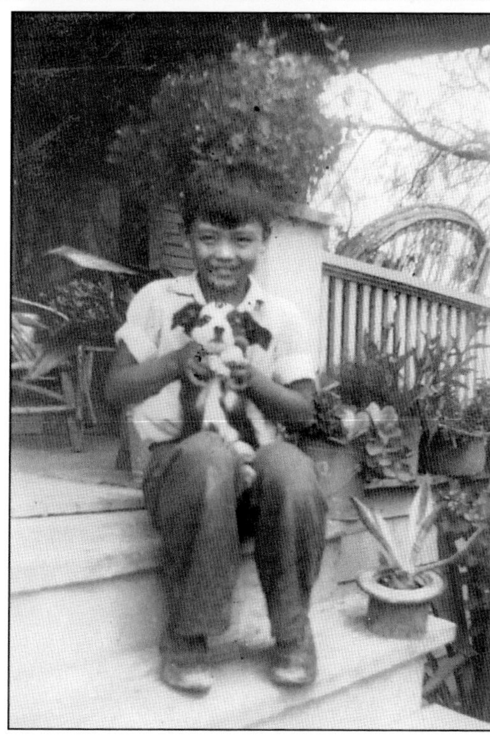

Carl Otsuki, shown here as a boy, recalled that when he was 15, his family was so poor that he would catch fish in the canal for supper. He says that those meals were as good back then as eating at Red Lobster today. In college, Carl says that he'd order chili and fill it with catsup to make it go further until the owner got wise and took the catsup off the table. Carl later married Faye Woods, daughter of Henry and Edith Adams Woods. (Courtesy Carl Otsuki.)

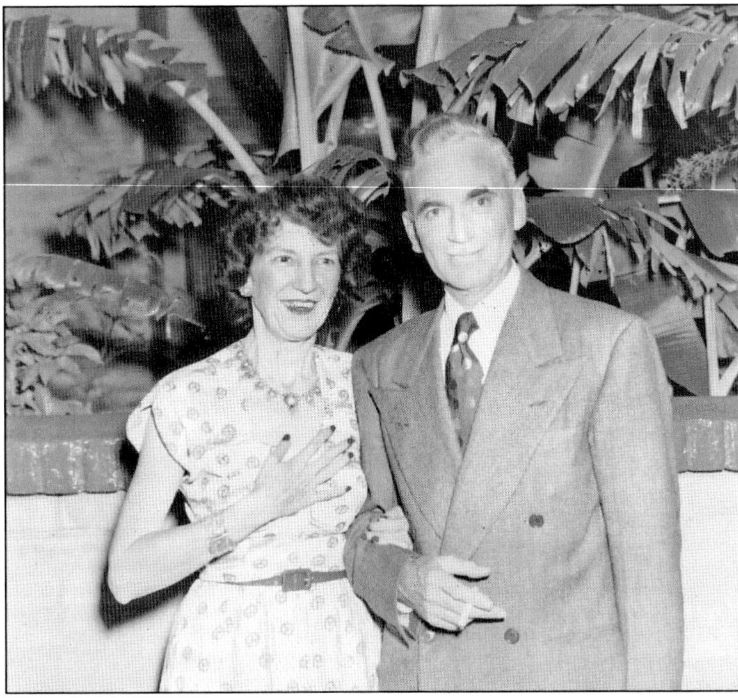

Shown here in the 1940s on the patio of the Stonewall Jackson Hotel is former Rhodes Scholar Charles Bowie, who served as exalted ruler of the San Benito Elks Lodge, was named Texas State Exalted Ruler, and was a candidate for the national post of grand exalted ruler. With Charles is his wife, Leona Bowie, a talented artist who volunteered her time to help with civic events and school functions. Charles and Leona were the parents of Patricia and Charles Jr. (Courtesy Pat Davis.)

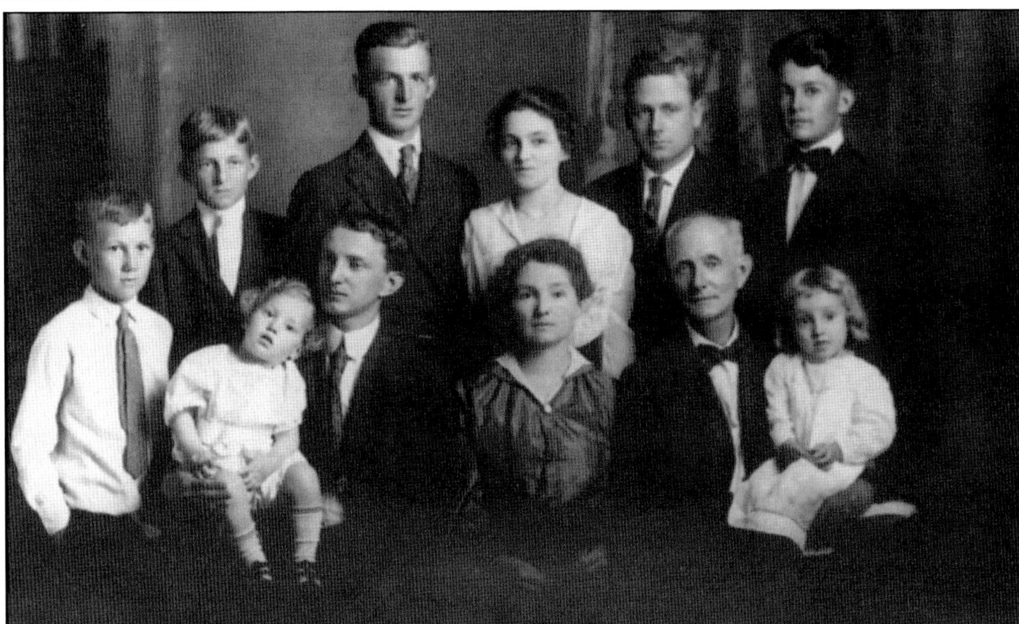

John Richard Collins and his wife, Sarah Catherine, arrived in San Benito in 1908 and lived in a tent until their home in the 300 block of North Sam Houston Boulevard was built. While John ran an insurance agency on South Sam Houston Boulevard, the Collins family grew. Pictured in this *c.* 1917 photograph are, from left to right, (first row) Richard P. Reese (being held), Olin C. Collins (holding child), Sarah Catherine Collins, John Richard Collins, and (on his lap) Catherine Reese; (second row) sons Robert M., William D., and Richard T. Collins, daughter Carrie Collins Reese, Erwin C. Reese, and James C. Collins. (Courtesy Mary Catherine Lovett.)

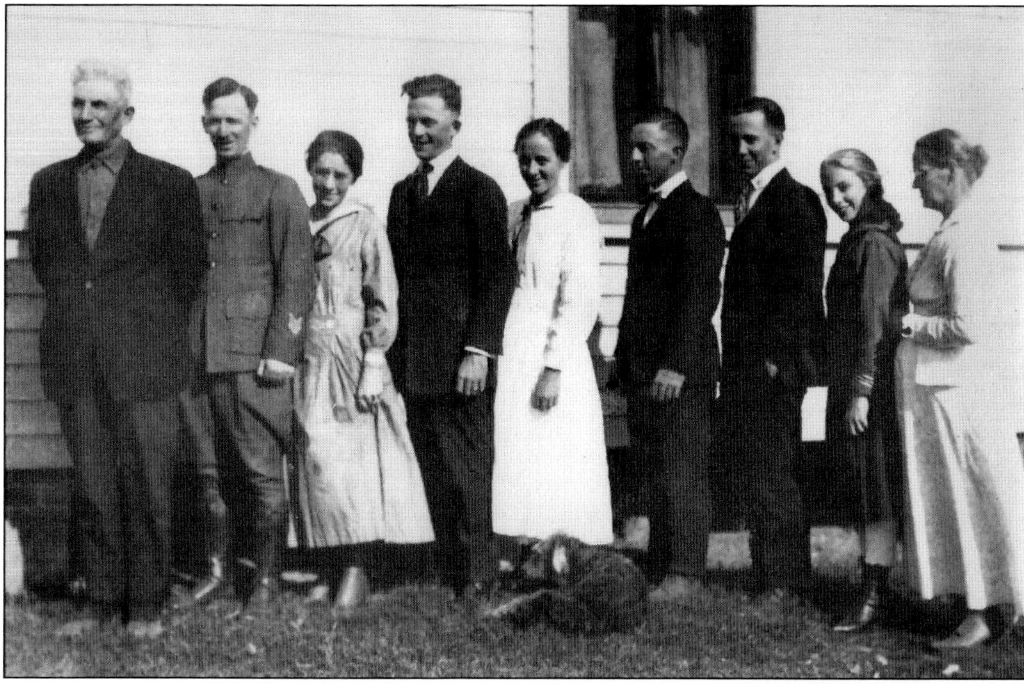

E. J. "Jake" Bohner family came from Kansas in 1908. Active in the development of the town, Bohner served two terms as city commissioner. When Bohner died in 1925, Mayor Scott Brown proclaimed that businesses should close during the funeral services. Shown are Ernest Jake, children Chauncey E., Ouida, Frost, Seeta Mayne, Pousette, Roswell, Cessarie, and wife Ophelia Ringey Bohner. E. J.'s son Frost and his wife, Ethel John Bohner, built a home at 844 North Sam Houston Boulevard, in which daughter Betty was born and where she still lives. The Frost Bohners also had another daughter, Jane. (Courtesy Betty Cashin.)

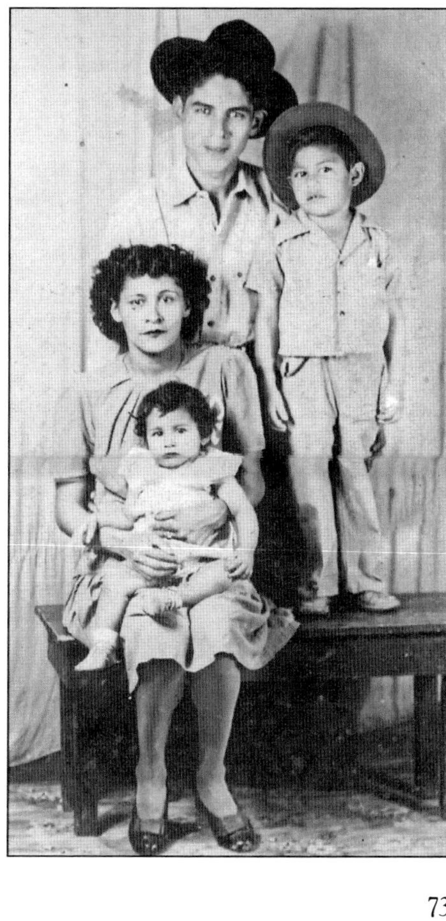

Forty years after Rafael Moreno suggested the name of San Benito, his granddaughter, Odilia, married Frutoso Gomez, and began to raise a family here. Odilia kept house while Frutoso worked as a laborer. Their children, Josefina and Atanacio are in their parents' arms in this photograph. The couple's other children were Amelia, George, Joe, Daniel, Ruben, Otila, Angelita, and Frutoso Jr. (Courtesy Frutoso Gomez Jr.)

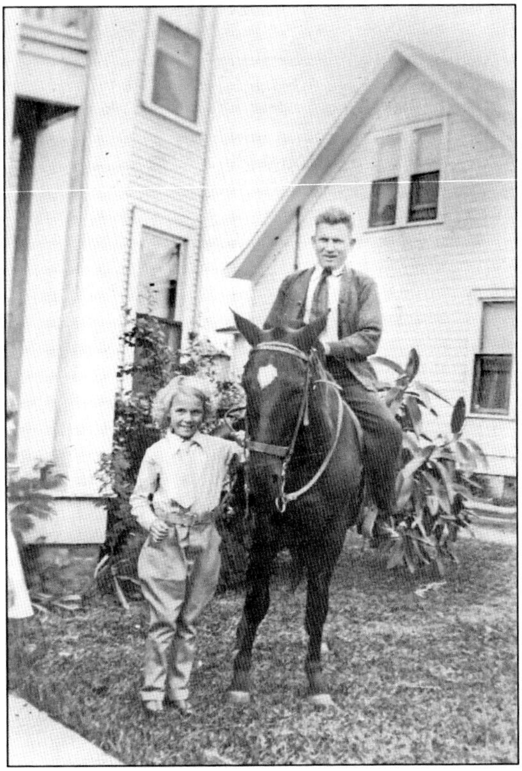

Anna C. Smith came to San Benito with her son, W. Ray, in 1909. She worked as a housekeeper for the Cowgill family until she had enough money to buy the already-existing boardinghouses at 335 North Reagan. Ray and Alice Sanderson Smith took over after his mother died providing meals and boarding as well as selling meals to the public. Marion Treadwell, the black cook, worked there until his death in 1951. In this photograph, W. Ray Smith and his daughter Marilyn stand in front of their two boardinghouses. Marilyn and J. R. Hight Jr. had three daughters, Janice, Judy, and Alyson. (Courtesy Judy Jennings.)

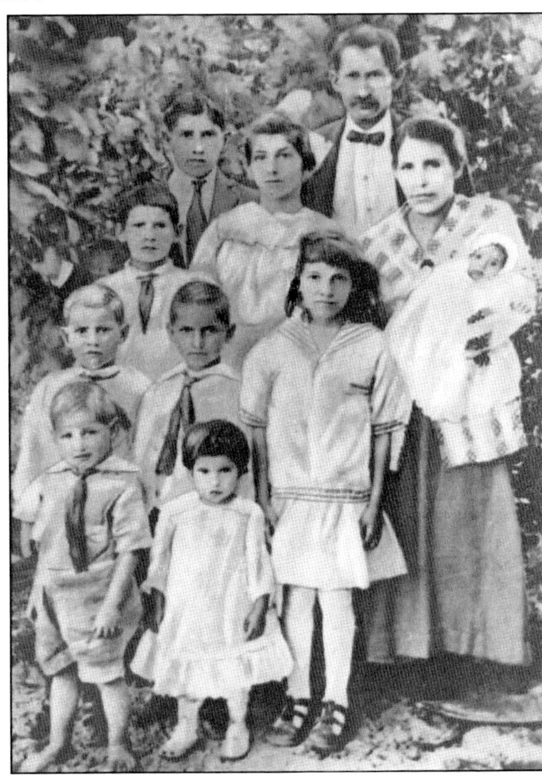

Ismael Montalvo, cattle rancher and entrepreneur, was born in Las Prietas, Cameron County to Antonio and Isabel Montalvo. He married Francisca Esparza and had 11 children, including the first baby born in San Benito, named San Benito Montalvo. Shown in this c. 1917 photograph are (first row) Fausto and Zoila; (second row) Jose, Ismael, and Frances; (third row) San Benito, Enriqueta, and Francisca, holding baby Herminia; (third row) Alfredo and Ismael. Henry and Rene were not yet born. (Courtesy Alfredo Montalvo Jr.)

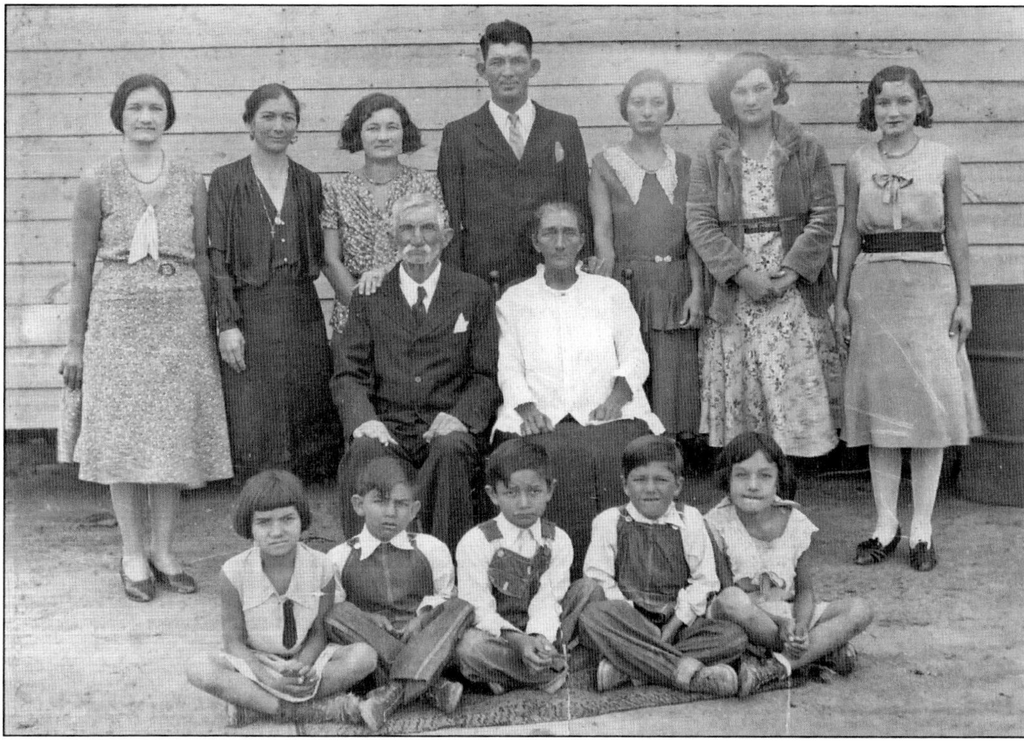

The Ramon Davila family commuted from their cotton farm in Willacy County to their town house at 142 Hidalgo Street, San Benito, which is still owned today by granddaughter Estela Davila Garcia. Their farm in Willacy County was part of the Quintanilla land grant. Three generations of the family members featured in this 1929 photograph are (first row) Celia, Mateo, Enrique Moreno Jr., Luis Banuelos, and Sulema Ramirez; (second row) Ramon and Rita Quintanilla Davila; (third row) Teodora, Teresa, Esperanza, Ramon Jr., Maria, Paula, and Consuelo Davila. (Courtesy Maria Elena Caparulo Martinez.)

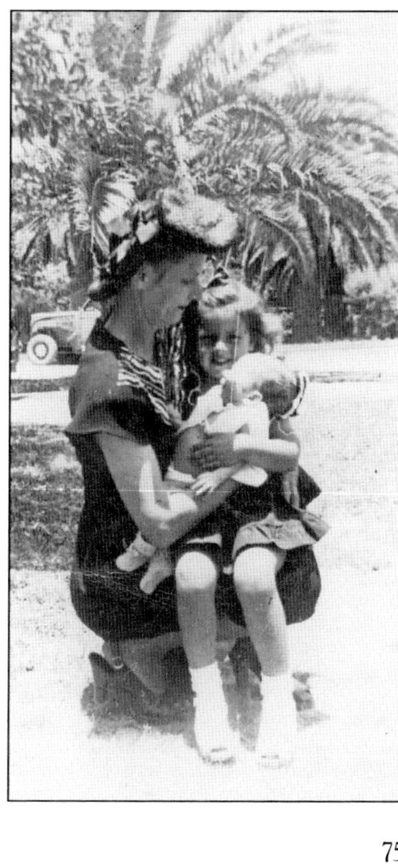

Stylishly dressed Katherine Rush Kennedy holds grandchildren Kay Bandy and Mike Kennedy in this 1940s photograph. Kennedy's hair, dress, and shoes epitomized 1940s fashions and made her a natural to work behind the cosmetics counter of the HEB on Sam Houston Boulevard. (Courtesy Mary Ann Frailing.)

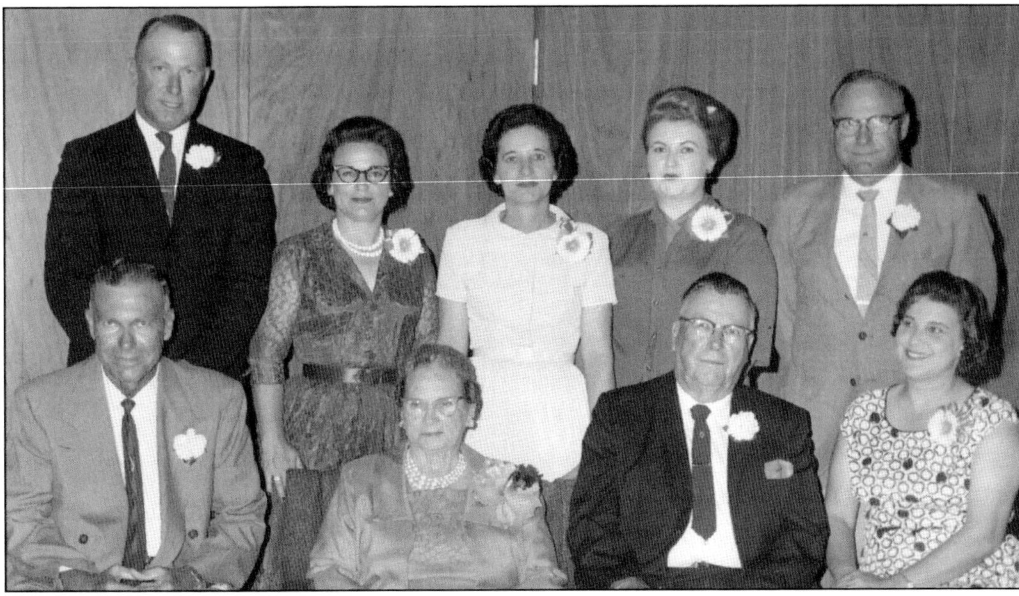

Denver and Eula Trimm Hance arrived in 1919 and farmed their land around Zillock Road until World War II. He worked for Department of Agriculture, served for 20 years on the Highland School Board and on the water district board. In this 1960s photograph, celebrating the Hances' 50th wedding anniversary are (first row, seated) Maurice Hance, Eula Mae Trimm Hance, Denver Hance, Wanda Hance McQueeney; (second row, standing) Norman Hance, Jean Hance Nesmith, Mildred Hance Witt, Rita Hance Crabtree, and Douglas Hance. (Courtesy Rita Hance Crabtree.)

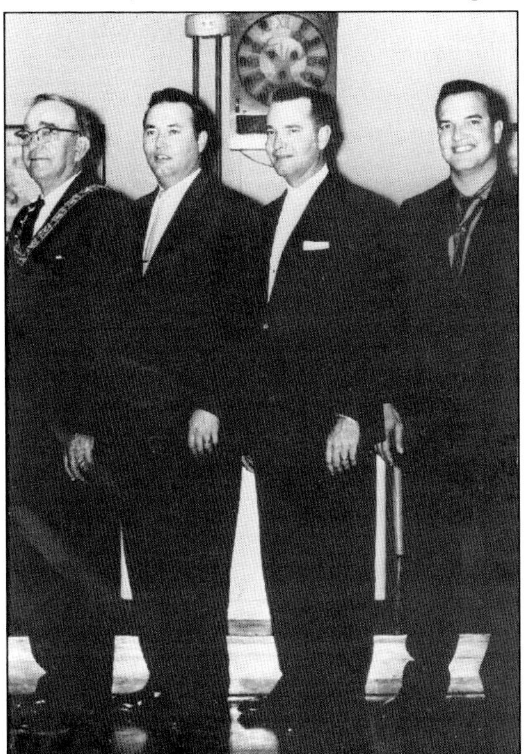

In 1927, after attending the University of Mississippi, Adolph Thomae Sr., an entomologist with the Department of Agriculture, was transferred here to assist in fighting the citrus Black Fly infestation. Adolph and Cumi Elizabeth Harrison "Bea" Thomae lived at 600 North Reagan Street. Shown here from left to right are Adolph Sr. and sons Adolph Jr., Edd, and Henry. Adolph Jr. farmed and served as a county commissioner for many years. Edd worked for the USDA, and Henry owned and operated the Thomae Funeral Home. (Courtesy Eileen Tyra.)

Five

How We Played

Sports, Dress Up, and Music

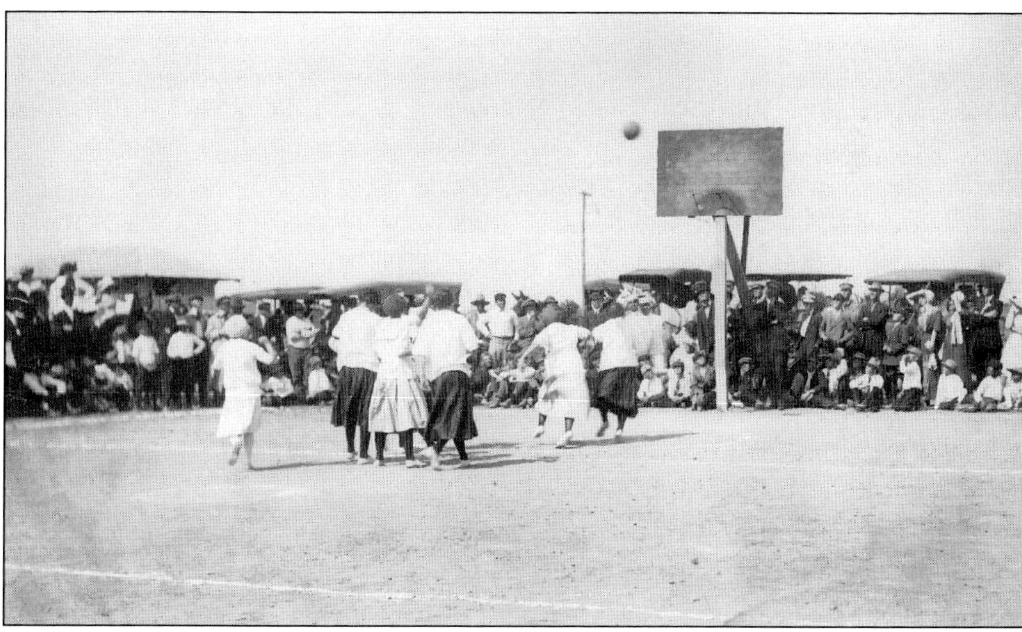

In long skirts, high socks, and hot sun: that's the way girls' basketball was played in 1910 at San Benito High School. The spectators seemed to enjoy the close proximity to the game, and the girls had fun. Carrie Collins was a team member. (Courtesy Mary Catherine Lovett.)

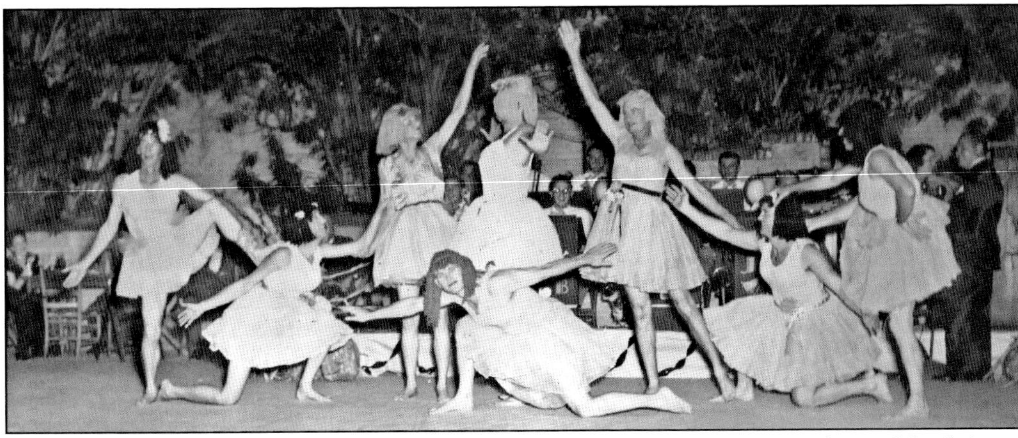

Wearing ballet costumes that defied description, the "Glamazon" troupe gave a beautiful exhibition and encored with an intricate leap frog number at the Stonewall Jackson Hotel patio. The proceeds from the Junior Service League performance benefitted the Well Baby Clinic. Jack Lomax was Master of Ceremonies, and the ballerinas included Hunter "Huntera" Scales, Ben "Benita" Shoemaker, Jack "Jacqueline" Zillafro, Ed "Edwina" Hatchett, Tom "Thomasina" Marchbanks, and John "Joanna" Benson. (Courtesy Tootie Madden.)

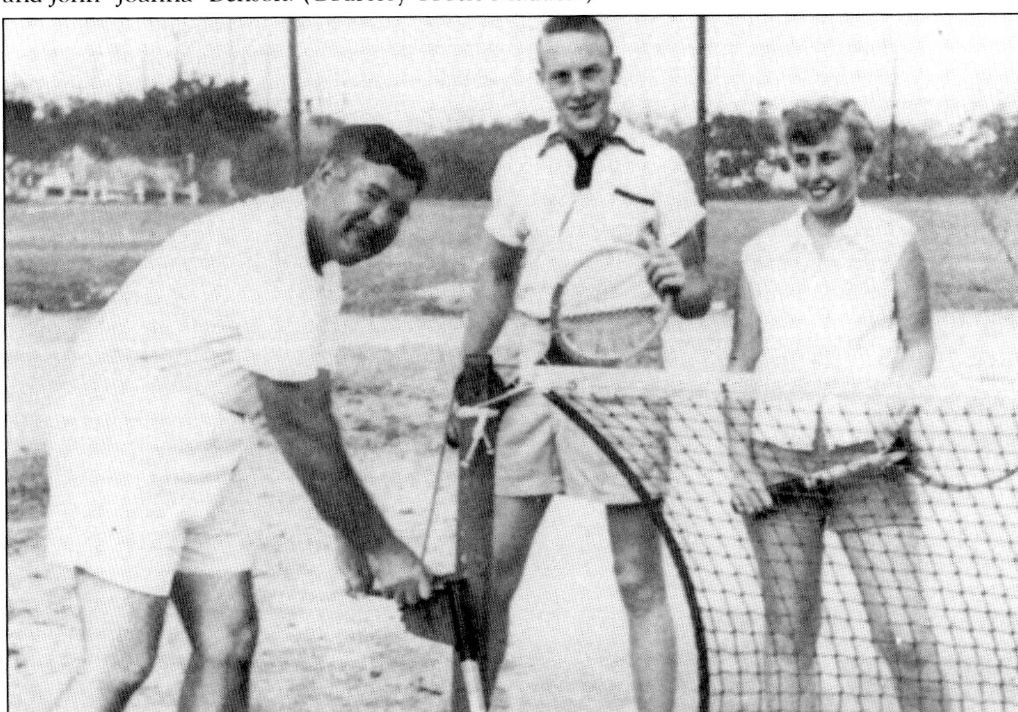

James C. Dobson, PhD., a 1954 graduate of SBHS, is the founder and president of Focus on the Family, a nonprofit organization that produces internationally syndicated radio programs, heard daily on more than 2,900 radio stations in North America and in seven languages on approximately 1,300 stations in more than 70 other countries. The Dobsons lived at 424 North Crockett Street, and James's father was pastor at the First Church of the Nazarene. While at SBHS, "Jimmy" Dobson played on the school tennis team; in this photograph, he stands between coach Harlan H. "H. H." Baker (left) and Meri Lolley. (Courtesy San Benito Historical Society.)

Even though betting was not legal in Texas, many Texans bred and owned horses to race in neighboring states. Trial races were held at a Mercedes track. Local dentist Dr. Edgar Lars "Bill" Sullivan and Ware McCall, owner of Electric Gin, co-owned Joe Dandy, the race horse seen here. Dr. Sullivan also served on the school board. (Courtesy Bob Duncan.)

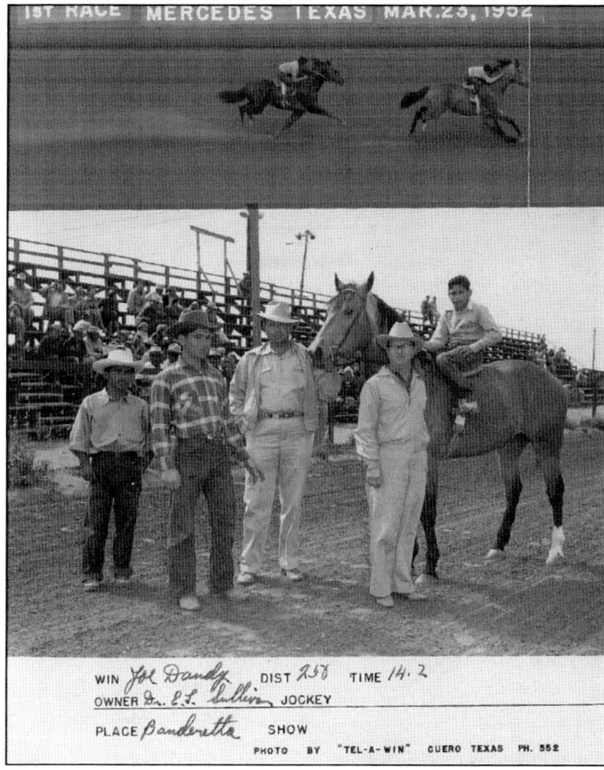

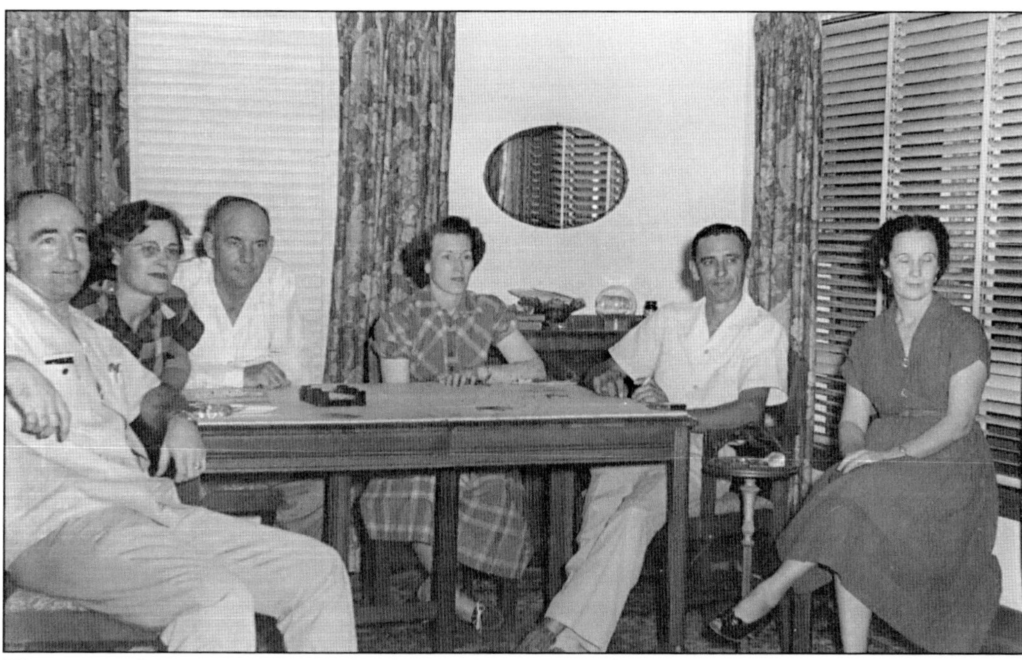

The game of Canasta was popular during the 1940s and 1950s. This Canasta group met every Saturday night for a game in the home of Leon and Grace Tumberlinson. From left to right, they are Dr. Earl E. "E. E." Dawson, Grace Tumberlinson, Jack Hays, Marie Dawson, Leon Tumberlinson, and Nora Hays. (Courtesy Bob Tumberlinson.)

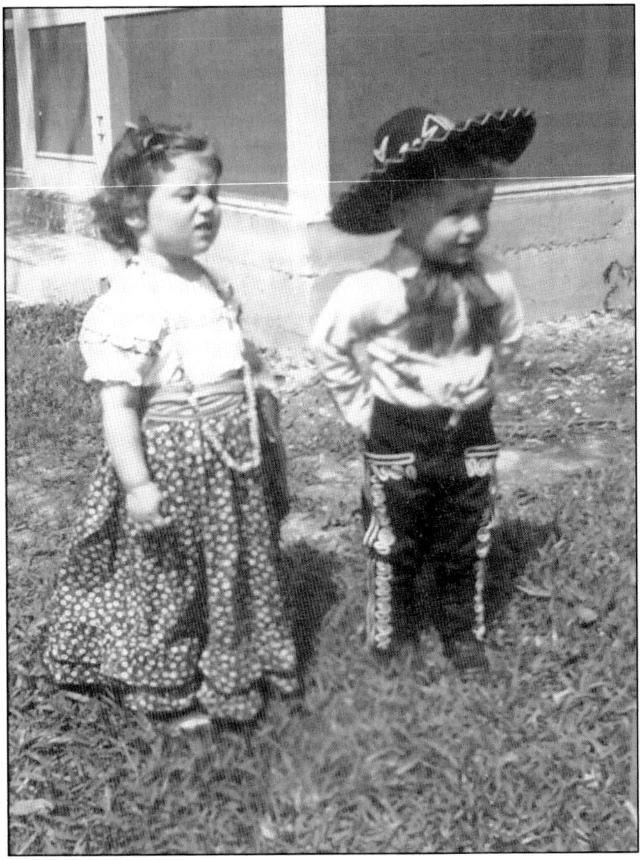

Future Miss San Benito Teresa Collins is seen here with buddy Bob Bowie, dressed for Charro Days in 1948. (Courtesy Mary Catherine Lovett.)

In 1952, Sam Lozano coached basketball players from the Fred Booth Elementary School neighborhood. Seen here with Lozano, the players are, from left to right, (first row) Jerry Amaya, Romeo Nuñez, Lionel Noyola, Ruben Noyola, Salome Martinez Jr., and Carlos Garza; (second row) Eugene Guetzow, Carlos Sanchez, Jim Corona, and Elias Gonzalez; (third row) Ernesto Gonzalez, Juan Aguilar, Ray Cortez, and Raul De Los Santos. (Courtesy Simon Cantu.)

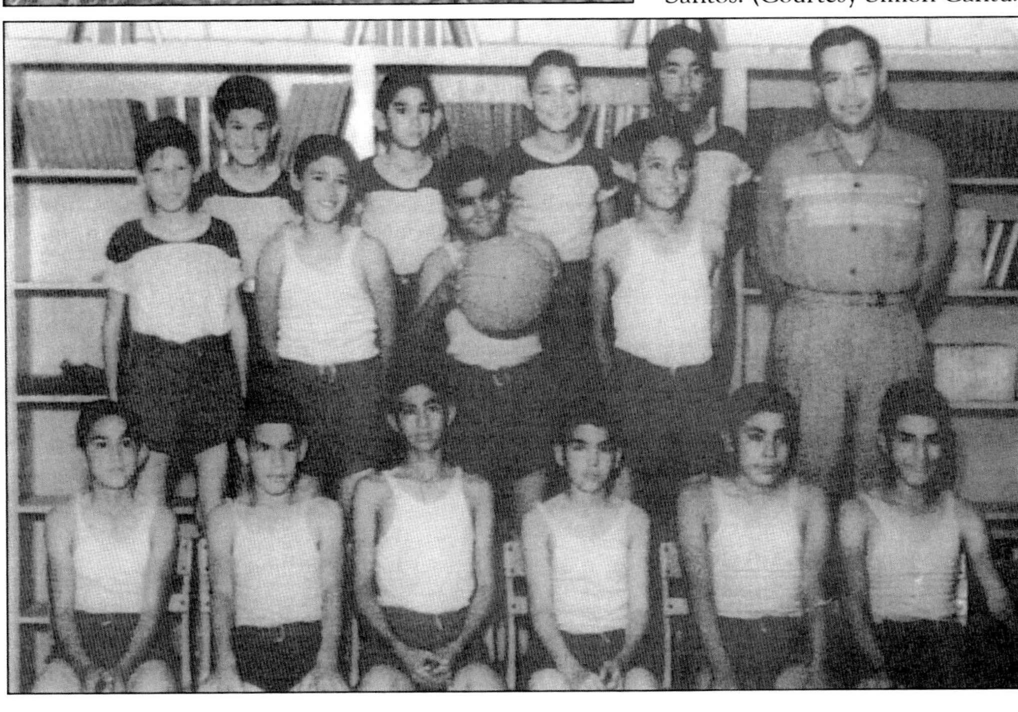

Elfego Esparza (1929–1991), born in El Ranchito, Texas, was a 1948 graduate of SBHS where choral teacher Ed Hatchett recognized his talent and encouraged him to study voice. Elfego went on to Trinity University in San Antonio and then continued at the Royal Conservatory in Brussels and the Academy of Music in Vienna. He sang in all of the world's major opera houses, including Italy's La Scala and New York's Metropolitan Opera House. (Courtesy San Benito Historical Society.)

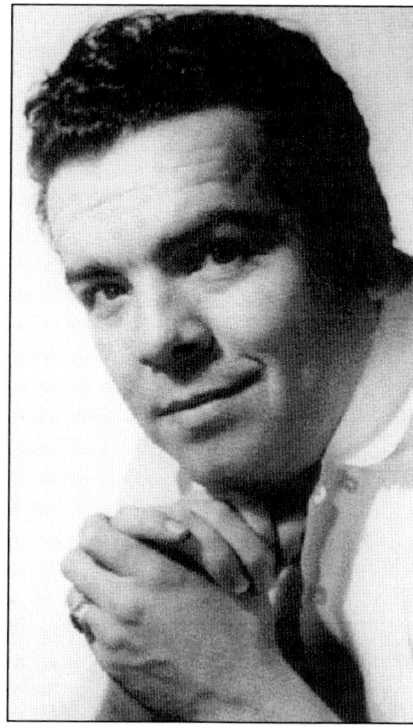

Decorating downtown windows and storefronts for the high school homecoming parade was a long-standing tradition. In 1955, Olga Corkill, at the top of the ladder, puts the finishing touches on Don's Photo Center at 107 South Sam Houston Boulevard, while Olivia Sifuentes holds the ladder. Helping out are, from left to right, Anita Rodriguez, Pat Treviño, and Librada Martinez. (Photograph Don Messer; courtesy Olga Corkill Rodriguez.)

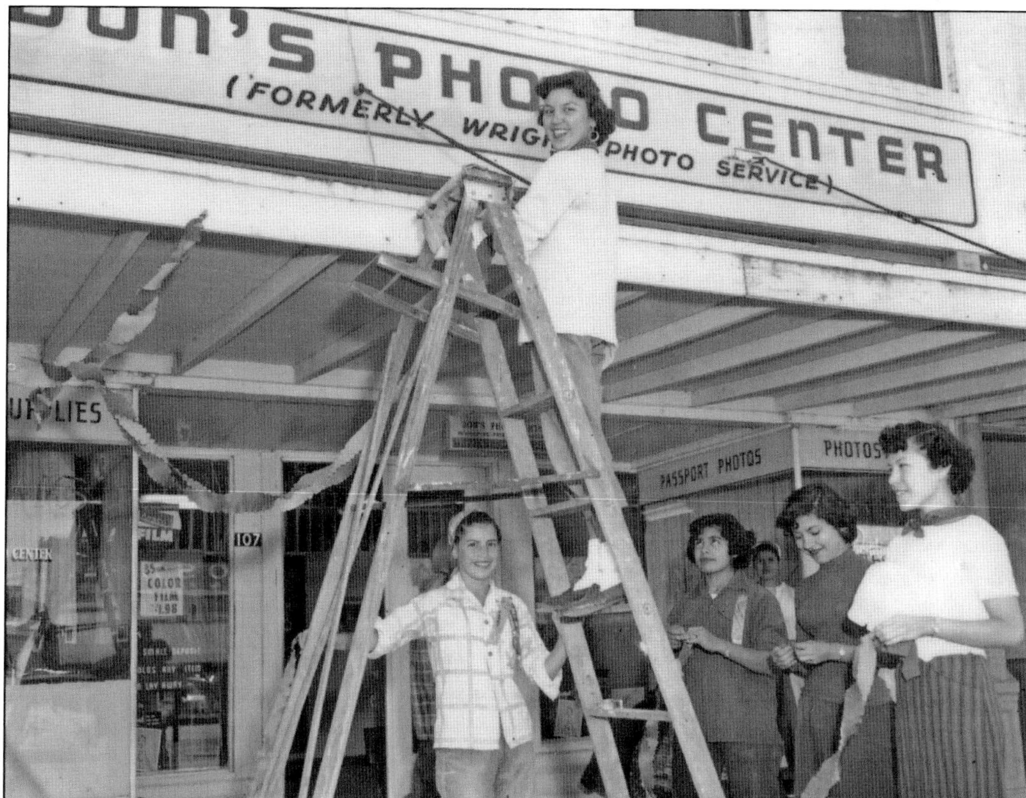

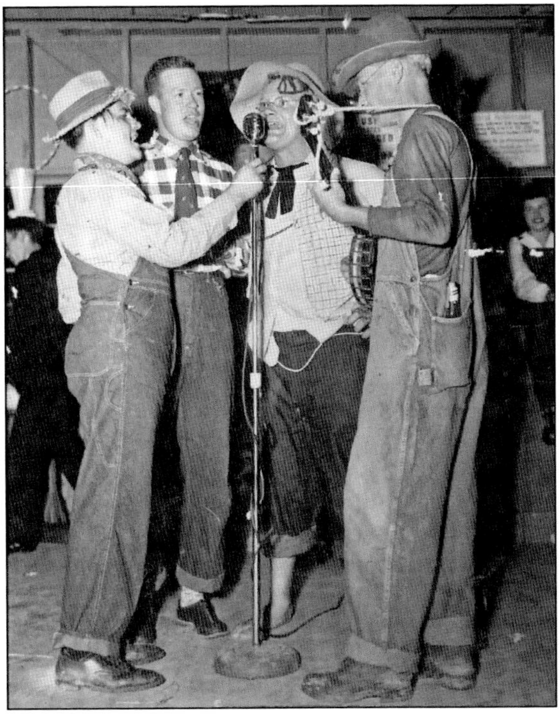

The Junior Service League held a barn dance in 1948 at the newly built Playland Rollercade. Singing for the crowd in this photograph are, from left to right, Tol Boswell Jr., Tom Marchbanks Jr., Jack Burke, and Ben Shoemaker. At the same show, Ruth Mix Hill, Tom Mix's daughter, performed rope tricks. (Photograph Jack Purnell.)

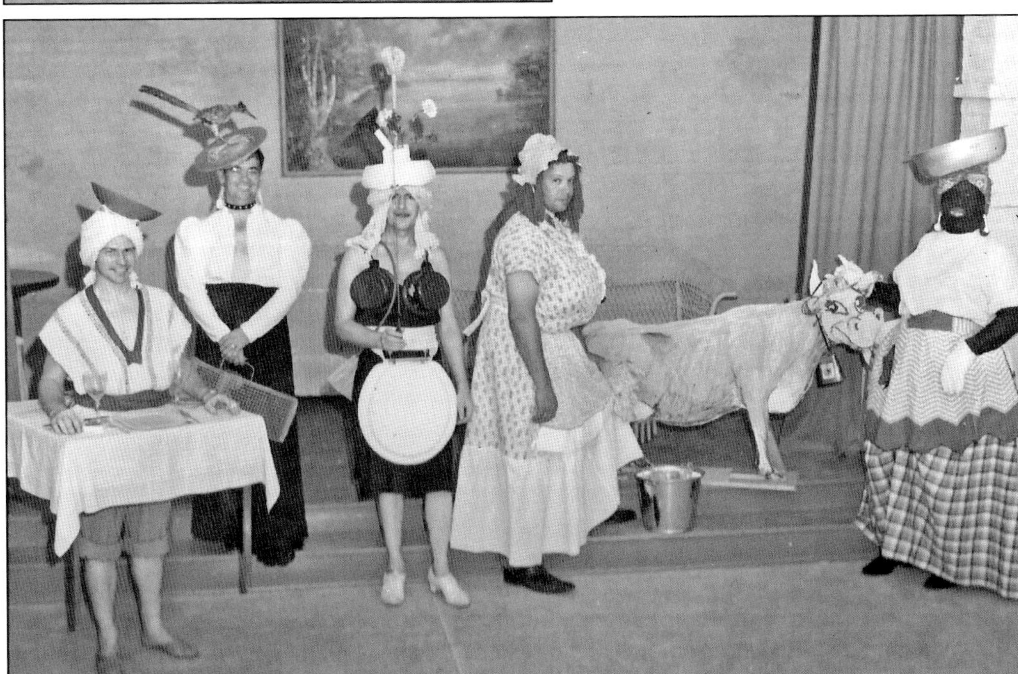

Junior Service League husbands were not above dressing in drag for a worthwhile project. In May 1948, "Five Sweet Maids" put on a show to benefit the Well Baby Clinic. From left to right, they are "table maid" James L. Mayer, "old maid" Martin Price, "chamber maid" Edward I. "Red" Bucklin Jr., "dairy maid" Dr. E. L. "Bill" Sullivan, and "kitchen maid" Bryan Long. (Courtesy Tootie Madden.)

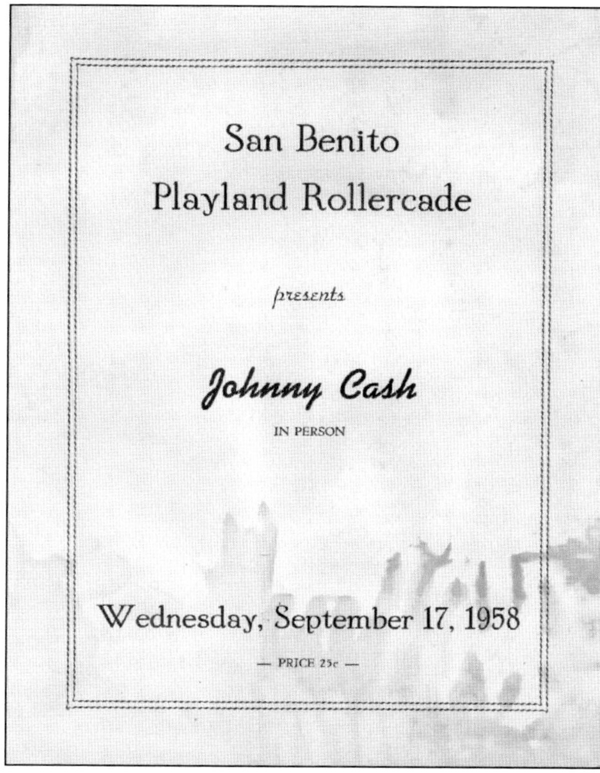

San Benito
Playland Rollercade

presents

Johnny Cash

IN PERSON

Wednesday, September 17, 1958

— PRICE 25c —

The Rainey family built the Playland Rollercade in 1947. In 1973, Charles and Bertha Wilson purchased the rink from a Rainey daughter, and the Wilsons operated the rink for another 26 years. Then their daughter Cynthia and her husband, Dave Cook, ran the rink for eight years. Four months after Karen Wilson took over management, the rink burned down in 2005, ending an era. As advertised on this program, Johnny Cash performed at the Rollercade in 1958. (Courtesy Charlie and Bertha Wilson.)

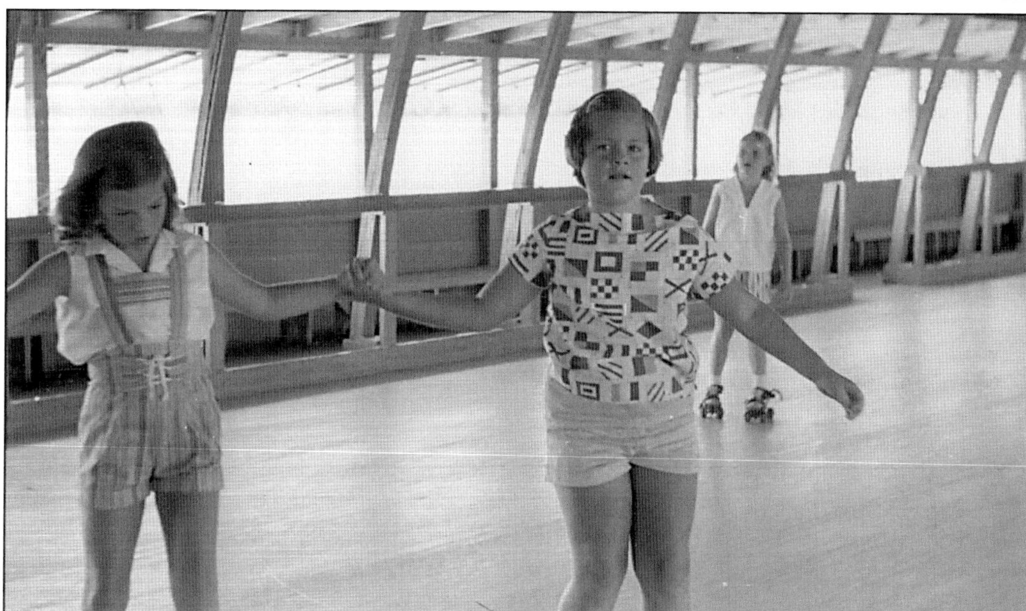

The quonset hut, open-air Playland Rollercade skating rink allowed the southern breeze to cool the skaters and, in the early days, helped cut down on the noise made by the roller skates' wheels. In this 1958 photograph, Katherine Scales and Tootie Boswell hold hands to balance themselves. Many birthday parties and weekend skating activities were held at the skating rink, and many children in San Benito learned to skate there. (Courtesy Tootie Madden.)

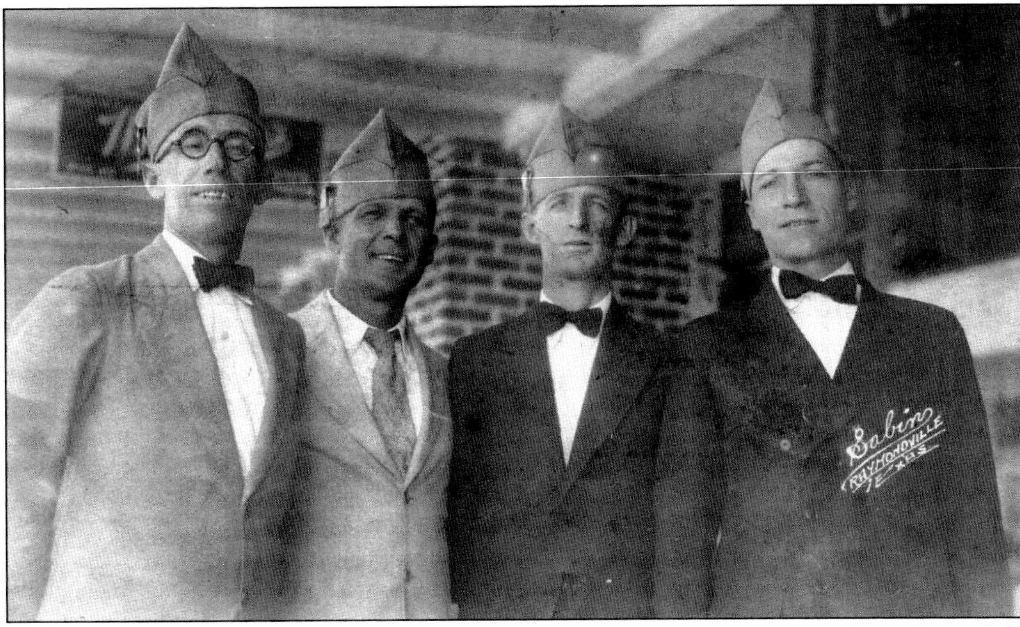

The "40 and 8" barbershop quartet consisted of four World War I veterans and members of the American Legion, who named their group for the European railcars they'd experienced during the war, each car holding 40 men and 8 mules. The quartet were in demand at functions throughout the Valley. Group members shown here are, from left to right, L. F. "Cotton" Boling, "Nappy" Chatelle, and Richard T. Collins. The fourth man here, Louis Hirsh, was temporarily substituting for the fourth member of the group, Bill Buck. (Courtesy Mary Catherine Lovett.)

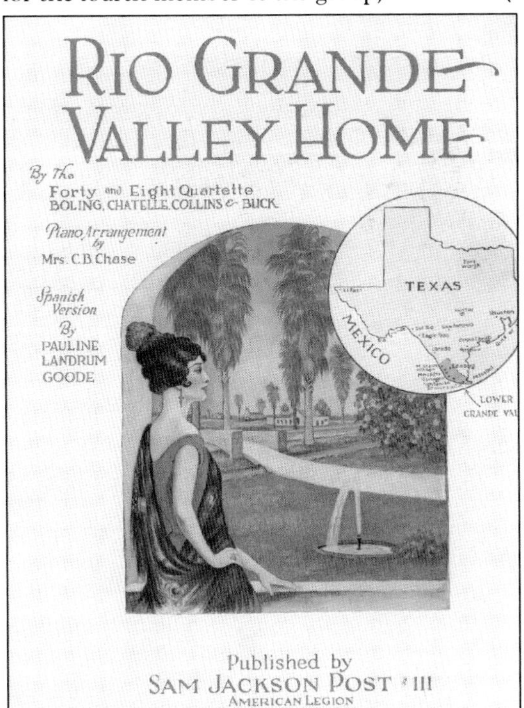

When in France during World War I, L. F. Boling heard a melody played by the French when Americans shipped home. When he got back to his job as manager of the San Benito Chamber of Commerce, he wrote the lyrics to "Rio Grande Valley Home," with help from the members of the quartet. The song, especially the chorus, was sung at service club meetings, school assemblies, and other public gatherings. Pride and optimism are reflected in the lyric's descriptions of the Valley, which began with "For we love our Valley home, way down upon the Rio Grande." (Courtesy Mary Catherine Lovett.)

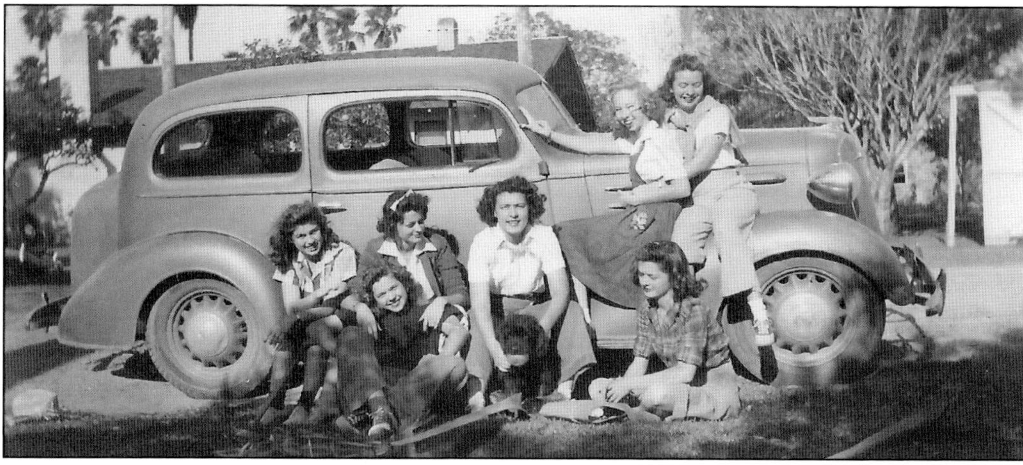

These happy young women dressed in their saddle Oxfords, bobby socks, and scarves, with sweaters worn around their shoulders and curls down to their shoulders, are Mary Minta Polly, Billie Joyce Lockmiller, Mary Lou Sweeney, Olive Polly, and unidentified, and on the ground are Jack Buesing and Helen Morris. (Courtesy Tootie Madden.)

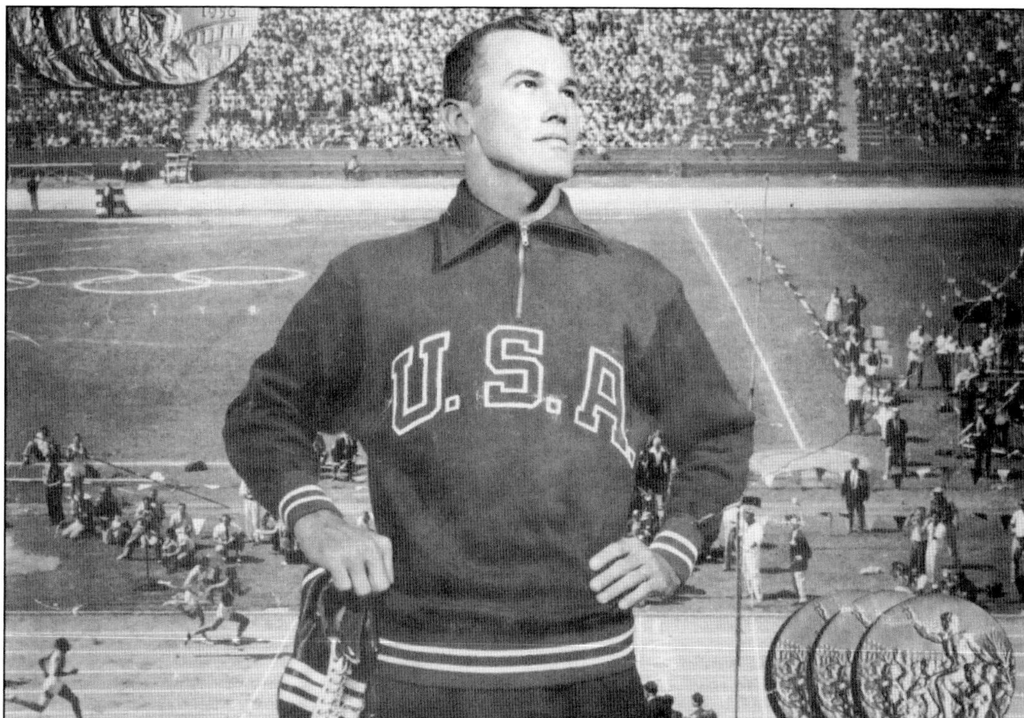

Bobby Joe Morrow, a 1954 SBHS graduate, won gold medals at the 1956 Olympic games in the 100-meter dash, 200-meter dash, and 400-meter relay. He anchored the mile relay team, which broke the Olympic record. Morrow was the first man to win three gold medals at an Olympics since Jesse Owens's 1936 Berlin performance. He was proclaimed *Sport Illustrated*'s Sportsman of the Year for 1956, was inducted into the Olympic Hall of Fame in 1989, and was on hand in 2006 when the San Benito Consolidated Independent School District named its new football stadium in his honor. (Courtesy San Benito Historical Society.)

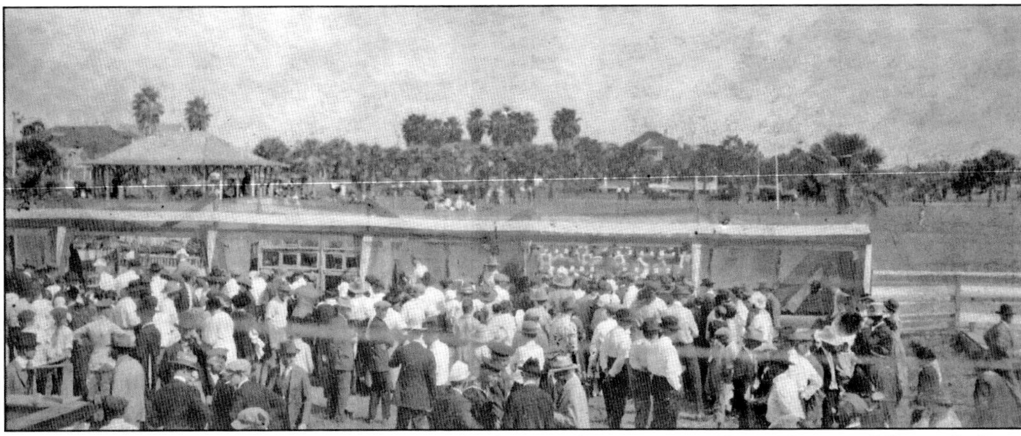

Kiwanis Ball Park, shown here in 1921, was built near the resaca on West Heywood Street behind San Benito Gin. During the Depression, the Kiwanis Club hosted triple bill: a bullfight, cockfight, and baseball game, all for 10¢. The park was filled with spectators. The Kiwanis later donated the park, grandstands and all, to the Civil Air Patrol, which later moved all the equipment to the airport. The Kiwanis Club hosted boys and girls softball teams for many years. (Courtesy Shirlee Thompson.)

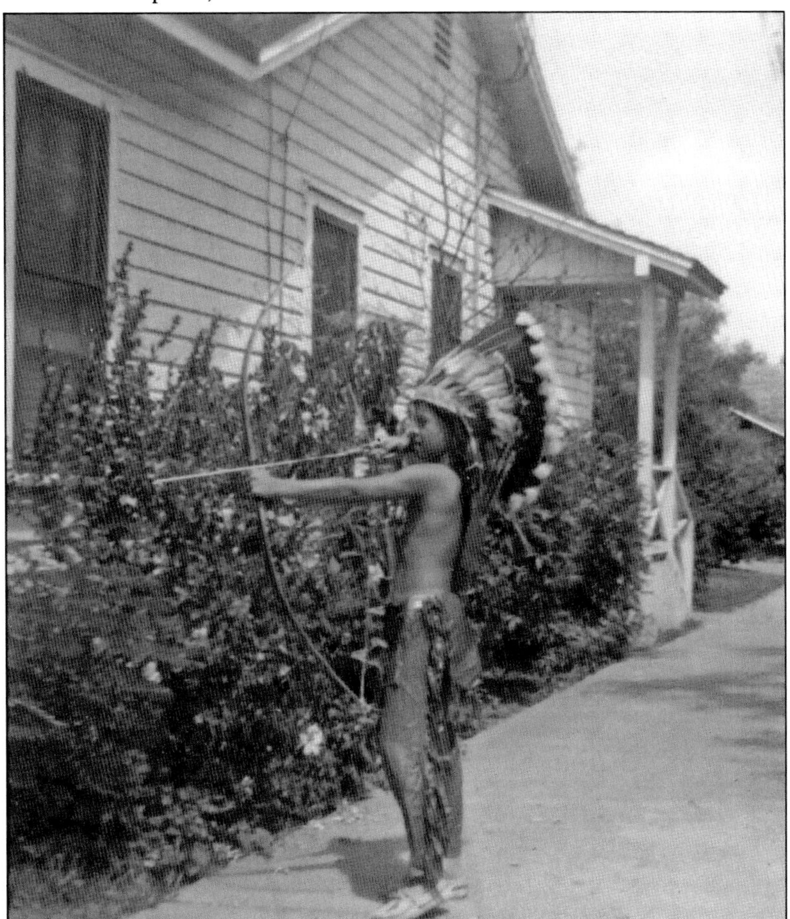

San Benito children loved to play cowboys and Indians—especially children growing up in the 1940s and 1950s when Hopalong Cassidy, Roy Rogers, and Gene Autry thrilled them at the Saturday matinees. Most of the time, kids wanted to dress up as cowboys, with their toy six-shooter strapped to their hip, but in this photograph, George M. "Monte" Gilbert wears a full Indian war bonnet, which he handmade, along with his quiver and leggings. (Courtesy Suzanne Gilbert.)

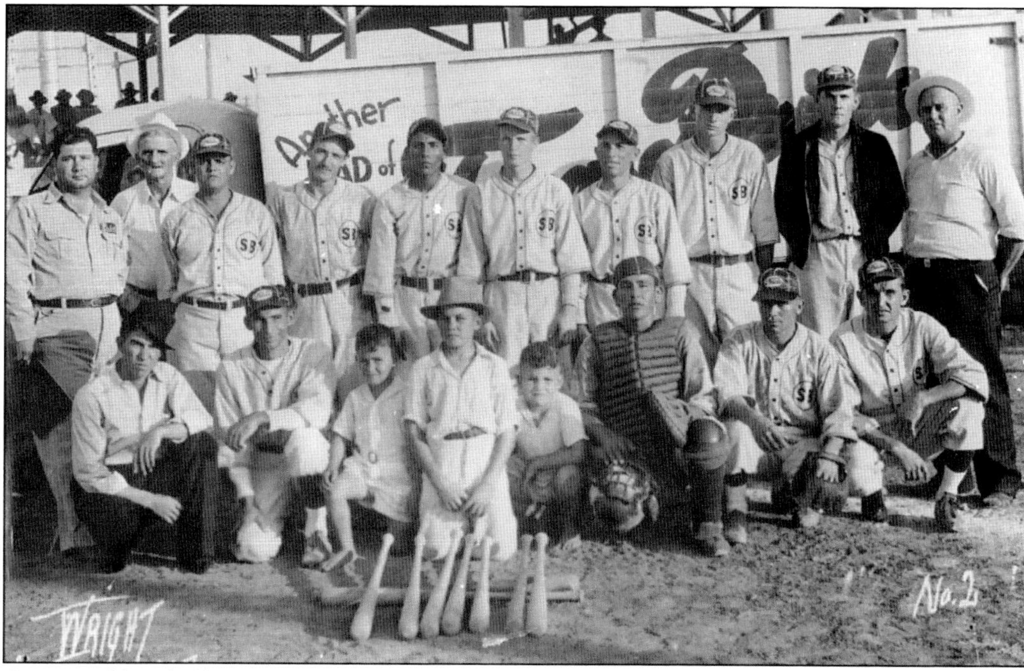

Organized baseball teams have played in San Benito for decades. The one pictured here is from c. 1937. From left to right, team members are (first row): Robert Cantu, left fielder; San Benito Montalvo, left fielder; Henry Sanchez Jr., bat boy; Hector Casas, bat boy; Benny Sanchez, bat boy; Jose Antonio Peña, catcher; Bill Carpenter, second baseman; and Robert ?; (second row) Thomas Garza, scorekeeper; Mr. Doan; ? Castillo, third baseman; ? Contreras, center fielder; T. Garcia, pitcher; Robert ?, second baseman; Alfredo Montalvo, catcher; ? Jackson, substitute; ? Jackson, pitcher; and Emilio Sanchez, manager. (Courtesy San Benito Historical Society.)

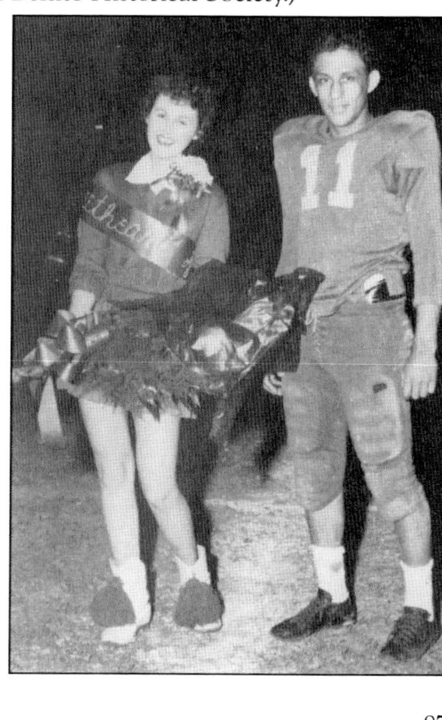

Carlos D. Conde (right), 1968 Pulitzer Prize nominee and 1955 SBHS graduate, served on Pres. Richard M. Nixon's Cabinet Committee on Hispanic Affairs and as a White House staff assistant. In a letter to San Benito students, Carlos wrote, "I was fortunate to grow up in a town like San Benito, during a transitional period that went from a highly segregated community to the homogeneous society it is today." In this 1954 photograph, SBHS homecoming queen Mary Jane Gause is presented a bouquet by Letterman Club president Carlos Conde. (Courtesy San Benito Historical Society.)

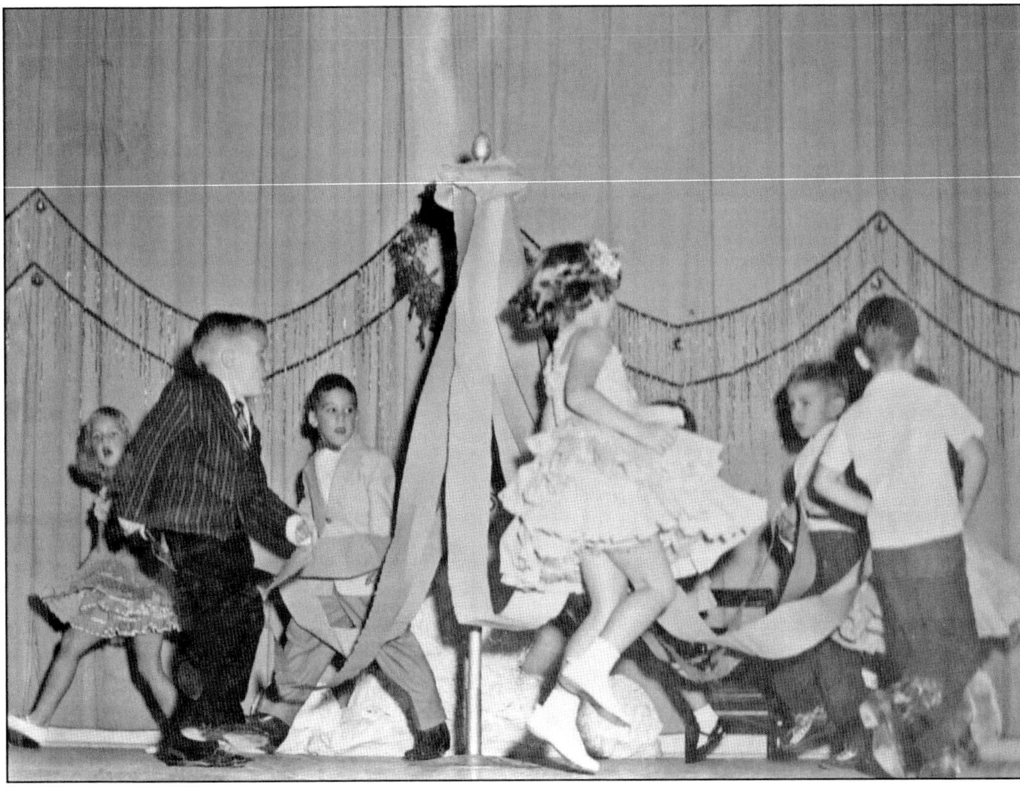

The May Pole Dance was one of the many annual programs performed by young students of Mama Crow's Kindergarten. This c. 1955 photograph features, from left to right, Deborah Medders, Lance Houghtling, an unidentified boy, Suzanne Gilbert, and four other unidentified children. (Courtesy Suzanne Gilbert.)

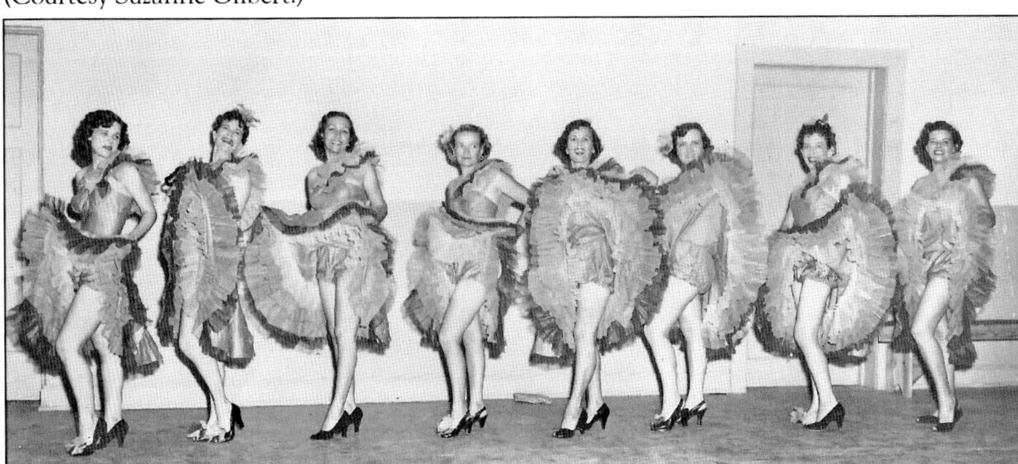

Junior Service League cancan girls performed at the American Legion Hall for a "Gay '90s" party benefiting the Well Baby Clinic. Music for the Glittering Palace–themed event was performed by the Palace Cavaliers. In this 1950 photograph, the dancers are, from left to right, "Jack" Boswell, Dorothy Huitt, Lorraine Mayer, Lois "Sissy" Landrum, Lorene Elam, Sue Marchbanks, Juanita Cook, and Kyle Cruse. (Courtesy Tootie Madden.)

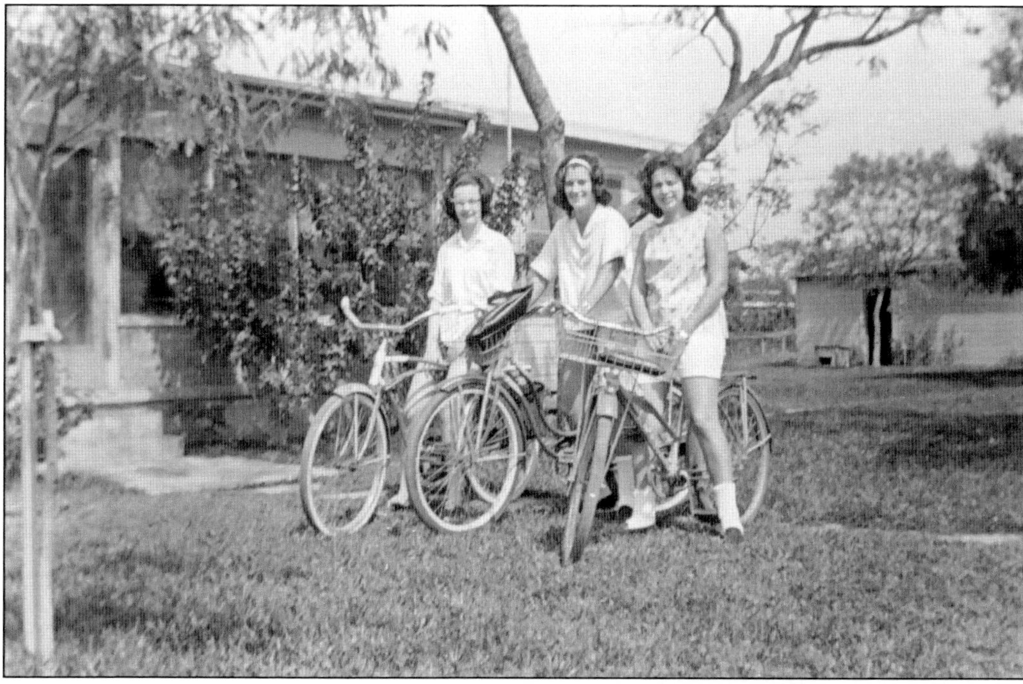

Before 10-speed bicycles were invented, girls and boys had bicycles that would go any speed the children could pedal. Bobby socks, tiger-eye glasses, and bicycle baskets were common. The three girls pictured in this 1963 photograph are Georgia Olive, Diantha Doan, and Carolyn Sanford. (Courtesy Carolyn Sanford Huesser.)

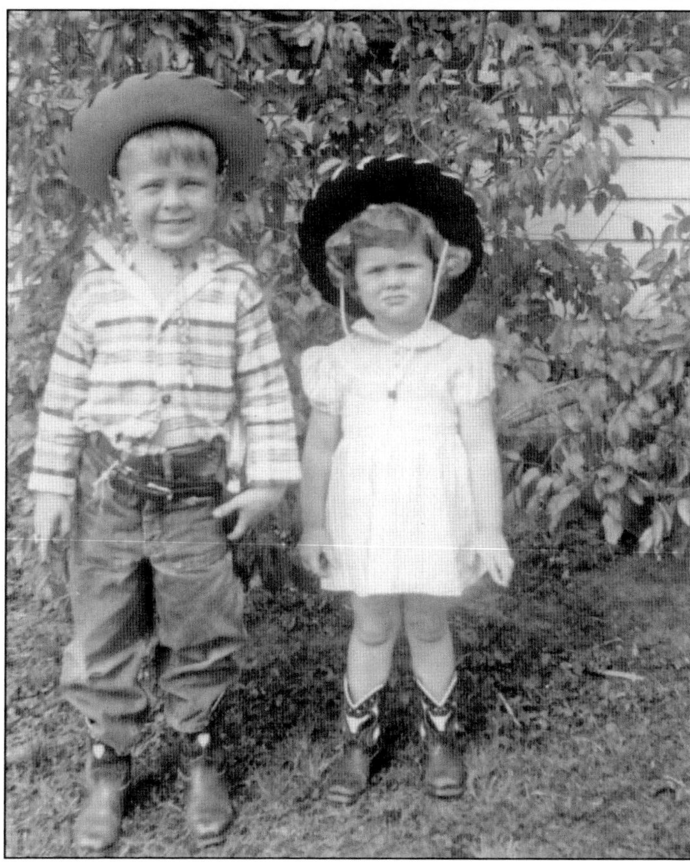

In the 1950s, cowboy and cowgirl dress-up was essential kids' fashion. Both Monte and sister Suzanne Gilbert have donned Western hats and boots for this c. 1953 photograph, but only Monte has a holster with a gun. The children are pictured here at their grandmother's house on Gamble Road. (Courtesy Suzanne Gilbert.)

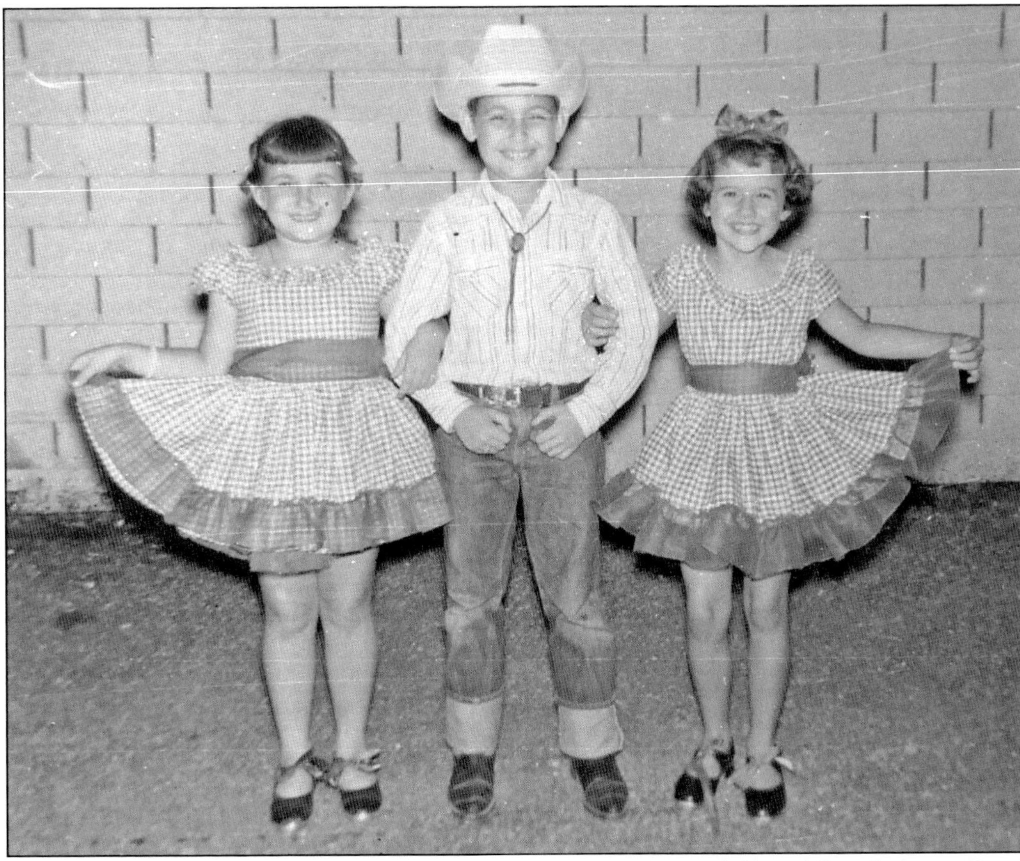

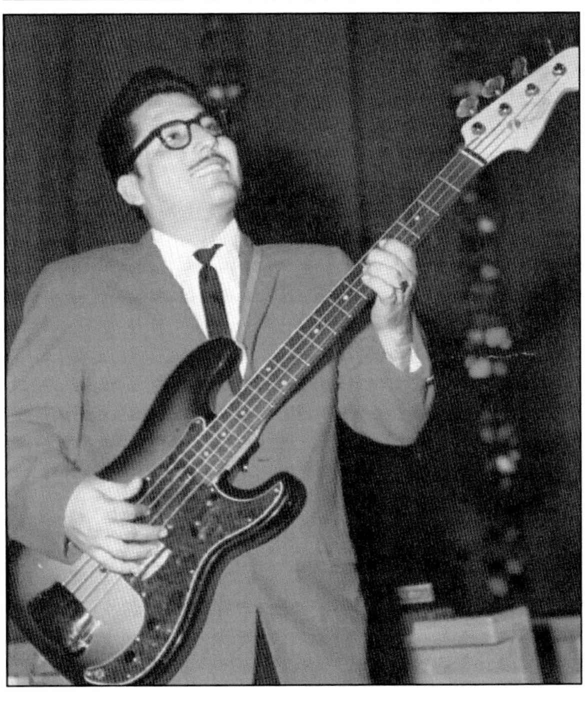

Judy Fry (left) and friend Sharon Reed are about to perform a tap number at the Jacob Brown Auditorium in Brownsville, and Judy's brother Ben has slipped between them for this picture. When asked if he'd also participated at the dance recital, Ben Fry replied, "No. This is how we always dressed in the Fifties." (Courtesy Ben Fry.)

In 1938, at the age of six, Alfredo "Freddy" Gomez, "El Ciclon Del Valle," began playing the guitar at El Rancho Carricitos, Texas, where he was born. In the 1940s, Alfredo's family moved to San Benito, where he attended Fred Booth Elementary and SBHS. Gomez went on to record over 25 albums in his career and acted in three Mexican movies. He was inducted into the Texas Conjunto Hall of Fame in 2003. (Courtesy Rey Avila.)

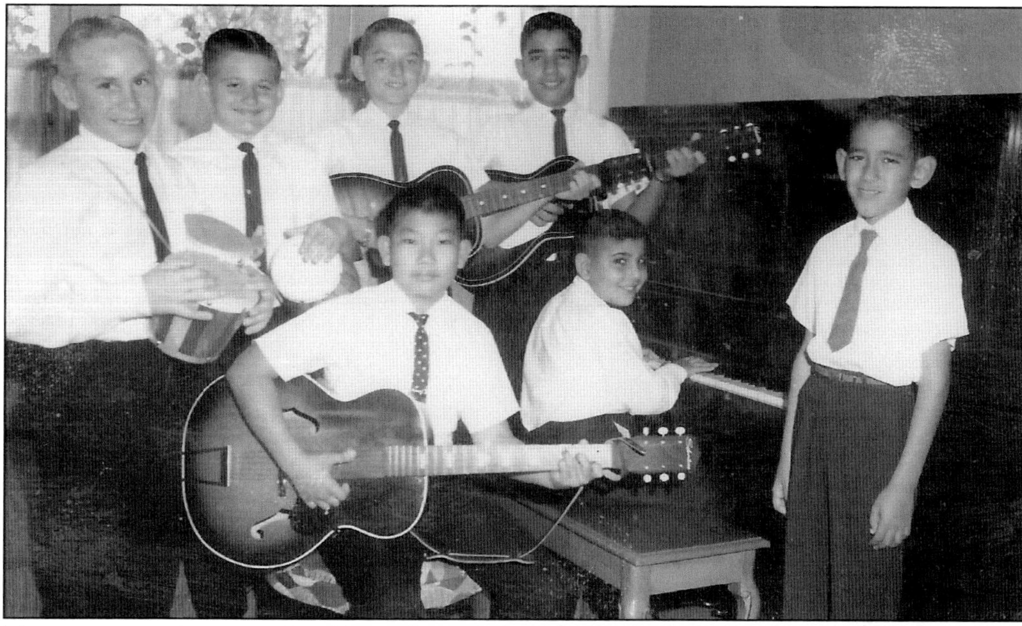

Musicians started young in San Benito. Pictured here from left to right are (first row) David Hanawa, Eddie Ogdee, and Omar "Bobby" Rodriguez; (second row) Ronnie Seals, Bobby Ledbetter, Don Nowakowski, and Barry Rodriguez. Four of the seven boys pictured here continued with music all their lives. The two Rodriguez brothers were taught music by their mother Amelia "Mela" Rodriquez, who trained many local residents on the guitar and piano. (Courtesy Tootie Madden.)

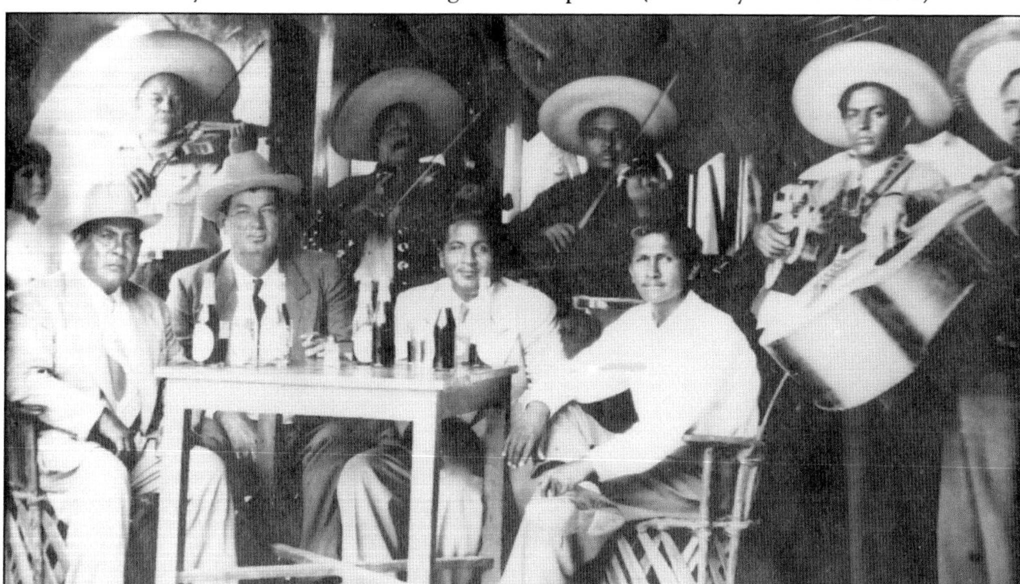

Although the roots of Mariachi go back hundreds of years, there were no Bachs or Beethovens in its early history because Mariachi music was the music of country people. Until the 1930s, Mariachi groups were local and were almost entirely unknown outside their own region. This began to change about 60 years ago. In this photograph, Hidalgo Street neighbors Jose Nuñez (seated, left) and Ramon Davila Jr. (to his right), enjoy mariachi music with friends. (Courtesy Maria Robles Nuñez.)

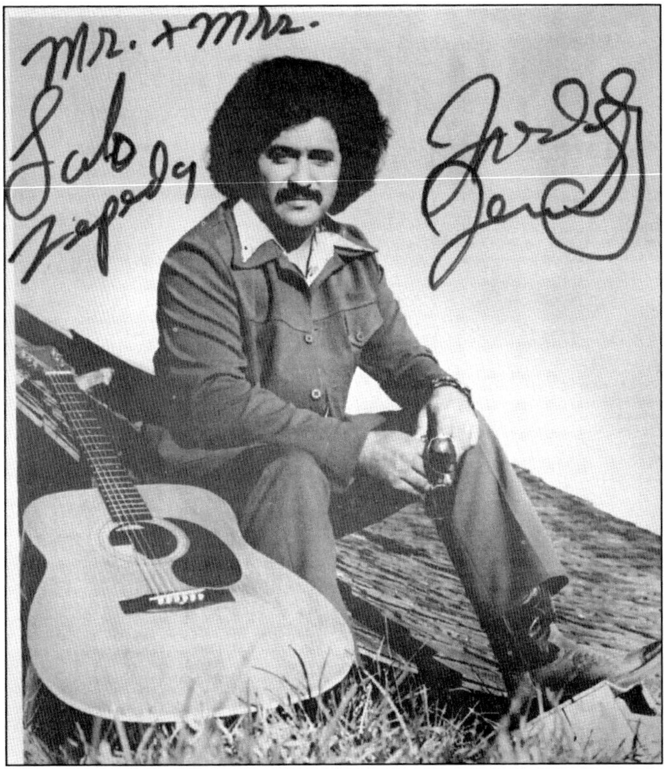

Country and rock musician Freddy Fender was born in San Benito. On one of his many visits back to town, he signed this photograph for Mr. and Mrs. Lalo Zepeda. Known locally by his real name, Baldemar G. Huerta, he played music from a young age and kept at it through hard times. Finally, beginning with 1975's "Before the Next Teardrop Falls," Fender began a string of four *Billboard* Top 40 hits and 16 Top 40 Country hits. Over the next 30 years, he earned 3 Grammys kept playing and recording until his death on October 14, 2006. Freddy Fender was buried at the San Benito City Cemetery. (Courtesy Celeste Z. Sanchez.)

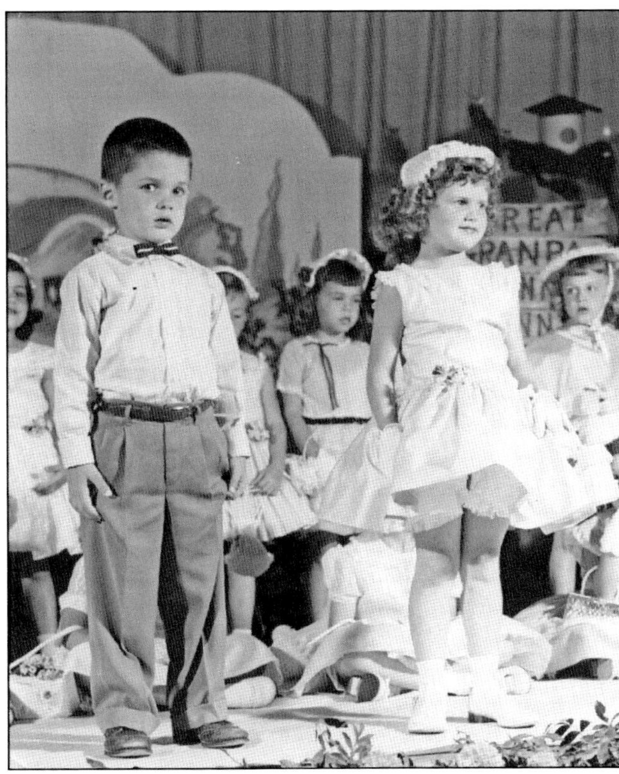

There were many private kindergartens in the 1940s and 1950s because pre-K and Kindergarten were not yet part of the public school system. Mama Crow's Kindergarten was located at the corner of Otho and North Dowling Streets, with a facade resembling the outline of the Alamo. Florence "Mama" Crow, owner, was also the great-aunt of Suzanne Gilbert, seen here with a classmate at the annual Easter Parade around 1955. (Courtesy Suzanne Gilbert.)

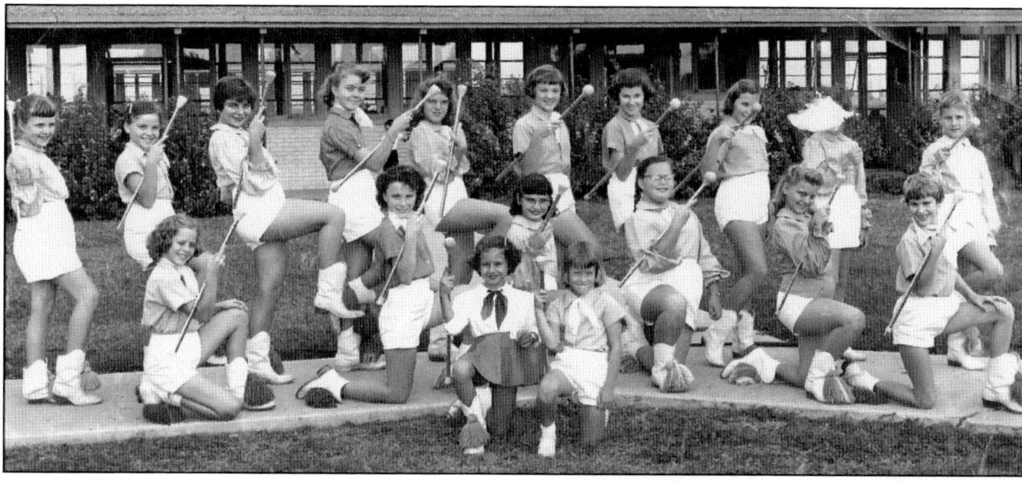

Because the Dr. Cash School and Ed Downs School didn't have enough boys to make their own football teams, they combined them into the Cash/Downs team, and did the same with their schools' twirlers, pictured here. From left to right are (first row) Sharon Reed and unidentified; (second row) Sharon Cornelius, Kay Bandy, Linda Ridgeway, Ann Lomax, Carolyn Huitt, and Bonnie Henderson; (third row) Nancy Phillips, unidentified, Diane Echols, Donna Dodson, Sandra Espey, Barbara Baker, Linda Hogan, Patsy Wenkstern, Dabney Scales, and Nancy Thompson. The schools also shared the same principal, Vola Prentiss. (Courtesy Katherine Scales.)

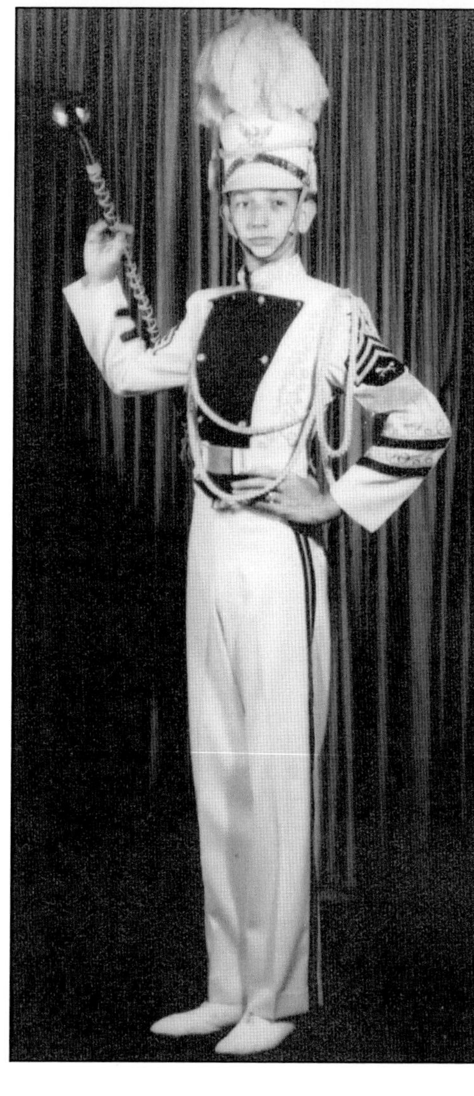

Future actor and San Benito native Ray Stewart was the 1949 San Benito High School Band drum major. He is best remembered for the character of Daryl Driscoll on television's *Barney Miller*, and was a regular on Barbara Mandrell's and Susan Anton's shows as well. He guest-starred on such major shows as *Dallas*, *Falcon Crest*, *Hill Street Blues*, *Hart to Hart*, *Fantasy Island*, *The Bob Newhart Show*, and *Benson*. He made his Broadway debut in the play *Postcards*. (Courtesy Ray Stewart.)

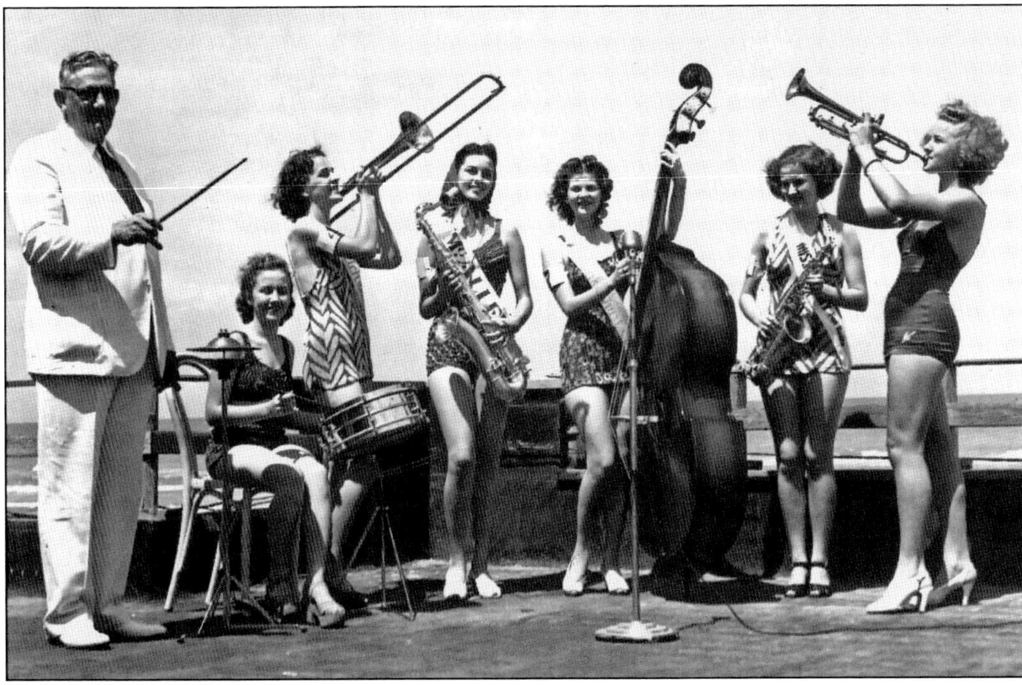

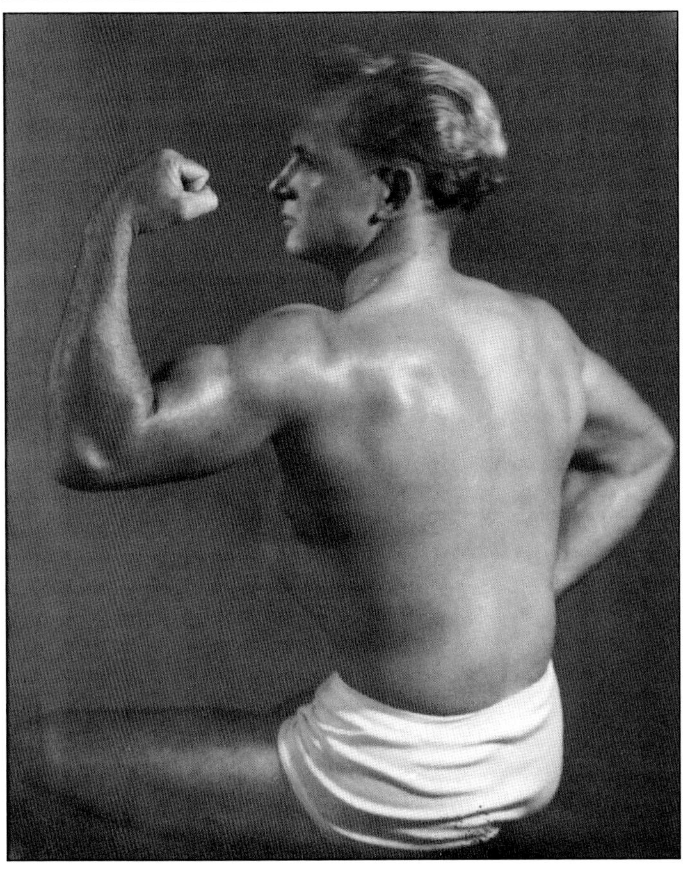

Pretty girls from all over the Valley have formed a Bathing Beauty Orchestra at one of the beach resorts. Ed Downs, who donated the land where the elementary school was built, conducts the band. Dorothy Dodds from San Benito plays the bass fiddle. (Courtesy Carolyn Gentry.)

Boxer Linard Gilbert was ahead of his time in the field of body building. He kept in shape for his Golden Gloves boxing matches by regular exercise. (Courtesy Suzanne Gilbert.)

When Narciso Martinez, "Father of Conjunto Music," teamed up with Santiago Almeida, a 12-string bass guitar (bajo sexto) player in 1935, historians say that Texas Mexican Conjunto Music was born. In 1983, Pres. Ronald Reagan presented Narciso with the National Heritage Award, the highest award given to folk musicians. He was inducted into the Texas Conjunto Music Hall of Fame in 2002. Martinez was born October 29, 1911, Reynosa, Tamaulipas, Mexico, and his family immigrated to La Paloma Ranch, about 7 miles southeast of San Benito, that same year. (Courtesy Rey Avila.)

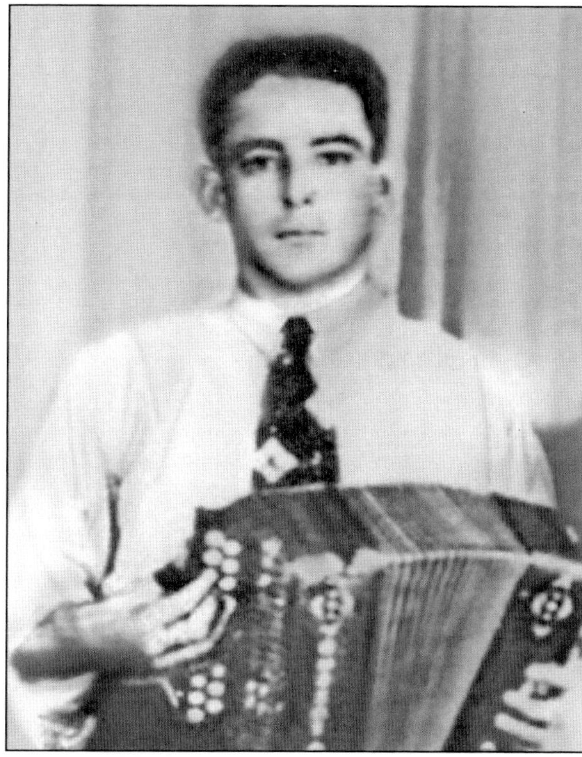

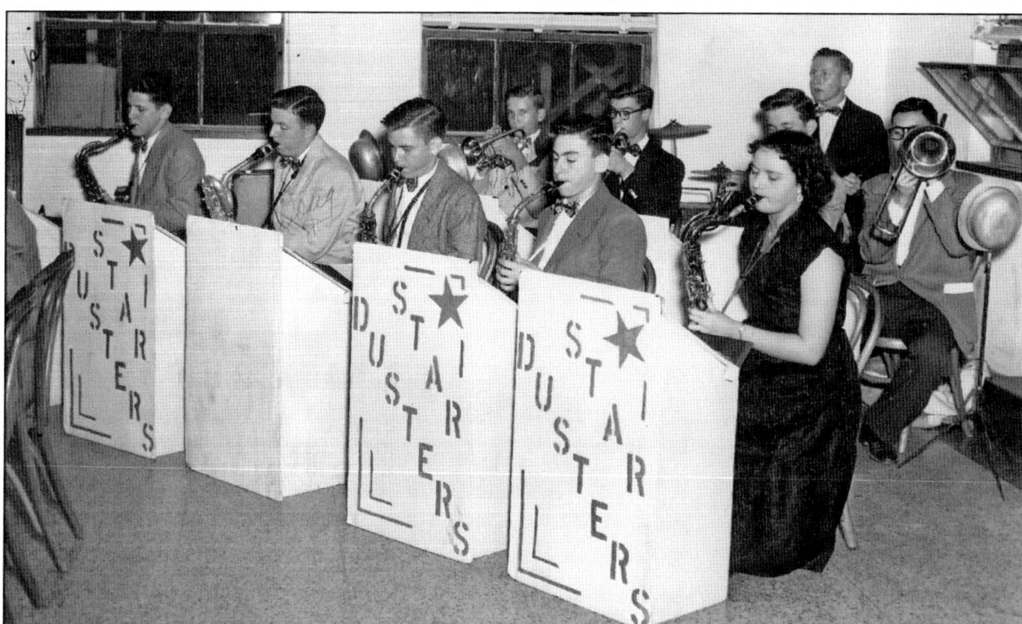

The San Benito High School Orchestra Star Dusters was one of the earliest dance bands in the history of SBHS. From left to right are (first row) Max Harris, Douglas Hutchings, Buddy Moore, Gregory Haas, and Mary June McIntosh; (second row) Ronnie Woods, Phil Shafer, Don Hood, and Lionel Betancourt; (third row) Melvin Allen on the drums. Dicki Nicholson and Patricia Bowie often played with the group, which was led by director Nat Alewine. (Courtesy Max Y. Harris.)

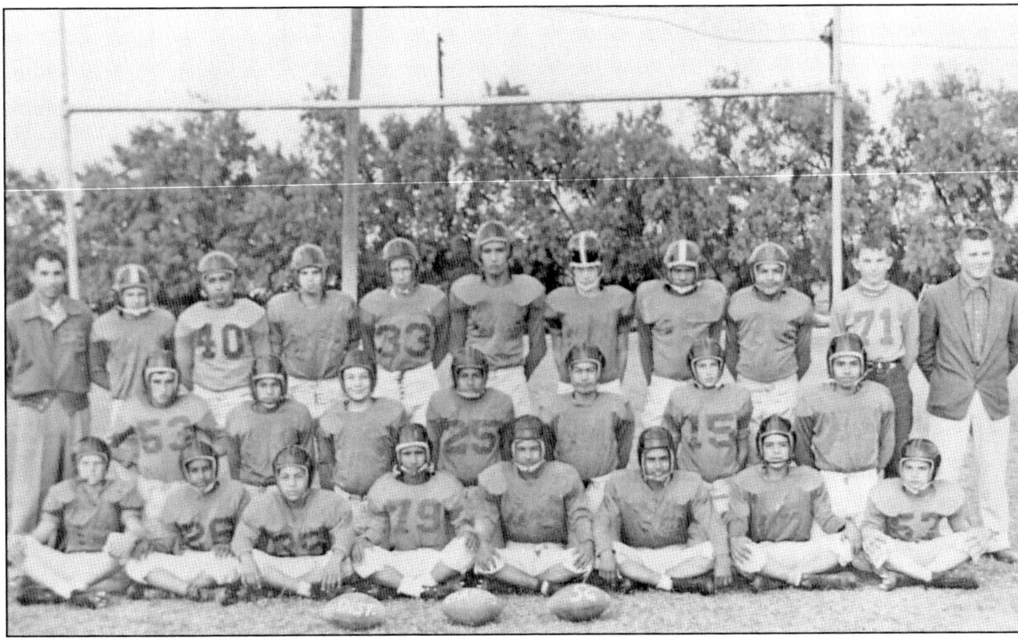

This San Benito Junior High football team won the AAA District Championship in 1956. The team was composed of seventh and eighth graders. A few years later in 1961, some of these same players took the San Benito Greyhounds to the state semi-finals round against Nederland High School. From left to right are (first row) Fred Christiansen, Agapito Rodriguez, Raul Saldaña, Rey Avila, Oscar Tamez, Jose V. Martinez, Marcos Lopez, and Jesus Perez; (second row) Robert Montalvo, Adolfo Huerta, Eddie Goldman, Demetrio Lucio, Uvence Galvan, Gene Uptegraph, and Juan Aguilar; (third row) coach Henry Montalvo, Emeterio Arellano, Oscar Ortega, Jim Lewis, Gene Guetzow, Carlos Garza, B. L. Foley, Felix Ybarra, Domingo Ramirez, Tommie Dodson and coach Joe Collins. (Courtesy Rey Avila.)

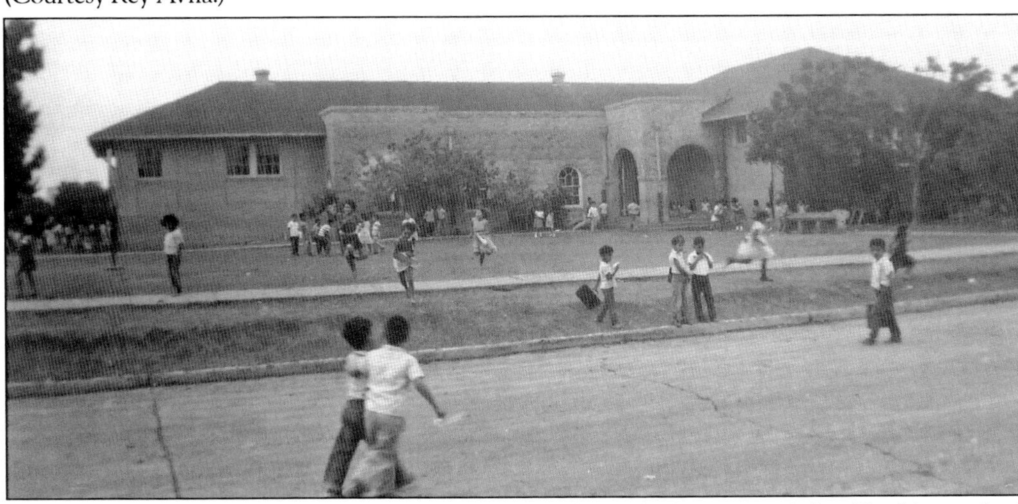

Seen in this early 1950s photograph is the original Fred Booth Elementary School building, which is still standing; it was used as a hospital during the 1918 influenza epidemic. Lupe Aguirre worked as a doctor's aide and said, "People that died, we'd just take them and put them in a wagon and take them out there to the old city cemetery . . . and just dump them in. Something you regret in those days." (Courtesy San Benito Historical Society.)

While San Benito's boys were out playing "cowboys and Indians," little girls like Mary Ann Kennedy and Deborah Medders were busily preparing for marriage and motherhood. In this c. 1954 photograph, these young "mommies" take their baby dolls for an afternoon stroll. (Courtesy Mary Ann Frailing.)

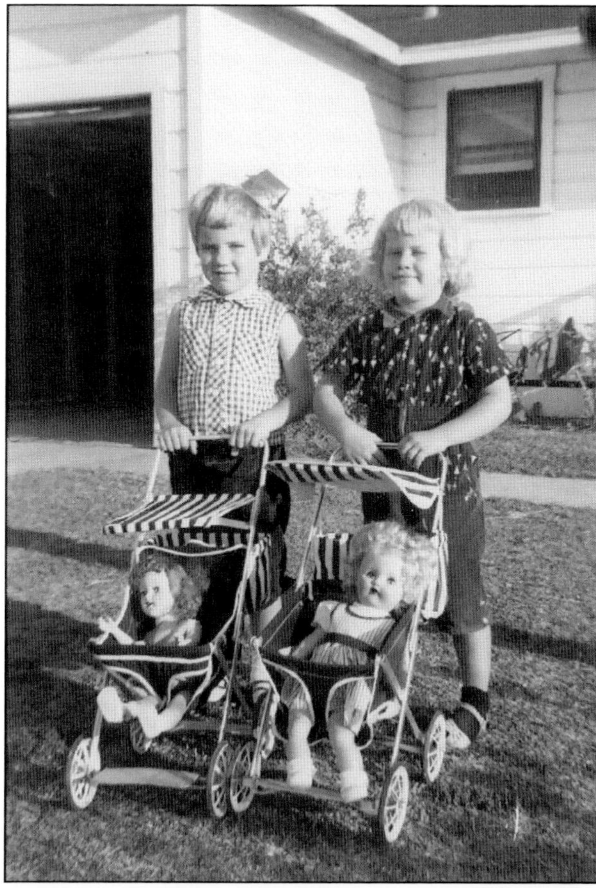

The Kiwanis Club sponsored boys' and girls' softball and baseball teams throughout the years, which played at the Kiwanis Ball Park. The softball team pictured here played other teams from around the Valley. At the end of the season, the club honored the girls with a luncheon at the Stonewall Jackson Hotel and presented each with a sweater emblazoned with the Kiwanis logo. Bill Collins, Erwin C. Reese, and Lee Roy Crawford Sr. are among the Kiwanis members pictured. (Courtesy Mary Catherine Lovett.)

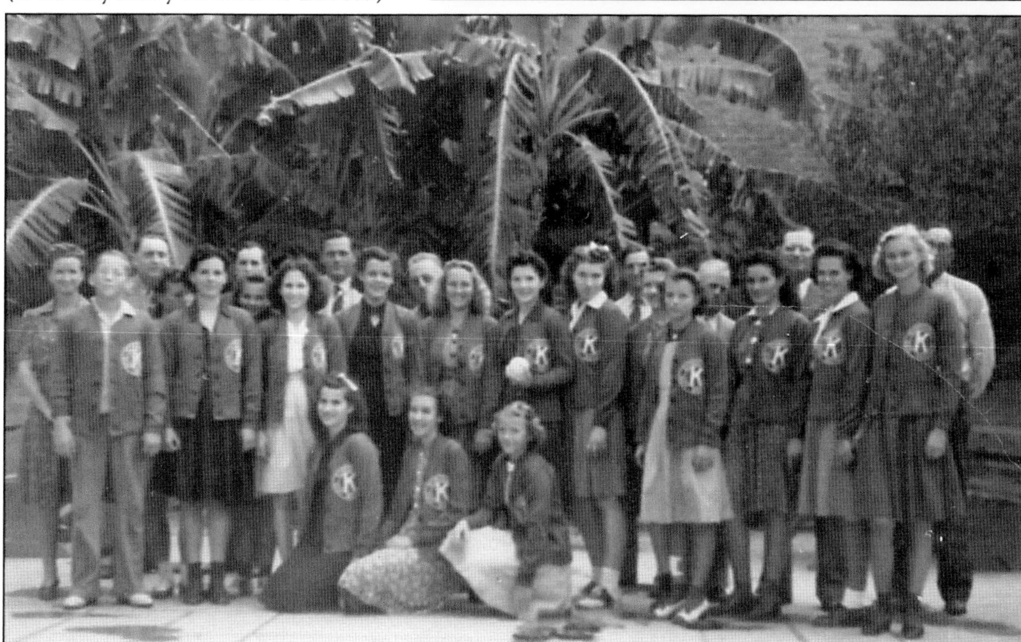

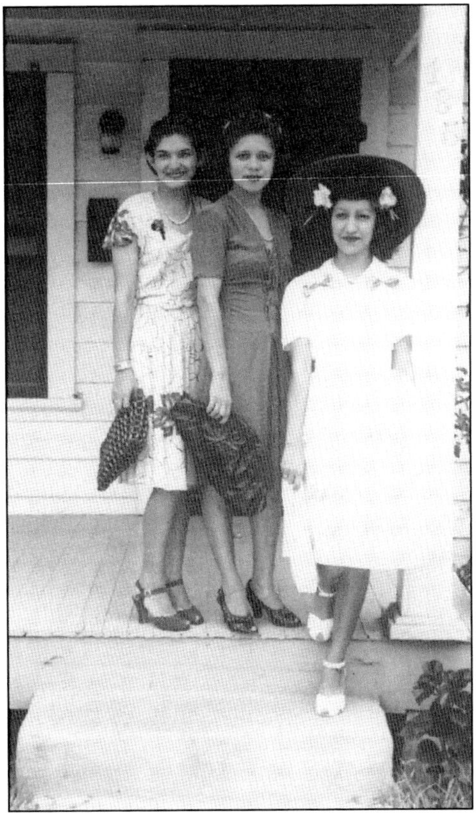

Sworn to remain best friends forever, Celia Moreno, Bertha Atkinson, and Sulema Argullin have their picture taken outside Celia's home at 185 Corral Street. According to Bertha's brother Ernie, these three women were always together and had a good time going places. During World War II, while many of the town's men were away defending the country, young women formed good, dependable friendships. Also evidenced here are the clothing styles popular during the war, which included big hats, strappy open-toed shoes, and large purses. (Courtesy Sandra Tumberlinson and Dolores Ramirez.)

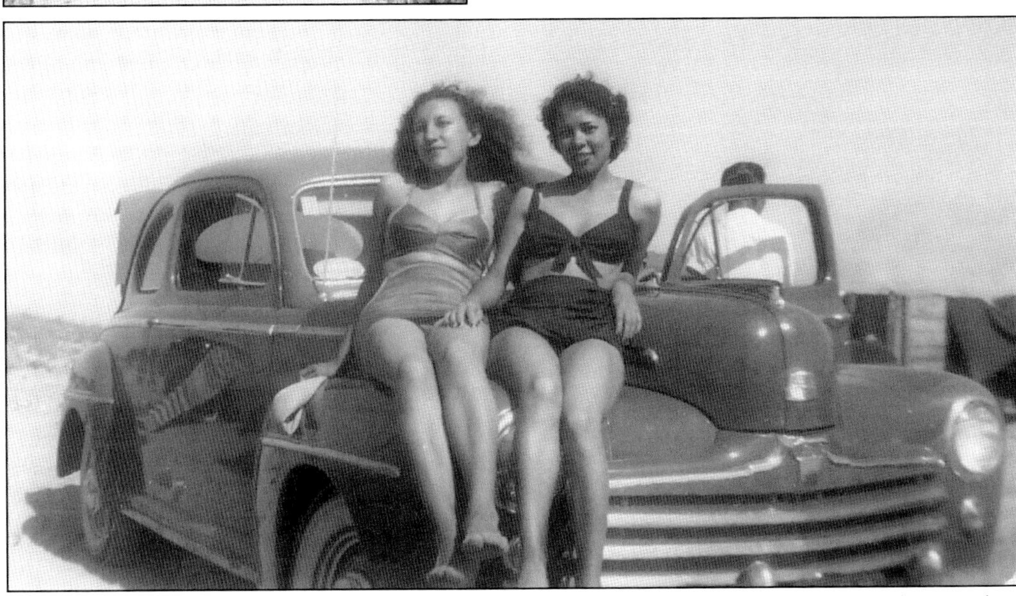

Before South Padre Island was developed and accessible to traffic, Boca Chica Beach was where people went to enjoy the gulf water, picnic on the sand, and spend the day relaxing. Boca Chica Beach is at the mouth of the Rio Grande River on the mainland, and directly on the Gulf of Mexico. In this photograph taken on July 4, 1947, bathing beauties Enriqueta Lopez (left) and Irene Ybarra enjoy the sun while sitting on Luis Moody's car. (Courtesy Enriqueta L. Ramos.)

Six

HOW WE CELEBRATED

PARADES, PARTIES, AND HOLIDAYS

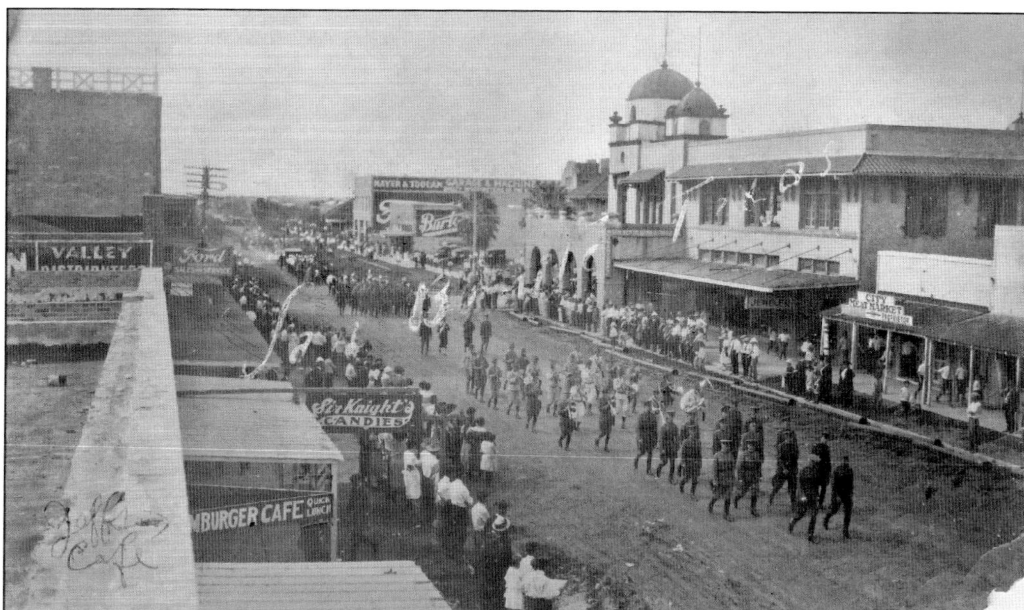

In this c. 1915 photograph, soldiers and their bands lead the parade through town along Sam Houston Boulevard. Note that although San Benito's main thoroughfare is still a dirt street, all of the stores along it are occupied. Jeff's Café, at bottom left, was owned by Jeff Thompson, father of Kenny Thompson, who himself served the town as a mail carrier for 25 years. Notice the words "San Benito, Texas," written in white across the postcard. (Courtesy Shirlee Thompson.)

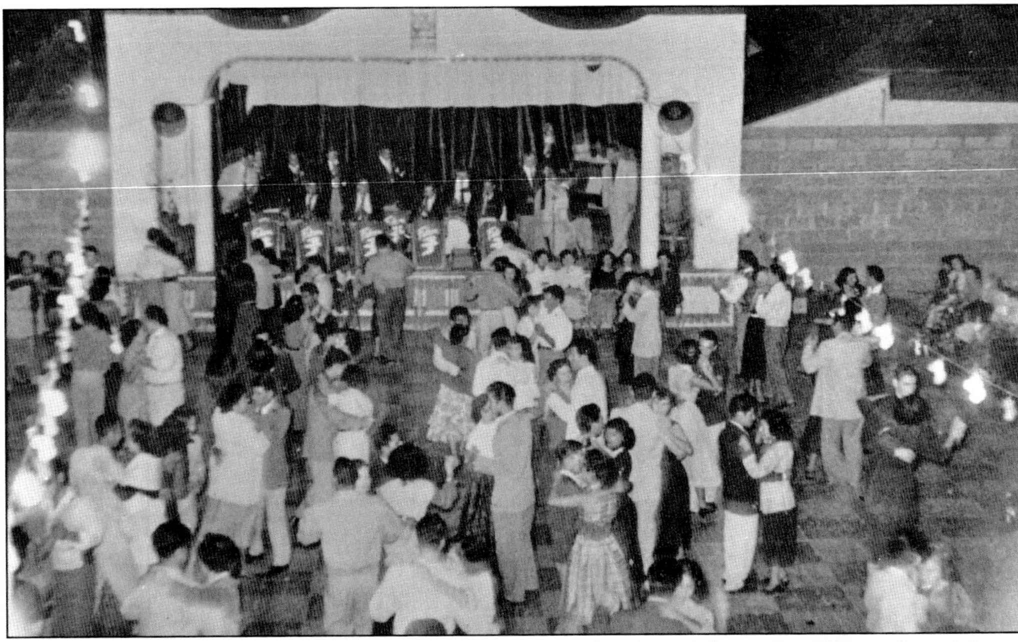

El que no conoce La Villita, no conoce San Benito. "He who doesn't know La Villita, doesn't know San Benito." This catchphrase, coined by La Villita co-owner Fernando S. Sanchez over 50 years ago, had much truth to it. In the early 1940s, Fernando and his wife, Eva, purchased property on West Robertson Street, and by 1948 had built a large complex with spaces for several businesses, including this open-air dance hall. "La Villita" was soon the most famous dance hall in the Valley. (Courtesy Rey Avila.)

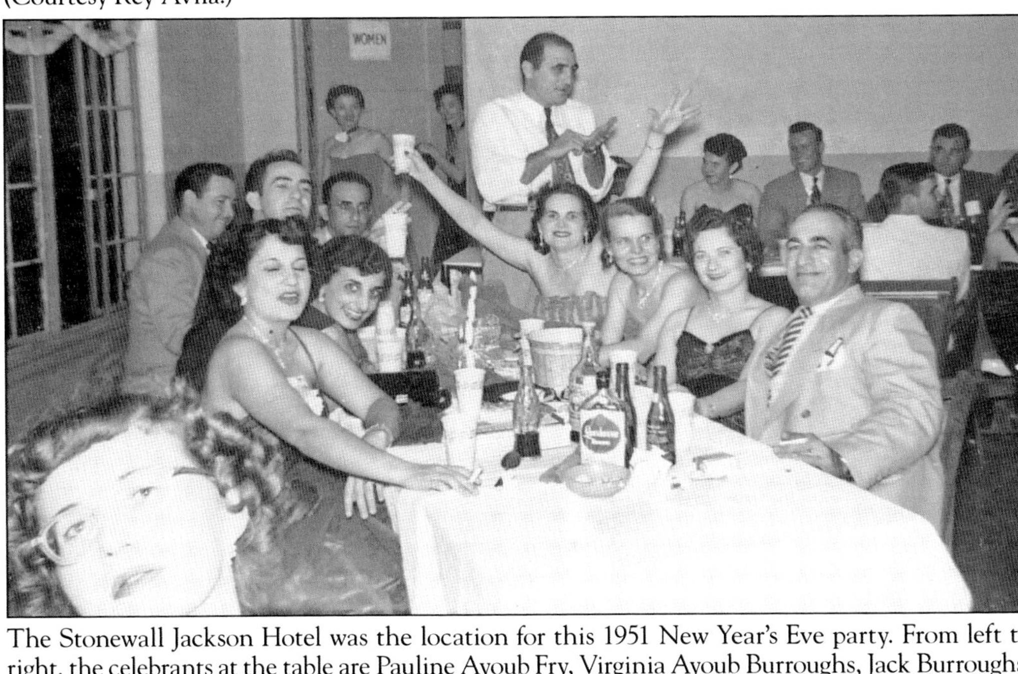

The Stonewall Jackson Hotel was the location for this 1951 New Year's Eve party. From left to right, the celebrants at the table are Pauline Ayoub Fry, Virginia Ayoub Burroughs, Jack Burroughs, unidentified, David Ayoub, Ed Ogdee (standing), Becky Ogdee, Cleo Ayoub, Cleo Johns, and James Johns. (Courtesy Ben Fry.)

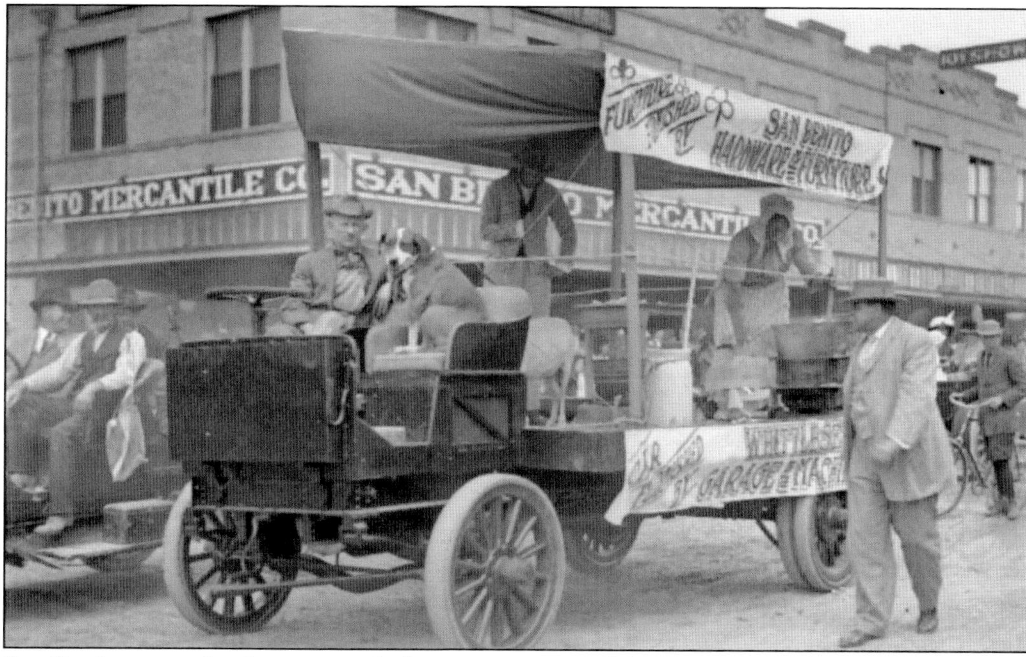

San Benito seemed to have a parade for every occasion. Most interesting about this photograph (aside from the primitive float with the dog riding shotgun) is the building in the background—201 North Sam Houston Boulevard. Downstairs was the San Benito Mercantile; the second floor handled overflow from the San Benito Hotel. (Courtesy San Benito Historical Society.)

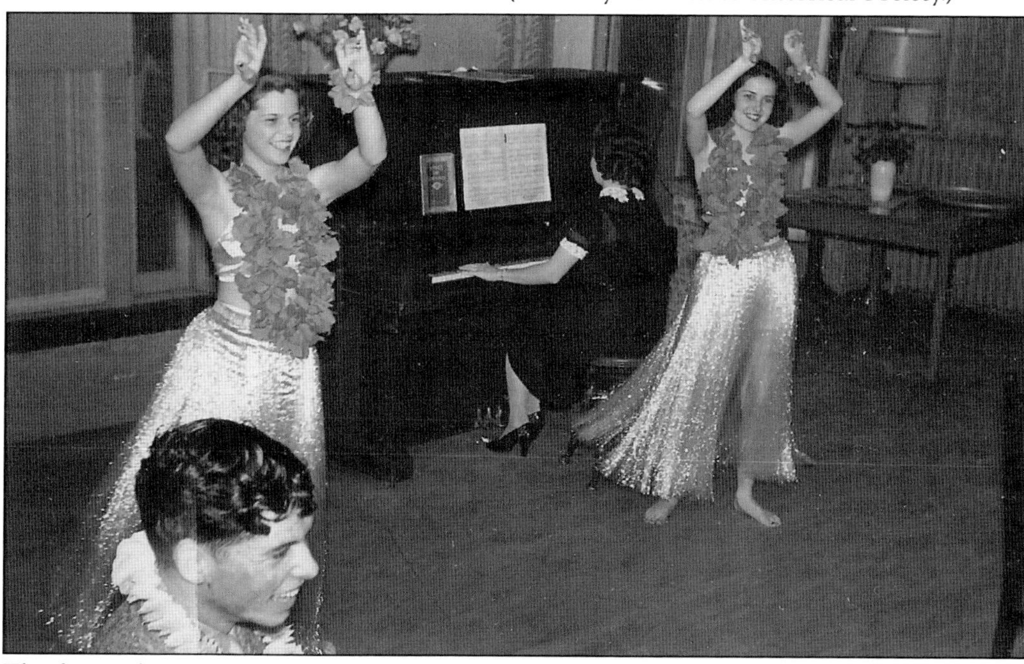

The featured entertainment for a Hawaiian-themed party were the beautiful Hula girls, "Jack" Buesing and Helen Morris. These girls were dance students of Markoleta Eltsner and were frequently featured entertainment for clubs, meetings, and banquets. Later, in the 1950s, Jack became assistant dance instructor for her mentor. (Courtesy Tootie Madden.)

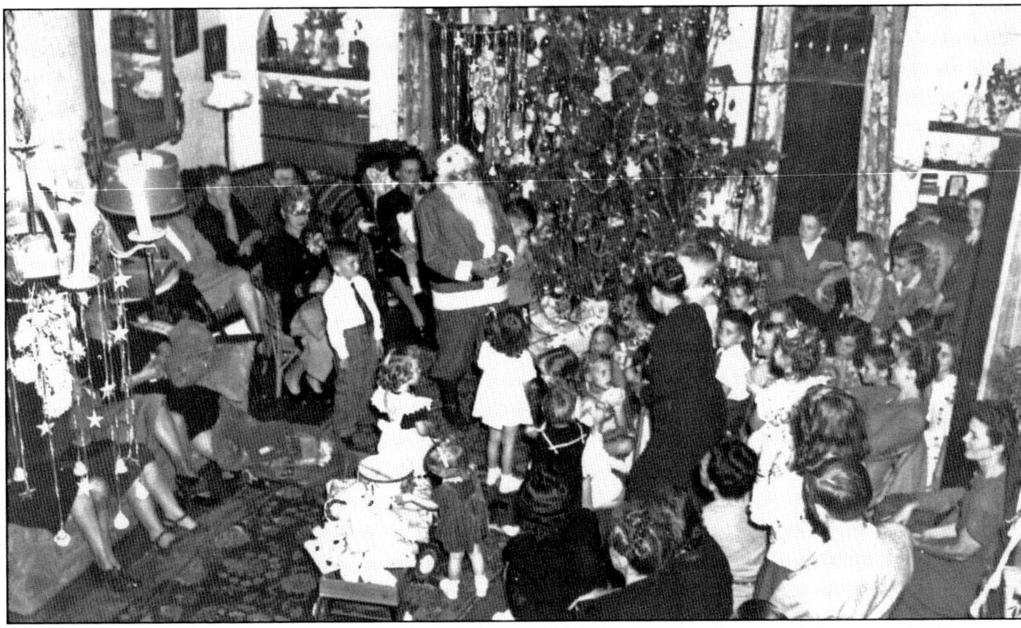

In 1945, over 200 guests pack Rae and Stanley Dodds's home for the couple's annual Christmas Eve party. By the end of World War II, this party had already been a ritual for 41 years, beginning in 1911. After the Christmas story was read and carols sung, Santa arrived with one toy for each child. Tamales, sandwiches, and cookies were served. The Dodds's daughter Dorothy Huitt revived the party for a third generation after a gap of a few years. (Courtesy Carolyn Gentry.)

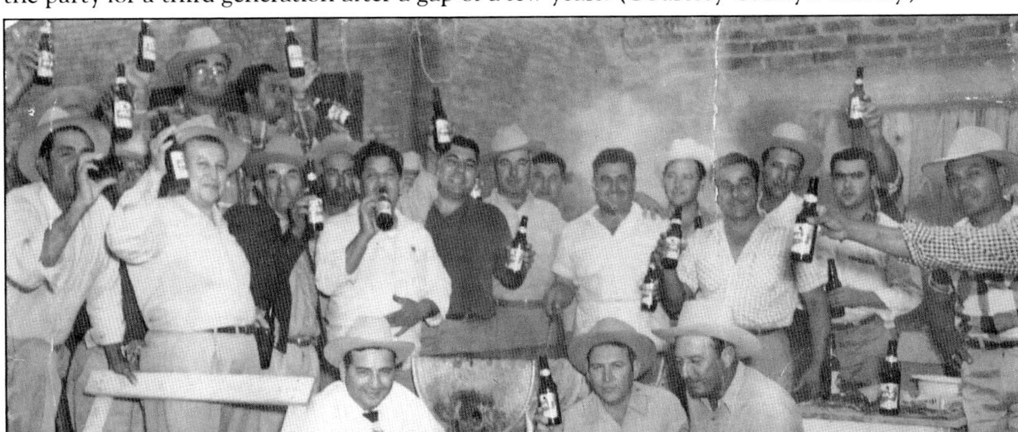

Celebrating Lalo Zepeda's birthday at the Buckhorn Inn on February 28, 1957, were a "few" of his friends and relatives. From left to right, they are (first row) Alberto Montemayor, Flavio Flores, and Jesus Contreras; (second row) two unidentified men, T. O. Ramirez (holding a beer to his ear), two unidentified men behind him, Beto Montalvo (black jacket), unidentified, Fernando Sanchez (holding his belly), unidentified, Lalo Zepeda (center, wearing hat), Lico Garcia, unidentified, Pancho Martinez, Eliseo Balli, Jesus Padilla, Richard Corkill, and an unidentified man. (Courtesy Celeste Z. Sanchez.)

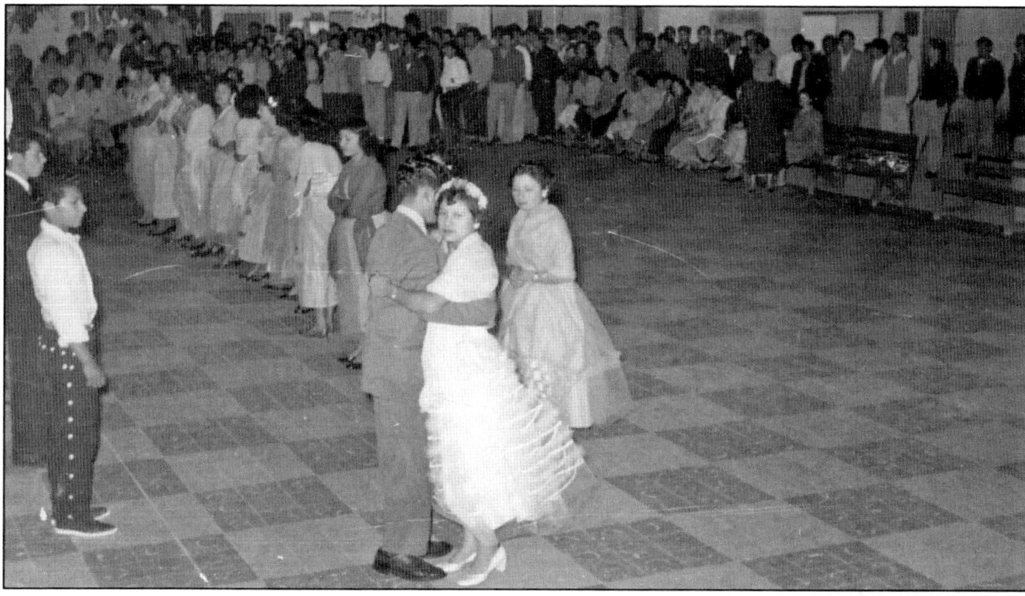

Wedding receptions were often held at La Villita. Notice the trademark checked-tile floor. In this late 1950s wedding photograph, Chano Lino is the young man standing at the left. Because he liked to sew white buttons on the sides of his pants, he earned the nickname "Chano Botones," or "Chano Buttons." (Courtesy Rey Avila.)

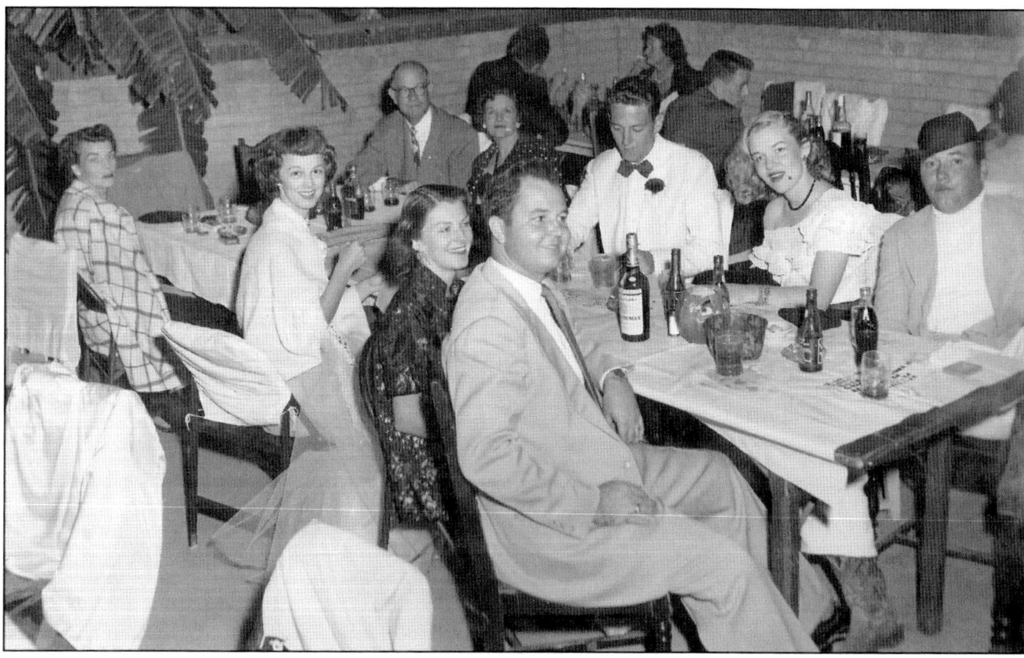

The Junior Service League held two themed charity balls a year at the Stonewall Jackson Hotel and usually drew some 300 people. Shown here enjoying a ball are, from left to right, (left side of table) Louise Lovett, Mary Catherine Lovett, Mary Ann Welch, Dick Welch; (right side of table) Tom Lovett, Patsy Thomae, Adolph Thomae Jr., and Jim Barnes and wife. Pink Ladies were the featured drink that night; prices ranged from 97¢ for a Pale Pink to a whopping $1.49 for Shocking Pink. Admission was $4 per couple. (Courtesy Tootie Madden.)

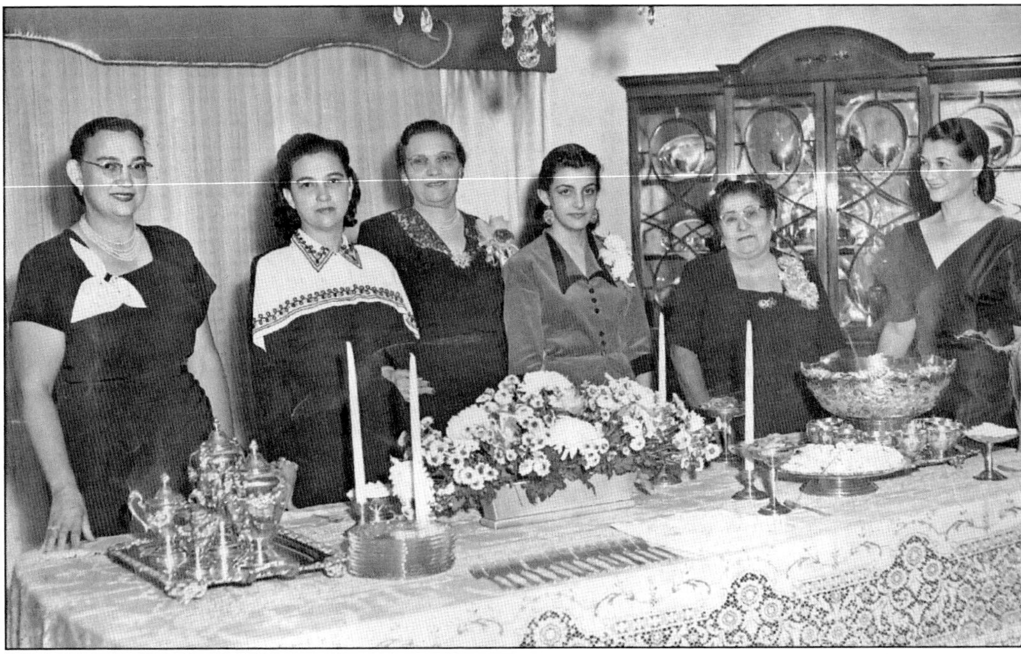

This bridal shower, held in the home of Ramon and Ester Ruenes, exemplified the art of fine living. From the left, the celebrants are Cristina Ruenes Brady, Francisca Cañas, *Doña* Ester Ruenes, two unidentified women, and Ester Ruenes. Cristina Ruenes was married to Phillip Brady. (Courtesy Carlos Cañas.)

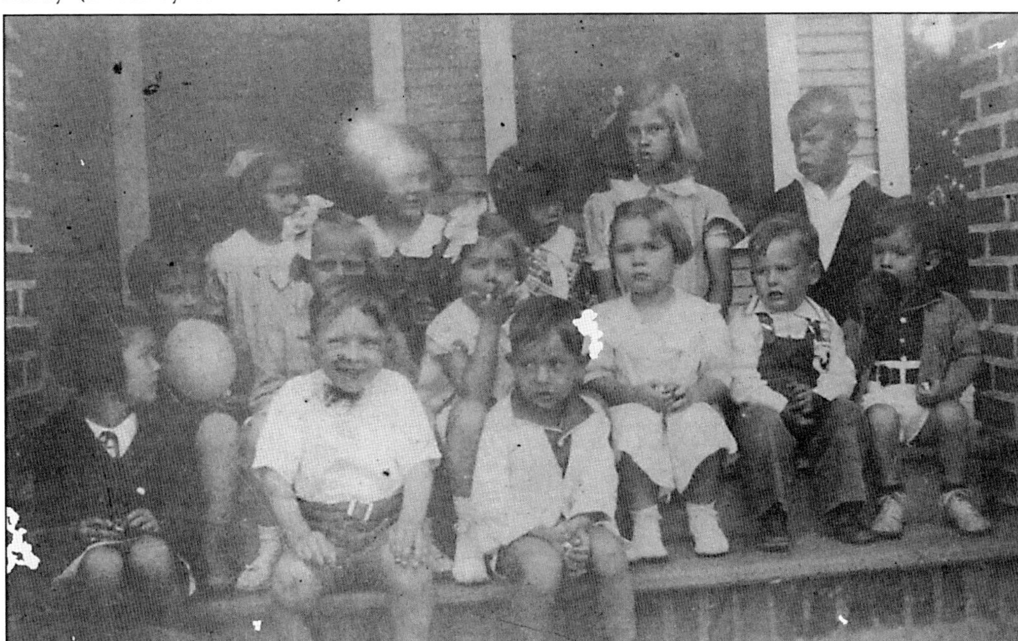

Celebrating a birthday in 1934 are (first row) Jo Ann Hamilton, Tipton Housewright, and Ray Stewart; (second row) unidentified boy and girl, Charlene Goolsby, Skipper Ehlers, Paulie Hill, Buddy Hamilton; (third row) Sis Morris, Helen Morris, Annette Stewart, Jo Ann Robertson, and her brother Ed Robertson. (Courtesy Ray Stewart.)

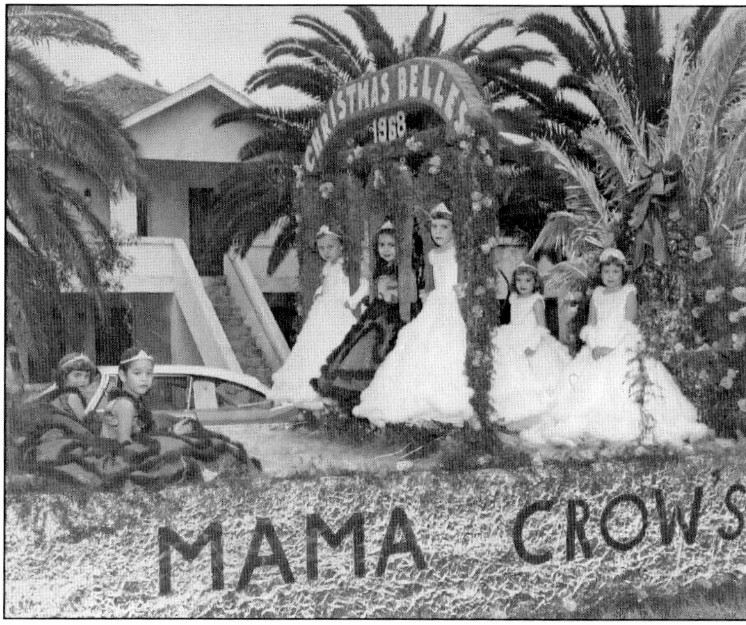

Mama Crow's Kindergarten entered this float in San Benito's and Harlingen's 1958 Christmas parades. The phrase *Christmas Belles 1968* suggests that in 10 years, the five-year-old girls will be beautiful belles. Seated are Barbara Parks (left) and Sandra Longoria. Standing on the swings beneath the arch are Judy Elam (left), Susie Casas (center), and an unidentified girl. The identities of the girls in back are not known. (Courtesy Judy Elam.)

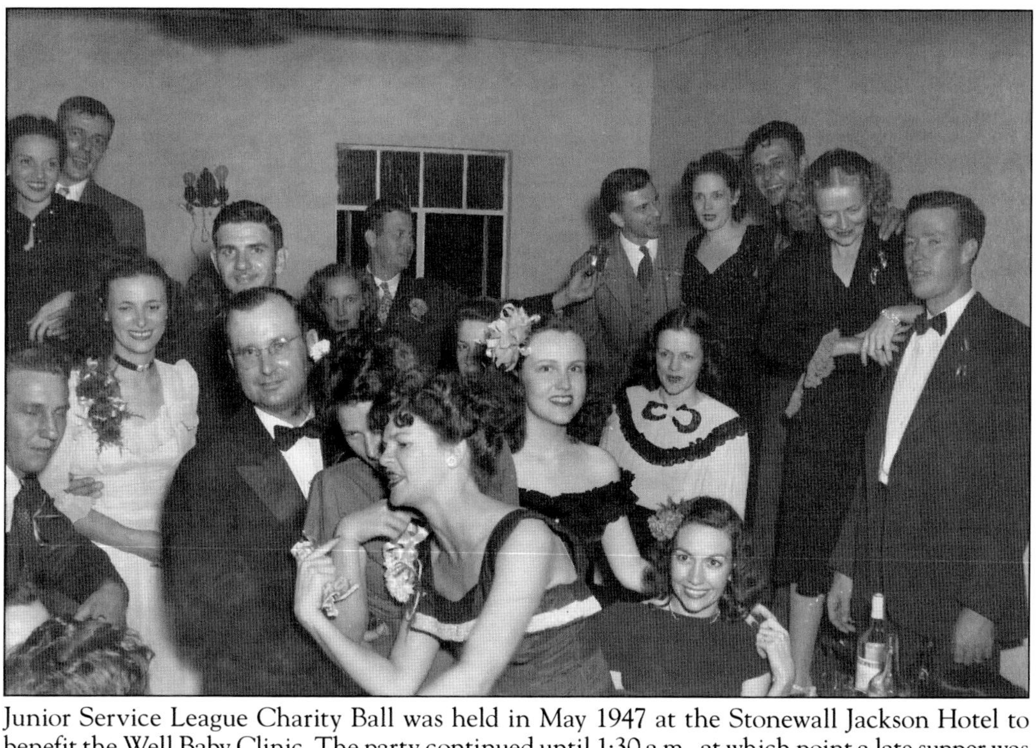

Junior Service League Charity Ball was held in May 1947 at the Stonewall Jackson Hotel to benefit the Well Baby Clinic. The party continued until 1:30 a.m., at which point a late supper was served in the dining room. The fund-raiser drew over 300 guests at $2.50 a person. Joe Bellamah's orchestra played. Some of those attending were Bill Huitt, Donnie Hood, Dorothy Huitt, Sue Marchbanks, Doris Ogden, Lorraine Mayer, Jimmie Mayer, Jimmy Landrum, "Sissy" Landrum, and Tom Marchbanks. (Courtesy Tootie Madden.)

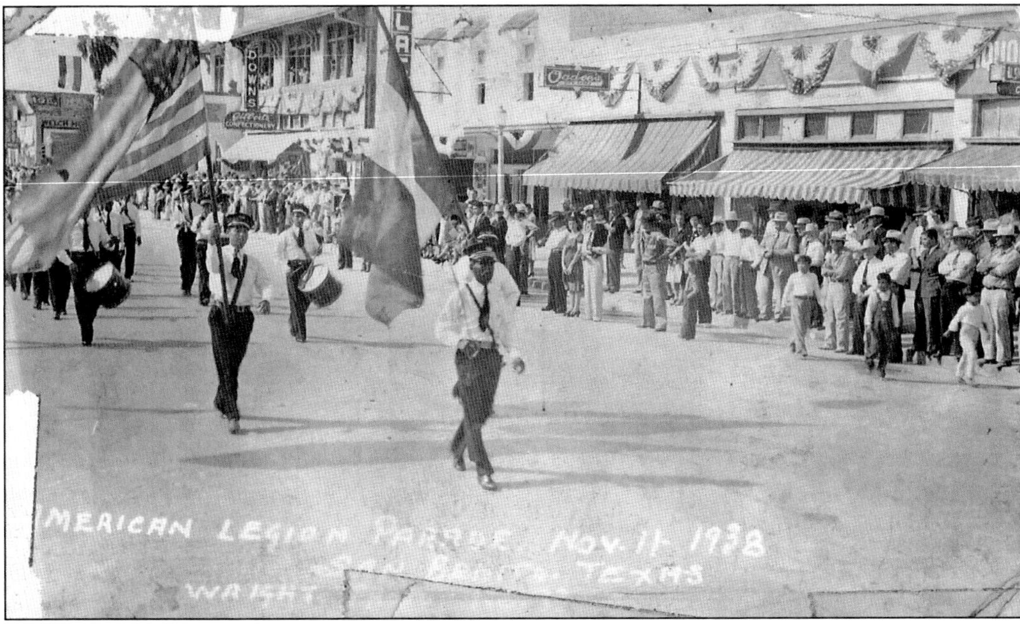

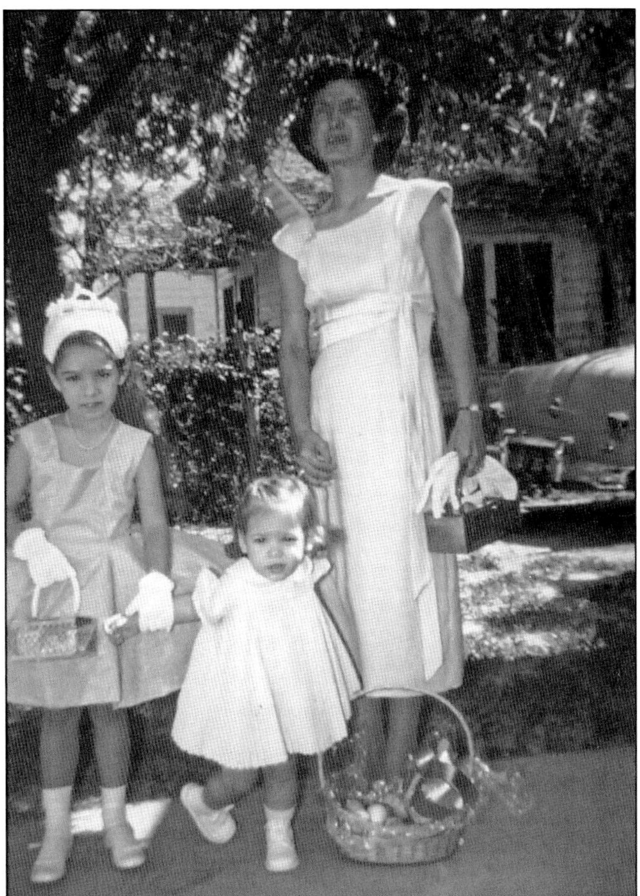

Armistice Day is the anniversary of the formal end of World War I on November 11, 1918. The cessation of hostilities took effect at 11 a.m—at the 11th hour of the 11th day of the 11th month. Armistice Day was celebrated in San Benito for many years with a parade down Sam Houston Boulevard. Pictured here holding the American flag in the 1938 parade is David Raymond De Leon. (Courtesy David De Leon.)

Celebrating Easter in the 1950s was always a "dress up" event for Sandra Longoria (left), Dolores Longoria, and their mother, Celia. Both mother and daughters wore hats, gloves, and matching purses to church. Sandra's pink dress, dotted with tiny rose buds, was made by her mother. In the 1950s, petticoats were always worn. Dolores, the baby, wore white high-top shoes. Celia, in the style of the season, wore a sleeveless pink crepe dress. (Courtesy Sandra Tumberlinson and Dolores Ramirez.)

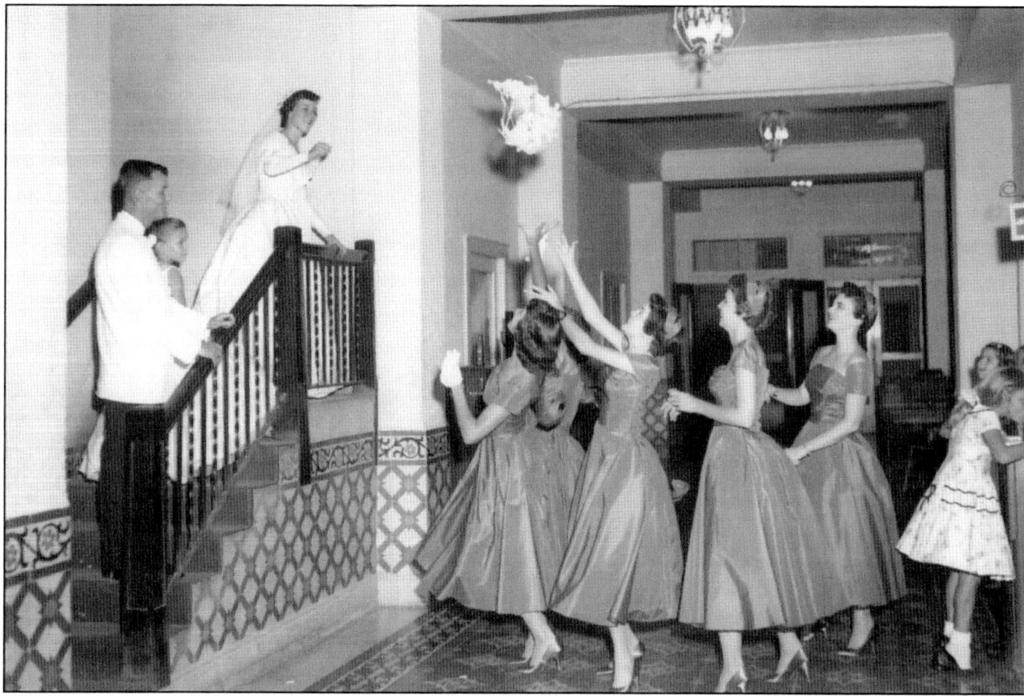

San Benito's wedding receptions were often held at the Stonewall Jackson Hotel. In this 1957 photograph, a newly married Pat Bowie Davis tosses her bouquet to her bridesmaids. From left to right, they are Connye Casey, Ann Spicer, Millicent Bleakney, Nancy Dobson, and Betty Blair. Groom Dick Davis and flower girl Kathy Davis watch from the stairs. (Courtesy Pat Bowie Davis.)

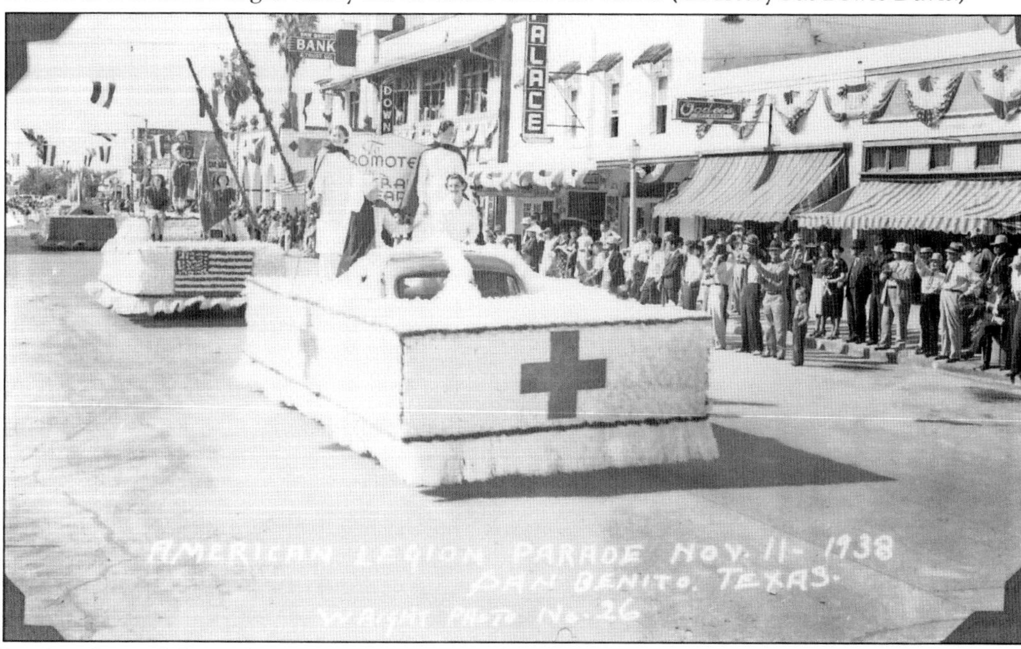

In this shot of the 1938 Armistice Day parade, the Palace Theater can be seen between the bank and Ogdee's. Notice that the float is not pulled by a car or truck, but encloses the vehicle. (Courtesy San Benito Historical Society.)

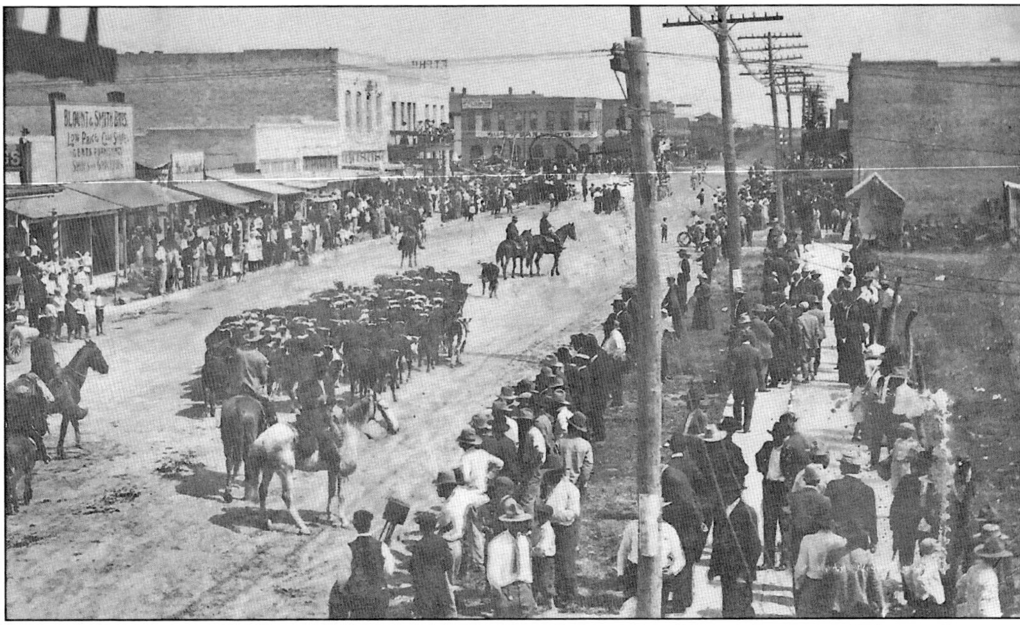

The distinctiveness of this early parade was that cowhands herded their cattle through the center of town, just as they did in cowboy times and movies. Notice the old wooden storefronts on the 100 block of South Sam Houston Boulevard. In the background, across the track, is the 100 block of North Sam Houston Boulevard, where Farmers State Bank, the San Benito Land and Water Company, and the San Benito Hotel were located. (Courtesy San Benito Historical Society.)

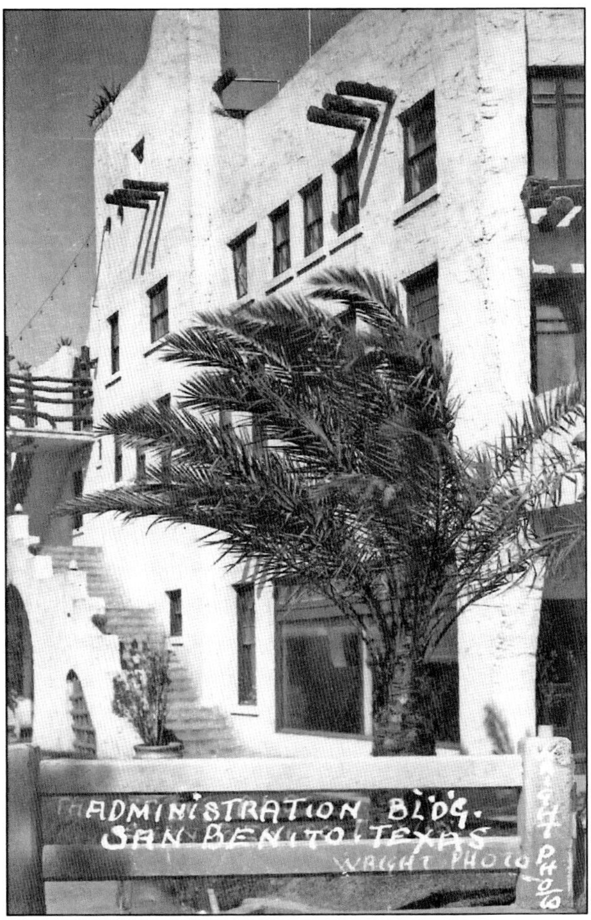

Many couples traveled up these stairs to hear the beautiful music of an orchestra, stand in the breeze of an open-air rooftop, and dance under the stars. The shell the orchestras played beneath still stands atop the Aztec Building. (Courtesy San Benito Historical Society.)

Seven

How We Served
Clubs, Churches, Children, and Country

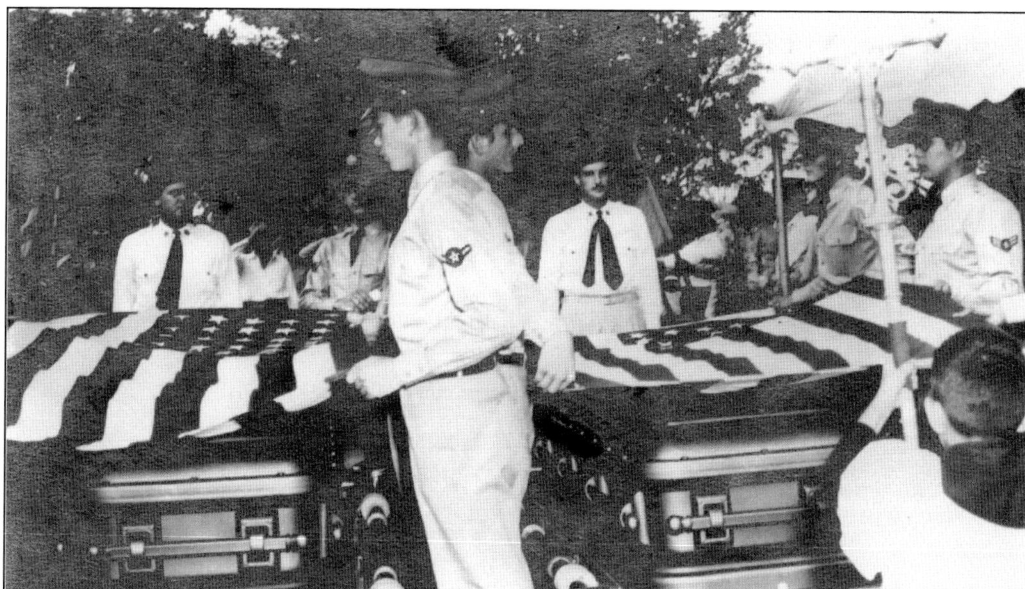

In April 1952, St. Benedict's Catholic Church held joint funeral services for two casualties of the Korean War who had once lived across the street from each other, attended school together, and worked together. Cpl. Florencio Pedraza and Pfc. Enrique Atkinson died in battle within three days of each other. Pedraza, 18, was the son of Mr. and Mrs. Nicholas Pedraza. Pfc. Enrique Atkinson, 19, was the son of Mr. and Mrs. Alberto C. Atkinson. San Benito stores closed from 2:00 p.m.–3:00 p.m. while the funeral mass was conducted. The men were buried side by side at Mont Meta Cemetery with full military honors provided by soldiers from Fort Sam Houston. (Courtesy Ernie Atkinson.)

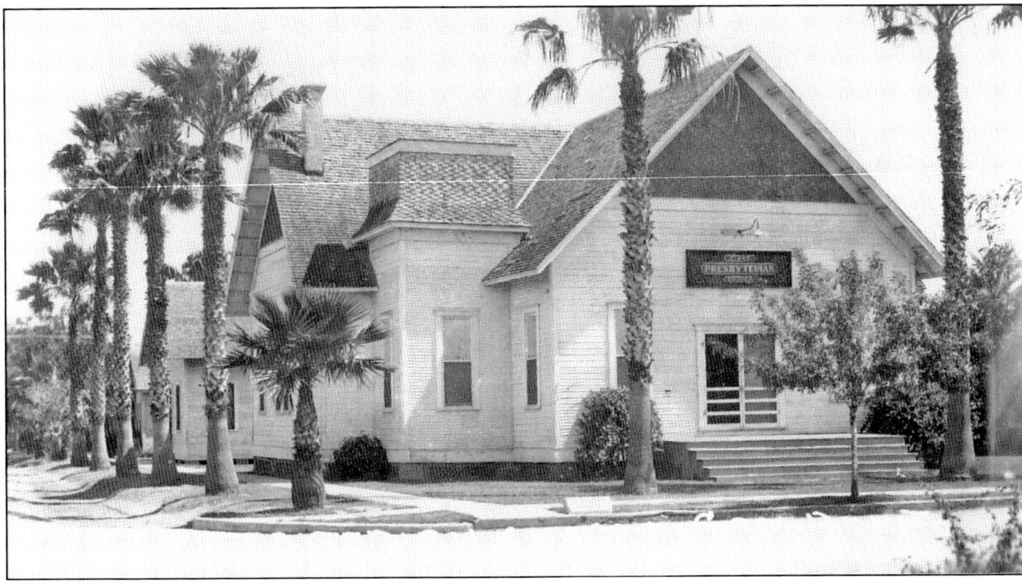

First Presbyterian Church was organized in 1910, three years after San Benito's founding. The first building, a frame structure completed in 1911, served the congregation until a hurricane destroyed it in 1933. The following year, a mission revival style building featuring arched gable parapets, was constructed. Funded in part by a loan from the federal government, it was known as America's first Public Works Administration church. (Courtesy Ed Robertson.)

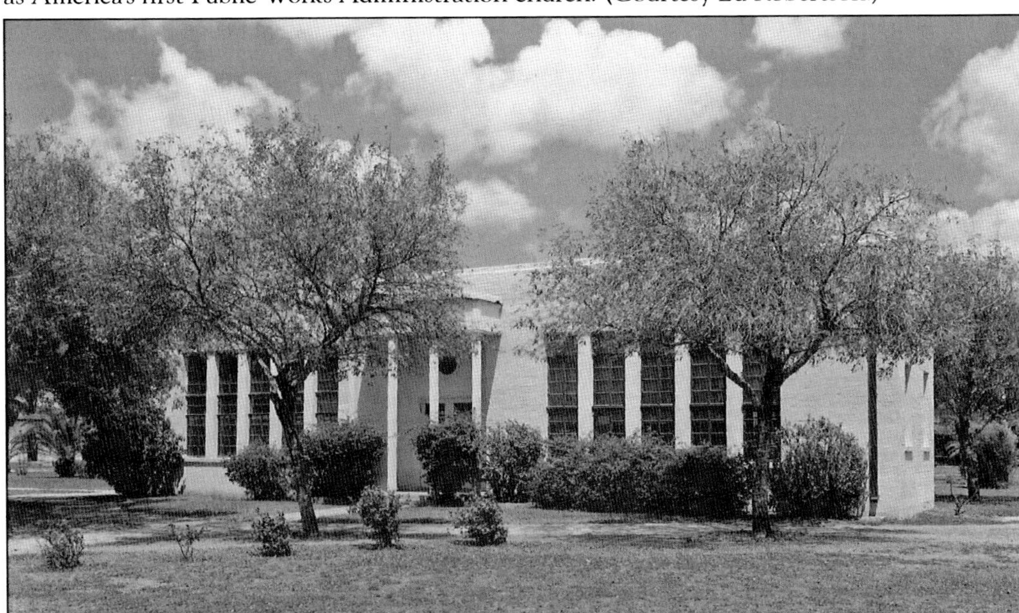

The first San Benito Public Library was started by Frances Turner Heywood after she called on citizens to observe Library Day, October 1, 1914, by donating books. The present-day library building was the result of the effort of the Council of Women's Clubs, with Chrissie Bucklin, president. The city commission granted the project a site in Heywood Park, opposite the Stonewall Jackson Hotel. Local architect Hadley Smith oversaw the planning. When completed, the building cost an estimated $10,000. (Courtesy San Benito Historical Society.)

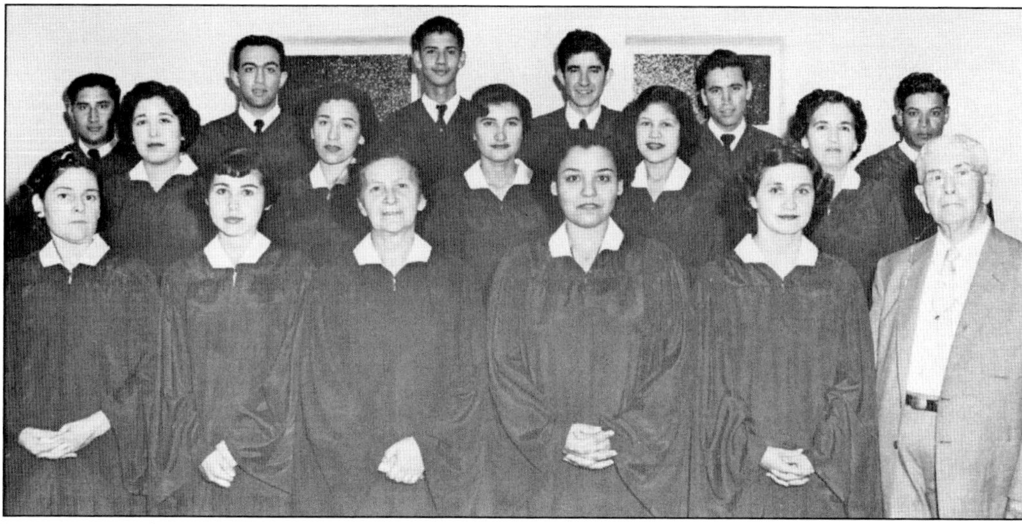

Hispanic Presbyterians in San Benito began meeting in homes to worship in 1909, and this early congregation formed the Mexican Presbyterian Church in 1910, known today as Getsemani Presbyterian Church. Pictured in this c. 1950 photograph are, from left to right, choir members (first row) Virginia Cavazos, Juanita Treviño, Lillie Vazquez, Susana Argullín, Estela Davila, and Rev. Juan G. Cavazos; (second row) Raquel Garcia, Rafaela Rodriguez, Elizabeth Lopez, Alicia Solis, and Lydia Garcia; (third row) David Gomez, David Cavazos, Rene Castillo, Jonathan Lopez, Abelardo Garcia Jr., and Ezequiel Reyes. (Courtesy Getsemani Presbyterian Church.)

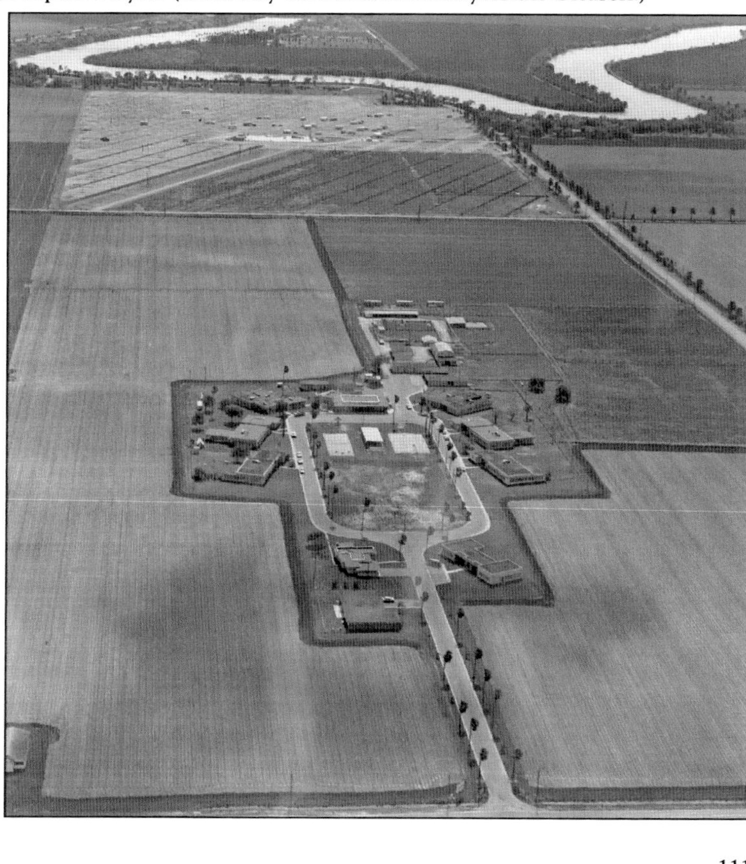

The present-day location of Sunny Glen Children's Home is on the Expressway 77/83 frontage road near Paso Real Road. Sunny Glen has occupied this site since 1948, when Henry Meyer donated 80 acres of land to the home. Initially, the home's six cottages housed 16 children each; in the mid-1980s, the state regulated the number of children allowed per cottage. This project is supported by the Church of Christ. In this photograph, notice the resaca in background. (Courtesy Jay Williams.)

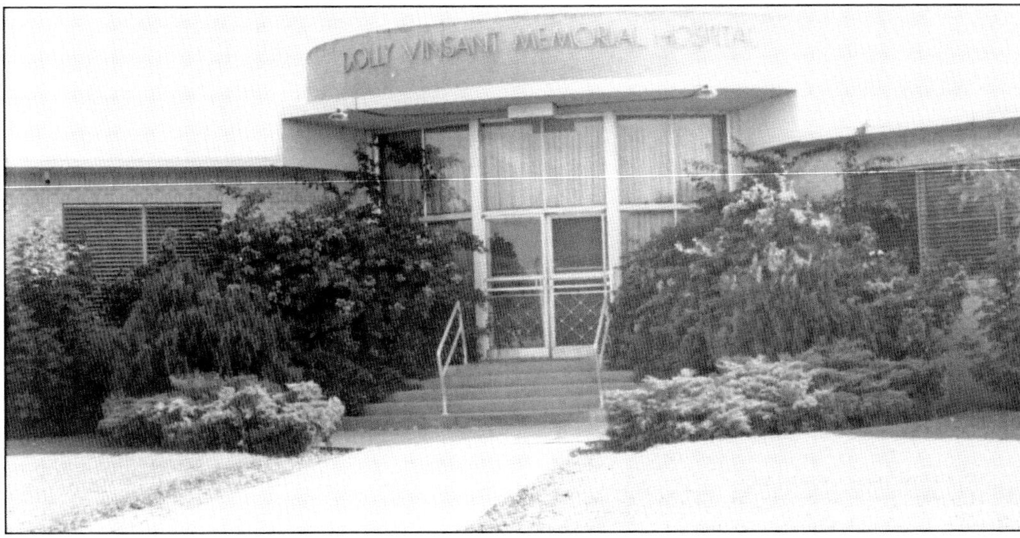

Headed by LeRoy Crawford, the Kiwanis Club's largest project ever began as an undertaking to raise $25,000 for a youth health clinic. The idea caught fire, other clubs joined in, and the enthusiasm was so great, project leaders decided to construct a full-scale hospital, Dolly Vinsant Memorial, named for the heroic San Benito–born U.S. Army nurse killed in the April 1945 crash of a C-47 in Eisenach, Germany. Dr. William J. and Nell Vinsant, Dolly's parents, were present for the May 1947 ground breaking. Every organization and group in the community had played a large role in obtaining the funds that built the hospital. Accordingly the original executive board included two representatives each from the Kiwanis Club, Rotary Club, Lions Club, and Elks Lodge. The general construction contract was awarded to J. B. Hughes of Brownsville, and two years later, the completed hospital welcomed its first patients. On November 13, 1949, Dolly Maria Martinez (Barrera) became the first baby born at Dolly Vinsant Memorial Hospital. In the photograph below, Drs. Mitchell Parker, Hunter Scales, and Cecil Simmons enjoy lunch in Dolly Vinsant Hospital's doctors' lunch room. (Above courtesy Enriqueta L. Ramos; below courtesy Katherine Scales.)

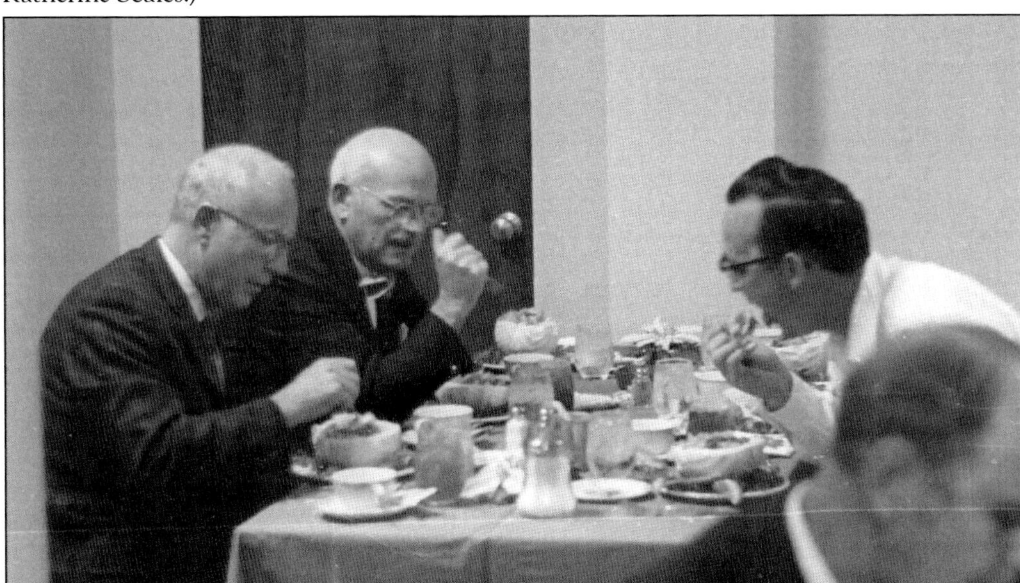

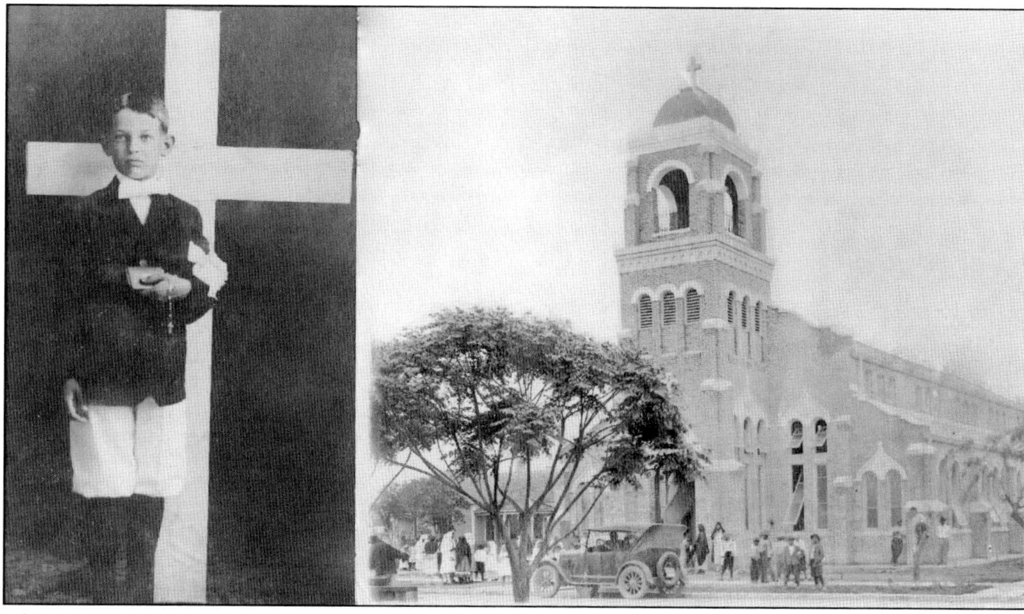

The original St. Benedict's Church was erected in 1910, two years before the fledgling congregation formally became a parish. In 1923, the building was destroyed by fire. Two years later, the brick structure pictured here was built to replace it, under the leadership of Fr. Yvo Tymen OMI, (1879–1977), who served the parish from 1921 to 1937. Pictured at left is Joseph Herbert Buesing, who took his First Communion here in 1911. Of German ancestry, Herbert's parents, Frederick and Emma Buesing, moved here in 1909 from Yoakum. Their home was on North Dowling Street, next to the railroad tracks. (Courtesy Tootie Madden.)

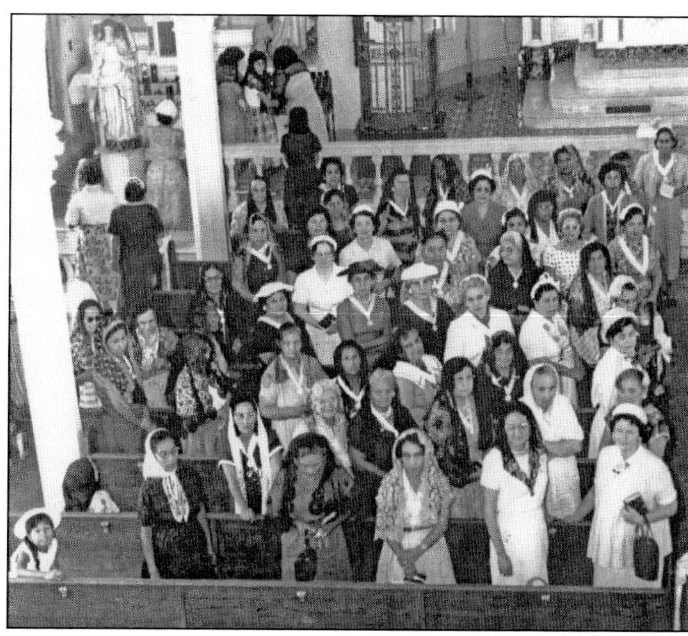

In 1955, a photographer snapped this picture of the St. Benedict's Catholic Church's Sacred Heart Society from the church balcony. Some of the women pictured here include Mary Conde, Berta Cabaza, Rebecca Gonzales, Fina Gonzales, Gonzala Noyola, Adela Lopez, Maria Zepeda, Francisca Perez, Isabel Rios, Maria De La Fuente, Zoila Reyna, Josefina "Chepita" Martinez, Manuela Guerra, Francisca Aleman, Ernestina Cavazos, Adelina Alvarez, Adelita Gonzales, Lina Alvarez, and Anita Zepeda. (Courtesy Celeste Z. Sanchez.)

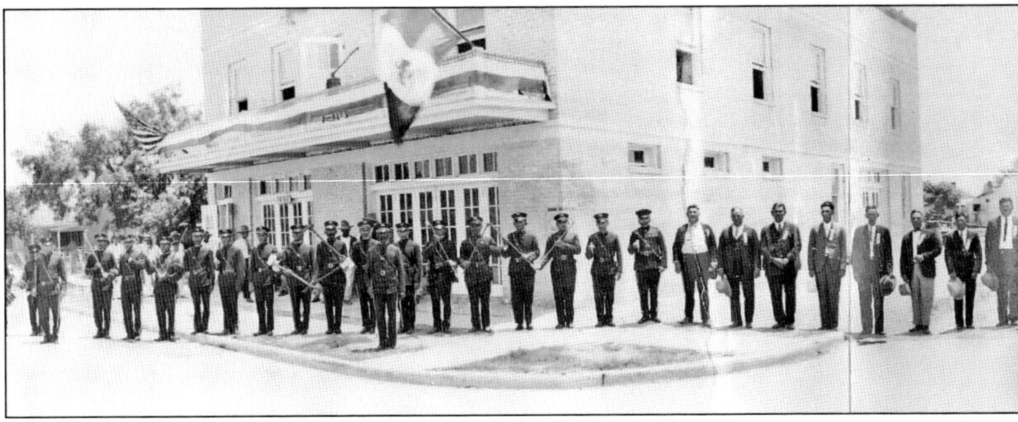

San Benito Woodmen of the World (WOW) lodge band members stand shoulder-to shoulder at the corner of Morelos and Hidalgo Streets in 1929 to pose for a panoramic photograph. WOW was the United States' largest fraternal benefit society with an open membership. Founded in 1890, the society grew into a financial services organization large enough to offer security, but small enough to still care about each member. In addition to providing life insurance protection, the society urged its members, through their local lodges, to serve as volunteer forces within their communities, helping those in need. (Courtesy Joe Hernandez.)

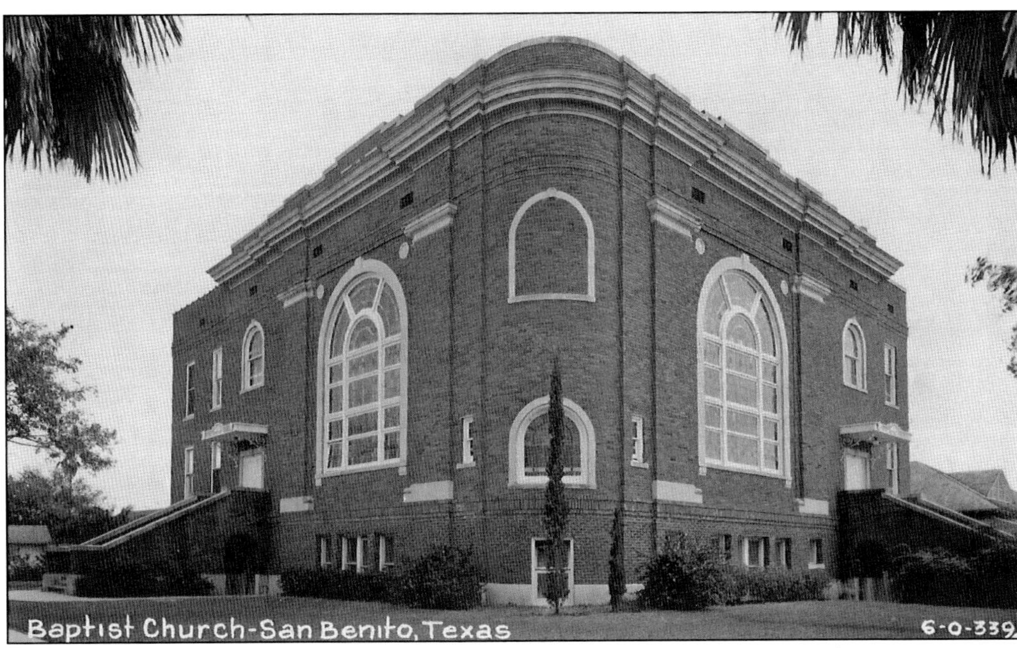

The First Baptist Church, located at the corner of Heywood and North Crockett Streets, was a beautiful building with one of the few basements built in San Benito. It was torn down in the early 1970s in an effort to modernize. The property was sold to HEB grocery chain. The stained-glass windows were bought by collectors. The site is now home to the administration building for the school district. (Courtesy San Benito Historical Society.)

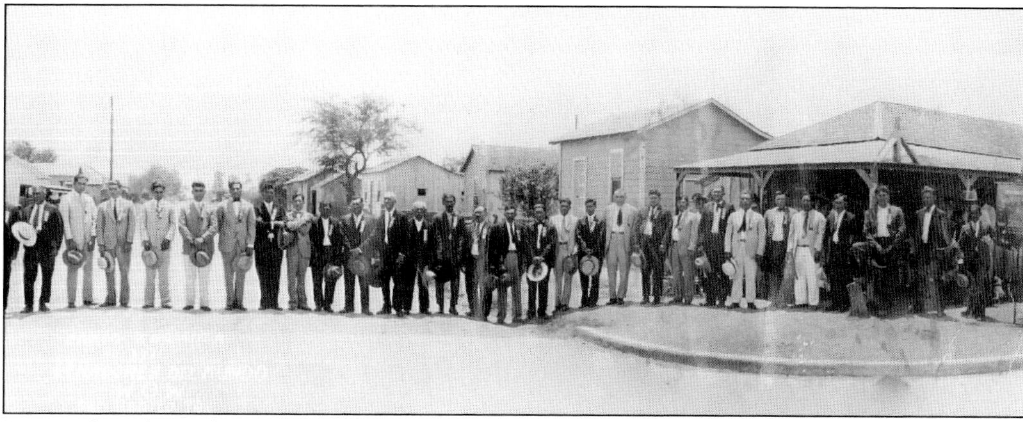

Los Hecheos ("woodmen") met on the second floor of La Colonial store, making plans to help their neighbors. Continuing leftward from the photograph on the previous page are the remaining members of the San Benito Woodmen of the World lodge. Damaso Zepeda, Virginia Ayoub's father, was an agent with Woodmen of the World, representing the interests of many Hispanics. (Courtesy Joe Hernandez.)

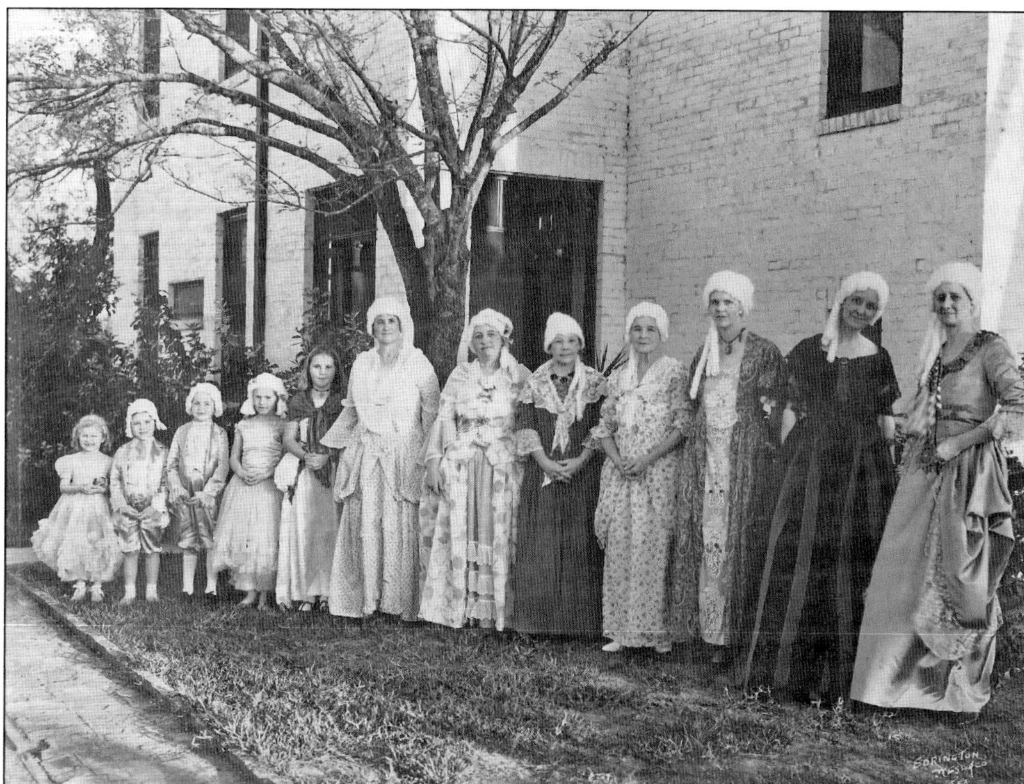

The Lt. Thomas Barlow Chapter NSDAR (Daughters of the American Revolution) of San Benito, chartered in 1914, is the first chapter established south of San Antonio. This *c.* 1935 photograph of members in period costume shows, from left to right, five unidentified children, Kathryn Chadick, Lee Kidder, Mrs. Richard Smith, Mrs. William Copeland, Mrs. Walter Swarrer, Mrs. Winn, and an unidentified DAR member. The chapter is still active. (Courtesy Susan Roland Francis.)

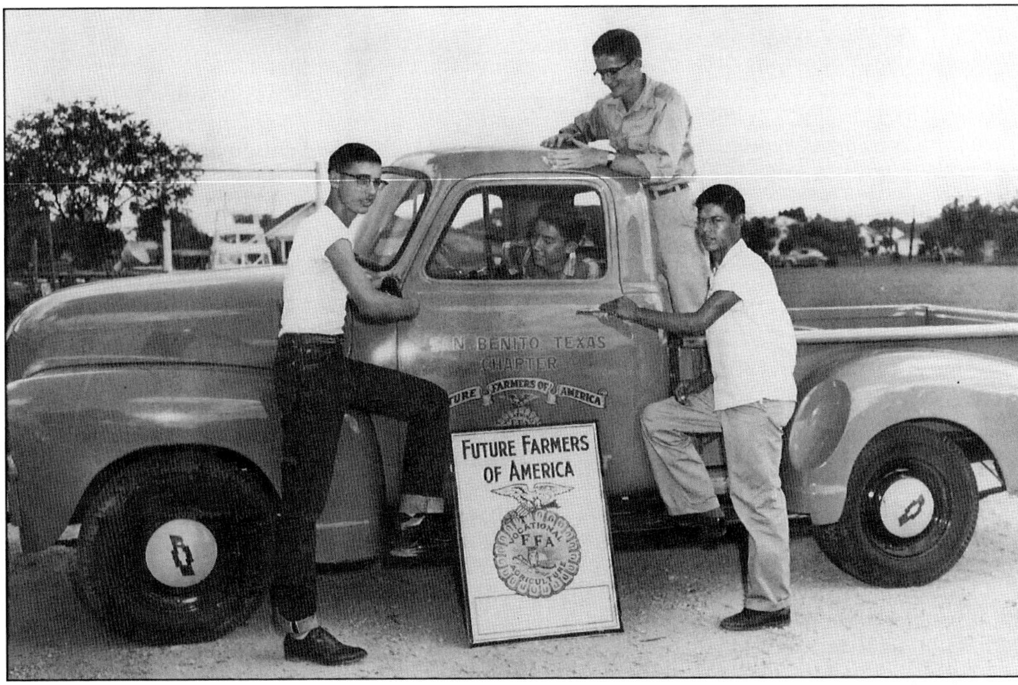

In 1955, Welch Chevrolet lent a half-ton Chevy pickup truck to the San Benito High School Future Farmers of America (FFA) chapter for use by the advisors to travel to the farms and check on the students' projects. The 1955 FFA officers shown here are, from left to right, Bob Tumberlinson, Billie Woolam, George Tamura (in the cab), and Cody Colchado. (Courtesy Bob Tumberlinson.)

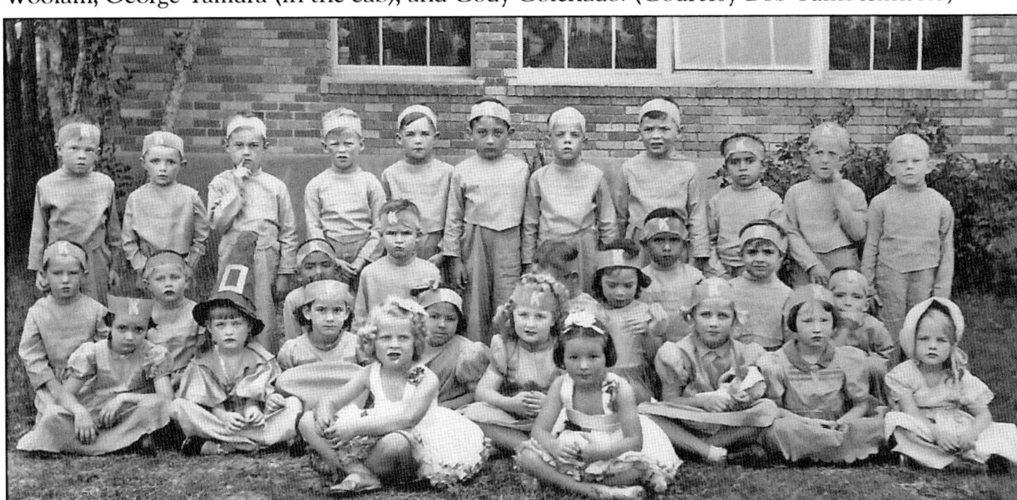

Landrum Elementary School didn't have a kindergarten in 1943. Therefore, all children attended North Ward Elementary, and afterwards, roughly half of them transferred to Landrum for first grade. The children in this photograph include, from left to right, (standing) Bobby Tumberlinson (third), Tommy Mendez, (sixth), Billy Brod (seventh), and Bobby Edwards (eighth); (kneeling) Beatrice Villarreal (sixth), Margaret Bendixon (seventh), and Hilario Garcia (eighth); (sitting) Ann Collins and Mike Palmer. And in the photograph but not identified are Billy Woolam, Taylor Ewing, Dickie Payne, Betty Jo Moxley, Wally Gilbert, Ariel Cantu, Mack Brown, Ben Yudesis, and Henry Garcia. (Courtesy Bob Tumberlinson.)

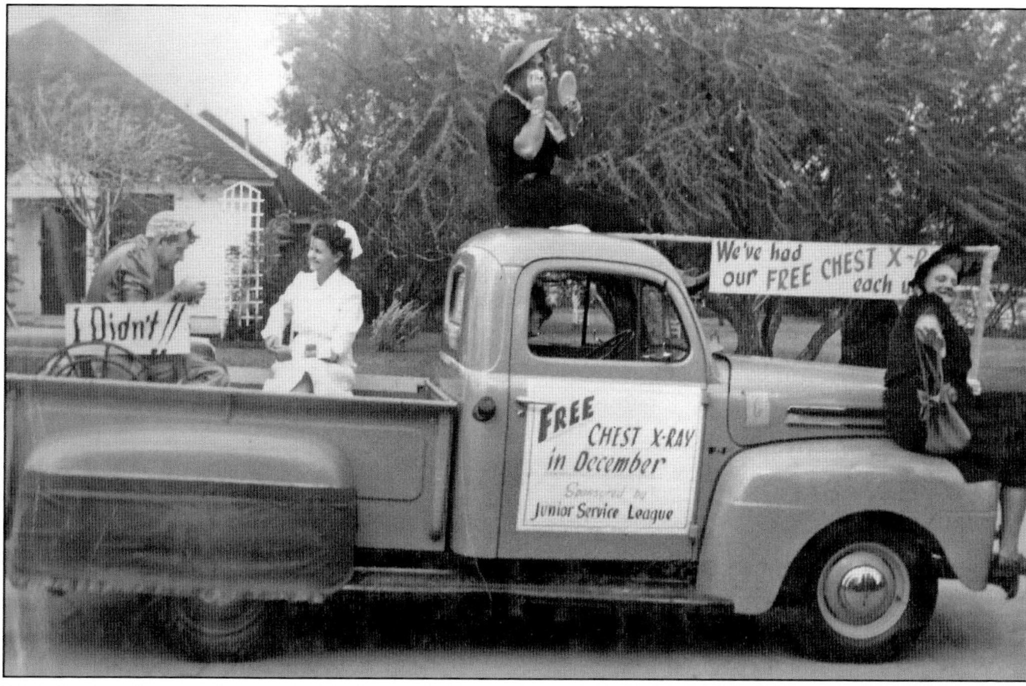

This Junior Service League's 1949 parade float advertised the group's Chest X-ray campaign. The parade started on Sam Houston Boulevard at Powers Street and snaked through the neighborhood to SBHS's Greyhound Stadium. (Courtesy Tootie Madden.)

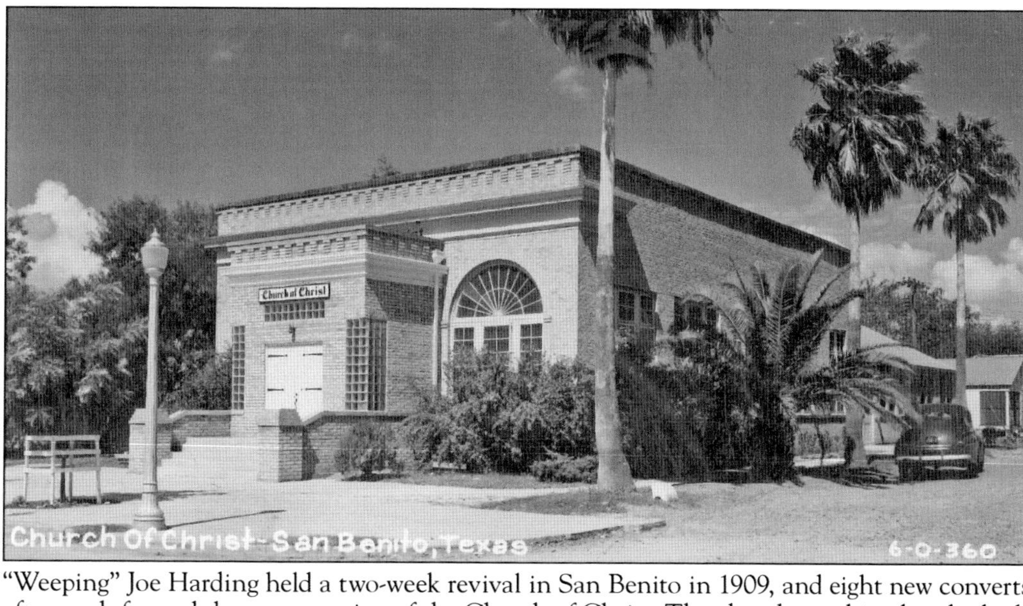

"Weeping" Joe Harding held a two-week revival in San Benito in 1909, and eight new converts afterwards formed the congregation of the Church of Christ. The church worshiped at the high school until 1916, then constructed a small building. In 1920, they erected a second building at 399 North Sam Houston Boulevard, and then replaced it in 1928 with the building pictured here. The present church was dedicated January 1975. In 1949, San Benito's Church of Christ accepted responsibility to oversee the Sunny Glen Children's Home. (Courtesy Charles M. Robinson III.)

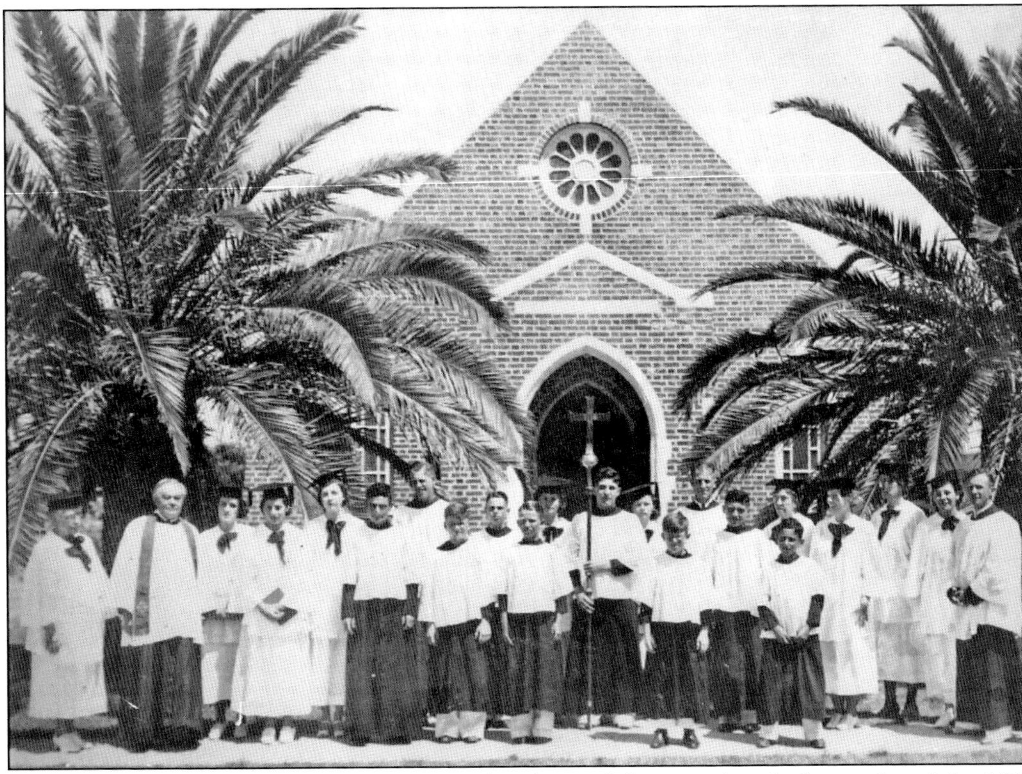

The All Saints Episcopal Church choir stood in front of the new church that replaced the 1911 building destroyed by the 1933 hurricane. On the left is "Mother" Johnson and Fr. Everett Johnson, the longtime priest who sponsored a traveling library and vocational education for Hispanic girls. Father Johnson owned the only barometer in San Benito during the 1933 hurricane, and he recorded the storm's changing barometric pressures from the Stonewall Jackson Hotel, to which he had evacuated. The crucifer was George Ogdee. George's sister Helen is the choir member standing beside Father Johnson. (Courtesy Tootie Madden.)

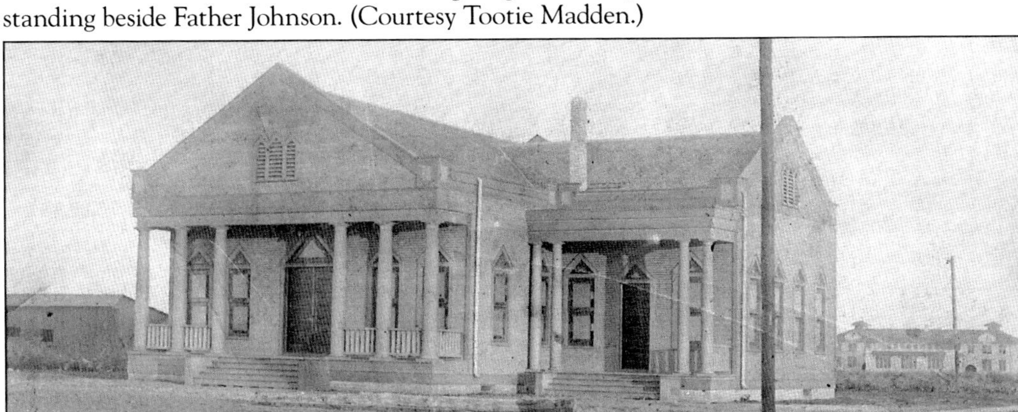

The First Methodist Church of San Benito was organized less than a year after the city was platted. On January 22, 1908, Rev. C. E. W. Smith, the Methodist pastor of Brownsville, organized the congregation in a one-room schoolhouse behind the Sam Robertson home. In the summer of 1910, at the cost of $6,000, this first Methodist church building was erected at the corner of Sam Houston Boulevard and Hicks Street. (Courtesy San Benito Historical Society.)

The Well Baby Clinic, sponsored by the newly organized Junior Service League, opened in February 1946, on the second floor of the Aztec Building, under director Rhea Monger. Drs. Hunter Scales, Clarence McClellan Cash, and Nelson W. Haas received a flat fee from the Cameron County Health Unit. Mothers were given canned milk, information on feeding, child care, and immunizations. In this photograph, Mary Scales weighs and measures a baby at the clinic. (Courtesy Tootie Madden.)

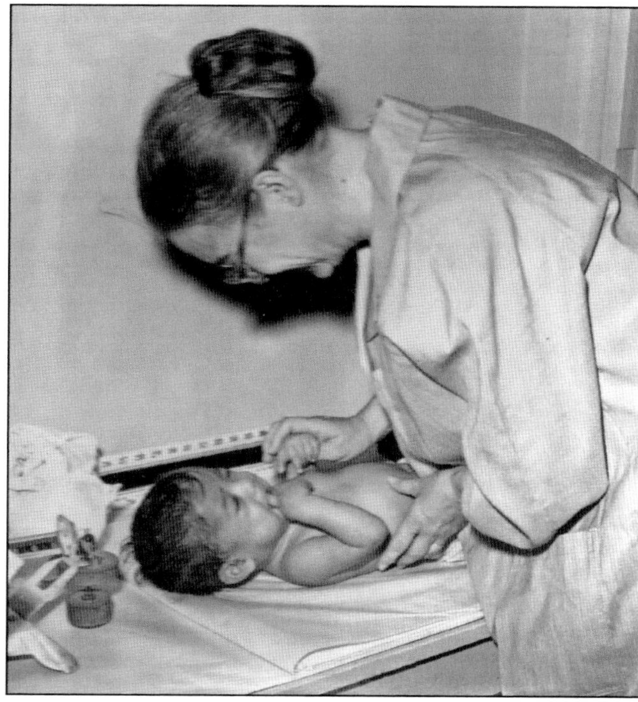

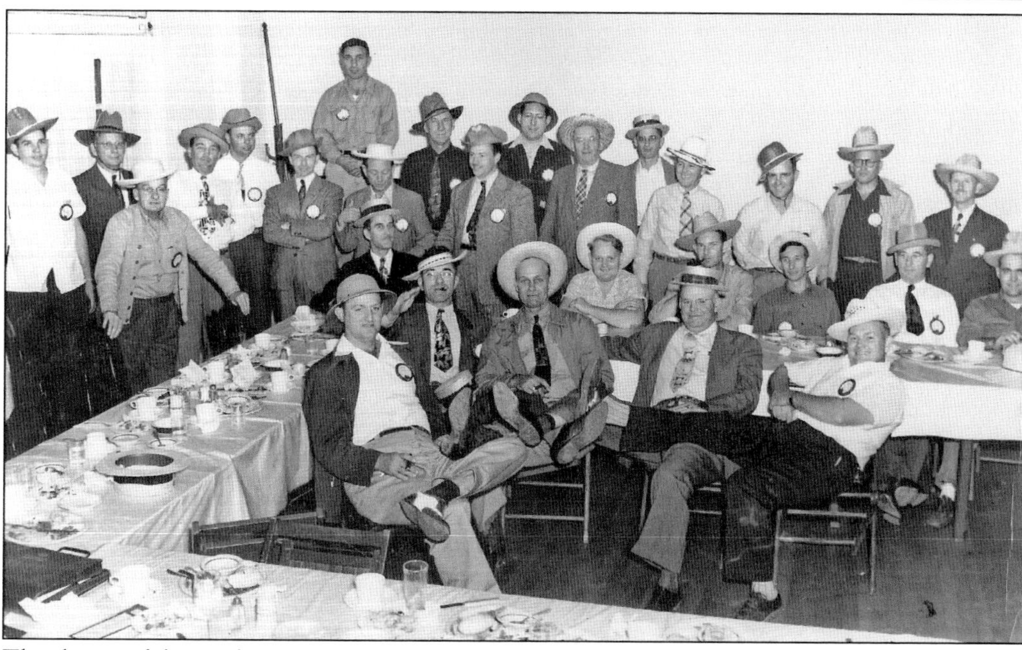

The theme of this mid-1950s Lions Club meeting was, "We wear many hats!" The Lions pictured here are, from left to right, (first row) George Finch, Kenneth Lake, Elmer Walk, Bill Brown, and Charles Schaudies; (second row) two unidentified, Bill Foust (with pipe), ? Cradit, unidentified, and Alison Mayfield; (third row, standing) Jack Merryman, Rudy Bendixon, C. D. Oakes, Ezra Dodson, Joe E. Smith, Jimmy Mayer, unidentified (without hat), Gilbert Crain, Carl Miller, Bill Simpson, Richard E. Bilbie, unidentified, Leon Tumberlinson, Flint Harris, William D. "Bill" Todd, unidentified, and Raymond Howard. (Courtesy Bob Tumberlinson.)

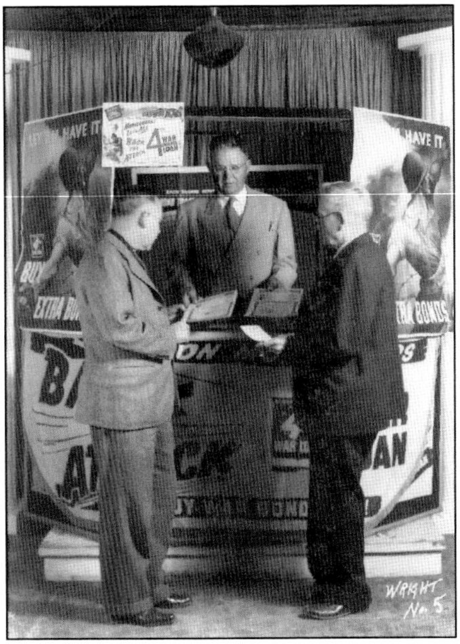

At first they were called defense bonds and issued by the U.S. Government, but that name was changed to war bonds after the Japanese attack on Pearl Harbor on December 7, 1941. Bond drives were emotional appeals to patriotic citizens to lend the government the money needed to fight the war. Here in San Benito, Leon Tolliver "Tol" Boswell Sr. and another man buy war bonds from Ed Brady at the Rivoli Theater. (Courtesy Tootie Madden.)

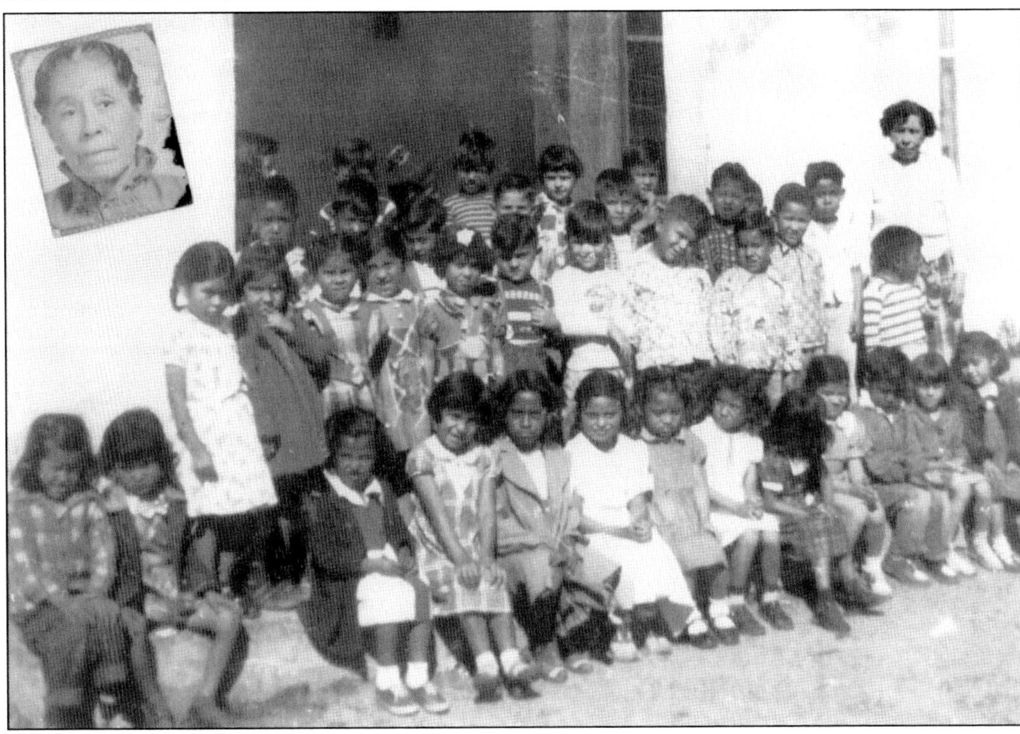

With the help of Sam Robertson, Fr. Isidro Chateau obtained a lot from the San Benito Land and Water Company for a parochial school. On September 9, 1912, the first Catholic school opened under the tutelage of Carmen Martinez and Beatriz Martinez. Later Catalina Huerta joined the faculty. They ran the two-storied, stucco La Escuela Guadalupe on Corral Street for Spanish speakers. After the nuns took charge in September 1924, Celia Longoria and Rodolfo Peña recalled being forced to kneel on uncooked rice or upside-down bottle caps as punishment for being naughty. (Courtesy Anita H. Garcia.)

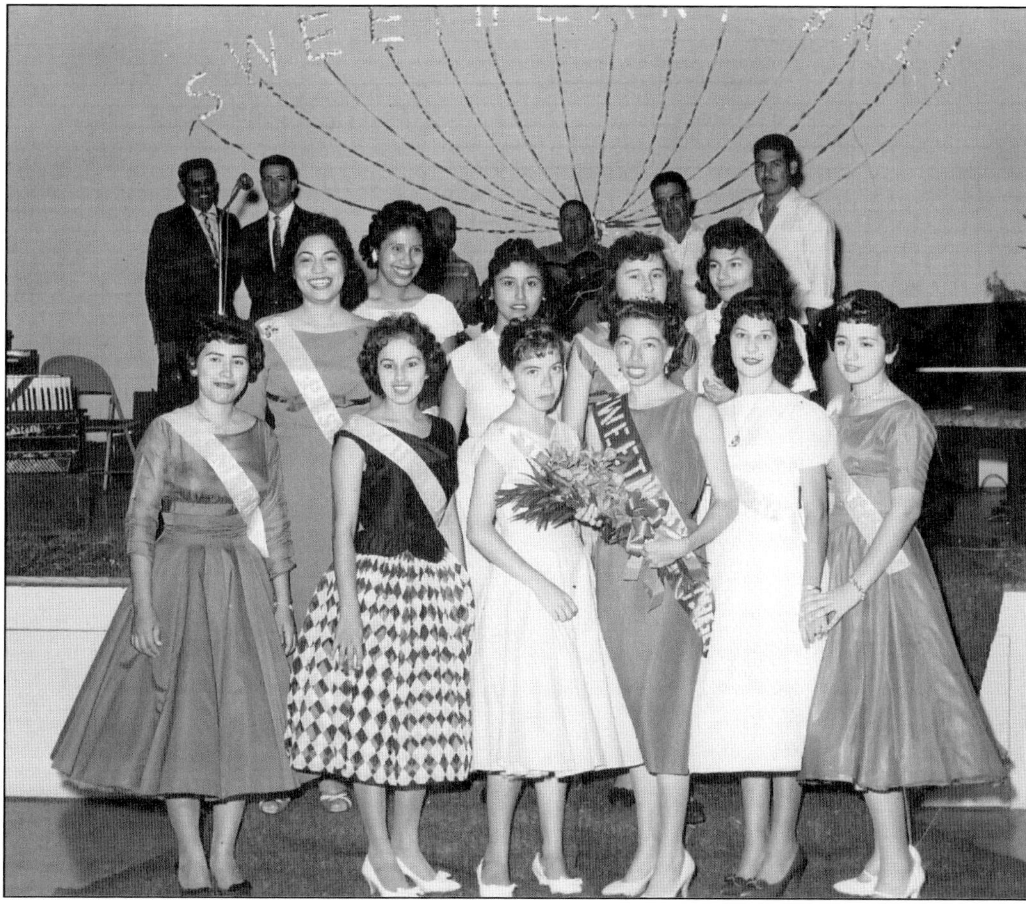

St. Benedict Church's teenage girls' organization, The Daughters of Mary, held its 1960 Sweetheart Ball at the Community Building. Seen here are (first row) an unidentified girl, Dolores Saldivar, Lily Flores, Oralia Flores, Mary Lou Ornelas, and Celeste Zepeda Sanchez; (second row) Berta Lara, Toni Vasquez, unidentified, Norma Garcia, and Alma Robles. (Courtesy Celeste Z. Sanchez.)

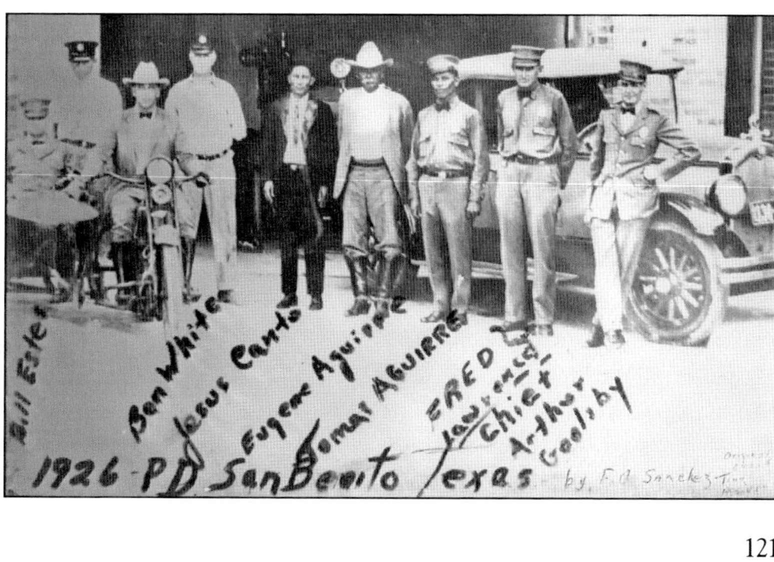

Standing in front of the police station in 1926 are Bill Estes, Ben White, Jesus Cantu, Deputy Sheriff Eugene Aguirre, Tomas Aguirre, Fred Lawrence, and Chief Arthur Goolsby. (Courtesy Maria Robles Nuñez.)

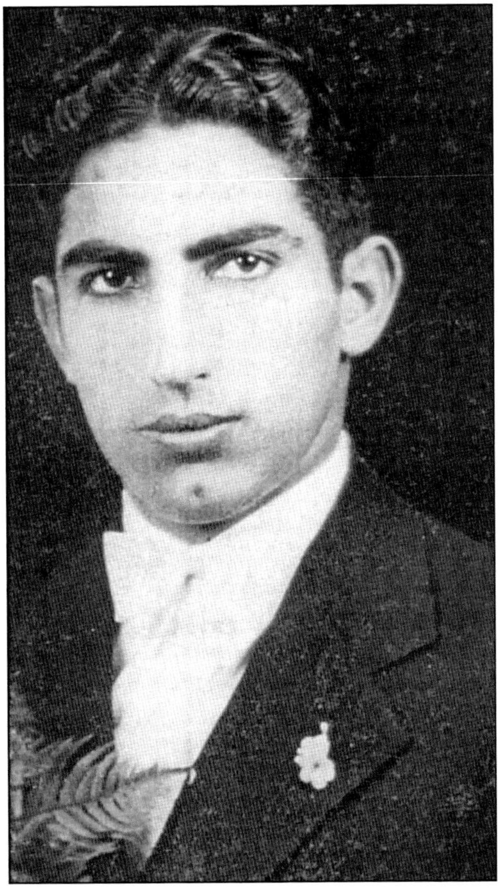

The town name was made official by the U.S. Post Office on May 11, 1907, and on September 20, 1907, parents Ismael and Francisca Esparza Montalvo gave birth to San Benito Montalvo—the first baby born in the newly christened town of San Benito. Col. Sam Robertson, in a 1931 letter to S. B. Montalvo, wrote, "You, Benito, were the first American child born in this town and you are more American than I am, and you should remain here among your friends as long as you live." Benny was considered a "good will ambassador" for the town, advertising its merits everywhere he went. He enjoyed telling this story: Upon returning to the United States from Mexico, customs officials would ask him, "Where were you born?" "San Benito," he'd respond. "Where are you going?" "San Benito," he'd respond. "What's your name?" "San Benito," he'd respond. He loved playing with the customs officials, and they always pulled him over. (Courtesy San Benito Historical Society.)

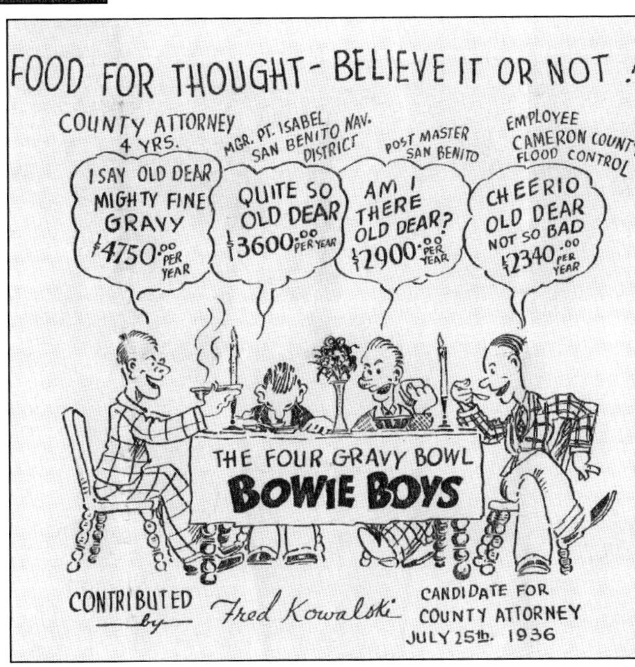

With this 1936 political cartoon, campaign opponent Fred Kowalski seeks to undermine Charles Bowie's bid for re-election as county attorney by fanning resentment over the significant number of Bowie Boys drawing salaries from the public "gravy bowl." The Bowies had undeniably achieved something of a political dynasty in the county: in addition to Charles's job as county attorney, Jim drew a salary as manager of the Port Isabel/ San Benito Navigation District; Alec as town postmaster, and Andy as a county flood control employee. Later Andy was elected county commissioner. The stretch of beach accessible to the public was named in his memory. (Courtesy Pat Bowie Davis.)

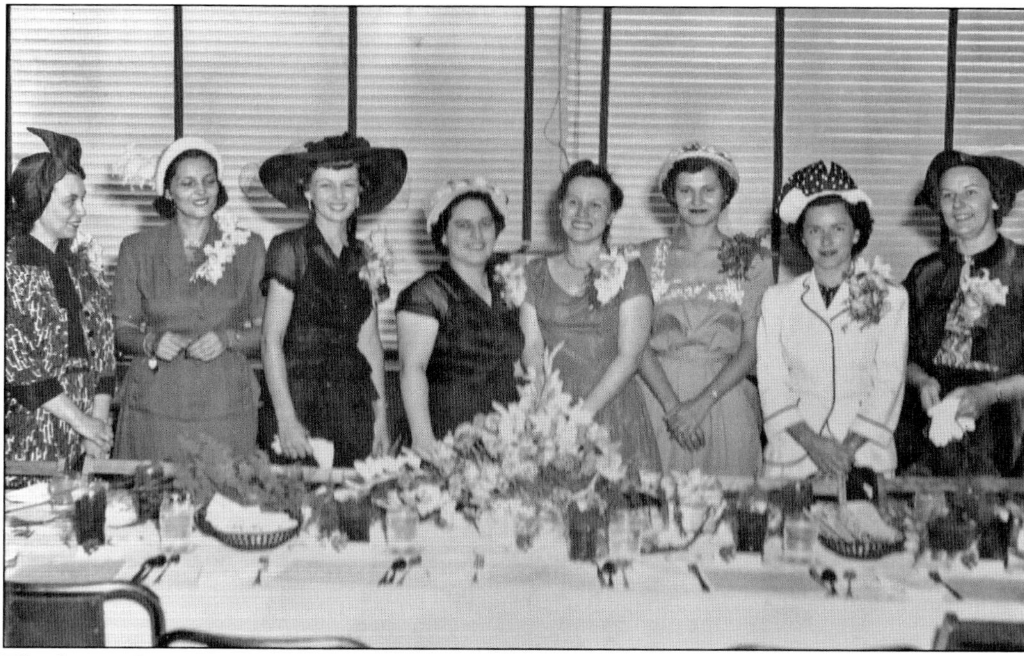

The Junior Service League honored its new members at the group's annual spring luncheon, held in May 1950 at the Little Creek Hotel in Harlingen. The women include, from left to right, Miriam Yudesis, Thelma Hiller, Jane Parker, Ann Brown, Irma Russell, Patsy Abbott, Kyle Cruse, and Danese Medders. (Courtesy Tootie Madden.)

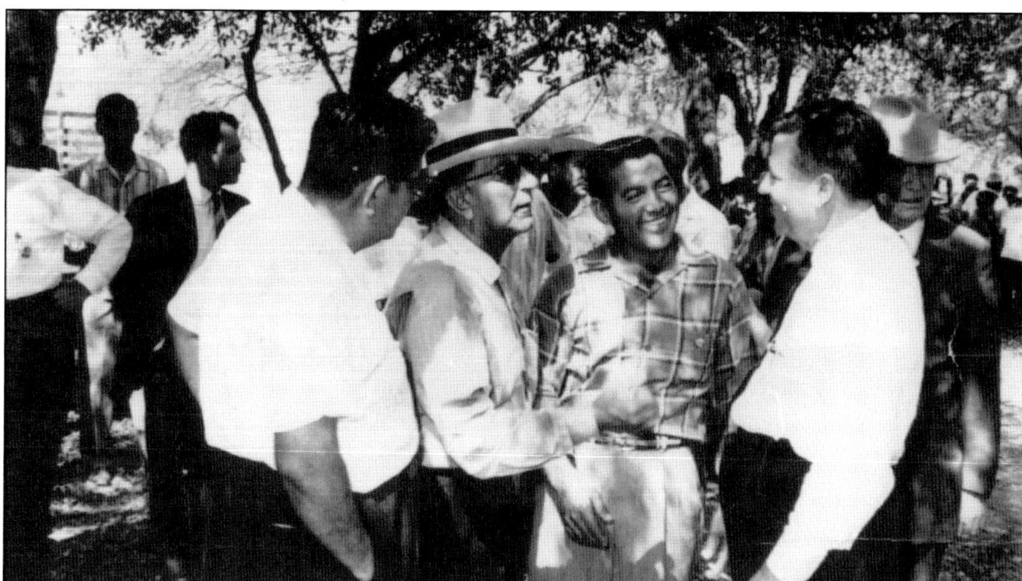

This 1960 *pachanga* (political gathering), organized by Francisca "Panchita" Domanski, included, from left to right, Fernando Sanchez, Justice of the Peace Joe E. Gerusa, Senon Garcia, and Sen. Ralph Yarborough. Yarborough was the only Southern senator to vote in favor of every civil rights bill from 1957 to 1970, including the civil rights act of 1964 and the Voting Rights Act. As senator, Yarborough got the bill passed that created Padre Island National Park. (Courtesy Mrs. Angela Leal to Rey Avila.)

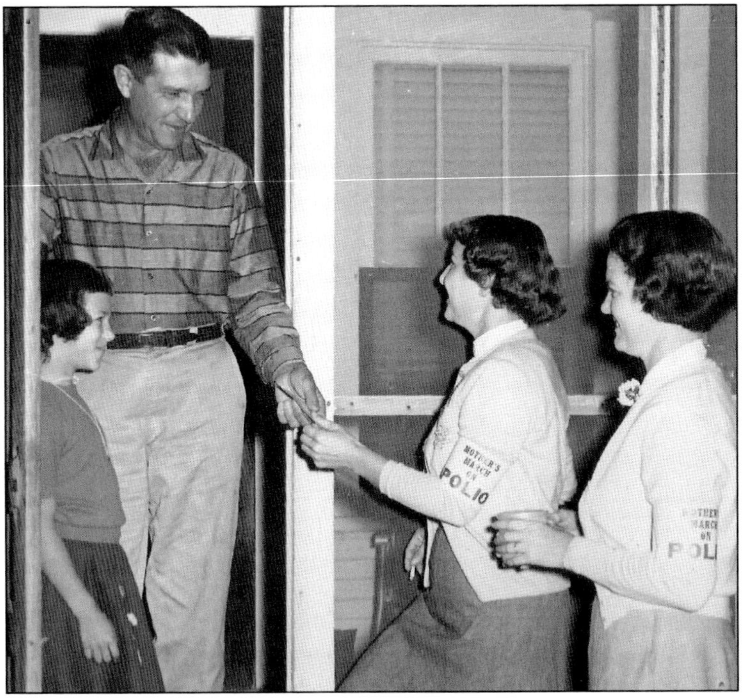

At the height of the polio epidemic in 1952, nearly 60,000 cases and more than 3,000 deaths were reported in the United States alone. The Mothers' March of Dimes was an annual door-to-door campaign that raised money to help stamp out polio. In this photograph, Susie and Bee Mobley greet canvassing Junior Service League members Ann Mobley and Jo Reese (far right). (Courtesy Tootie Madden.)

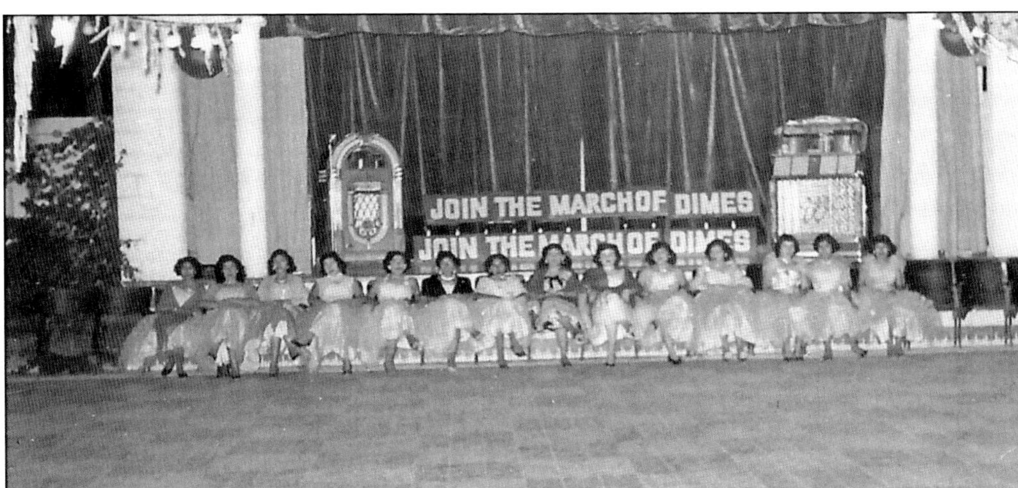

The Mothers' March began in 1950. Women carried "coin folders" door-to-door, collecting dimes to fill the folders in a campaign to fight polio. This group of women, together with their families, had a kick-off party at La Villita. Some of the women involved with this effort were Lydia Peña, Emma Garcia, Celia Longoria, Tina Valenzuela, Lupita Gonzales, Yolanda Ramirez, Eva Sanchez, Eliza Alvear, Elida Villarreal, Mary Conde, and Marie Bolado. (Courtesy Rey Avila.)

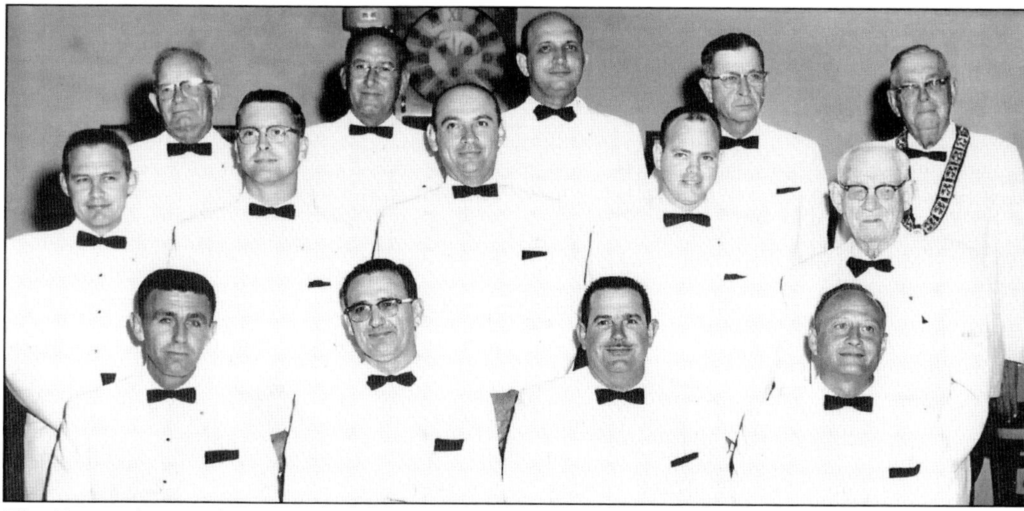

The Benevolent and Protective Order of Elks Lodge No. 1661 included, from left to right, (first row) Alvin Ripps, Leon Tumberlinson, Pete Hall, and John Phillips; (second row) two unidentified, Art Nowakowski, two unidentified; (third row) Troy Henderson, ? Stevenson, Kenneth Hill, Mark Gardner, and unidentified district officer. (Courtesy Bob Tumberlinson.)

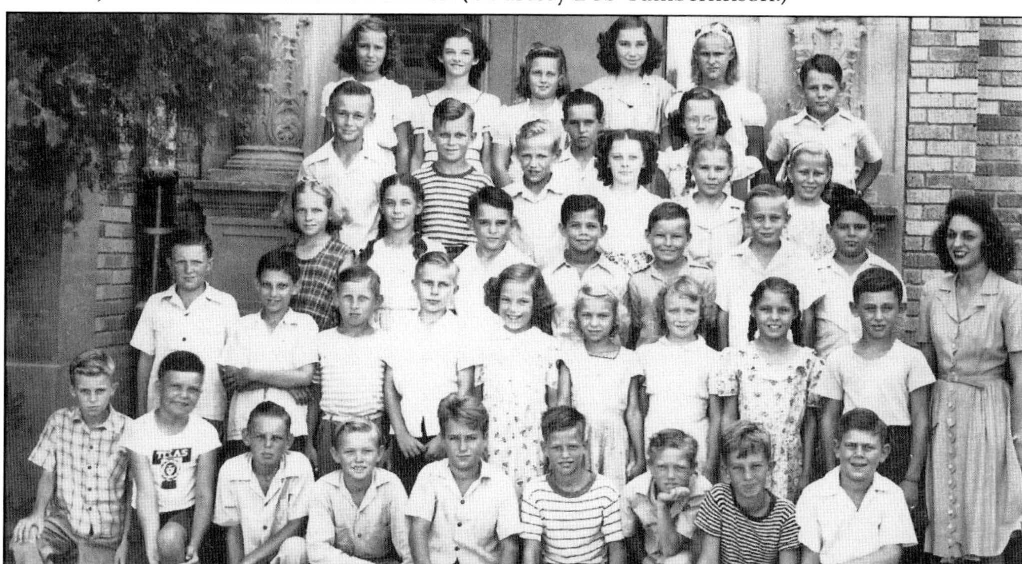

North Ward Elementary School's 1945 fifth grade class included the following students: (first row) John Scaief, Lucius Hill, Jake Kennedy, Carl Moore, David Cliborn, Kent Zimmerman, George Day, Harlan Baker, and Earl Moore; (second row) Douglas Hutchins, Franklin Mead, Melvin Allen, Robert ?, Erlyne Moore, Mary Slayden, Truella Roberts, Althea Oden, and Gregory Haas; (third row) Shirley Kennamer, Johanna Hitt, Bill Aldridge, Richard Bridges, Cecil Woods, Lee McNabb, Oscar Gomez; (fourth row) Vernon Hallbeck, Kenneth Mayfield, David Hines, Louis Valle, Jo Ann Strickland, Gladys Lynch, Patty Richardson, and Betty Daughtrey; (fifth row) Nancy Dobson, Dorothy Bruns, Lynda Gay Taylor, Nila Lou Moore, Carol Walk, and Max Harris. Standing far right is teacher Joan Hagar. (Courtesy Max Harris.)

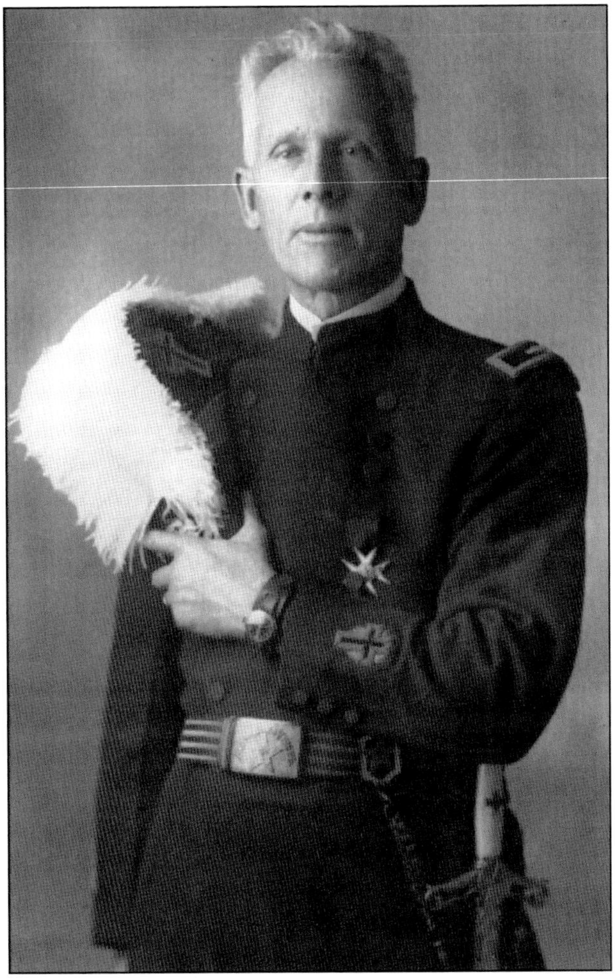

A product of the old-time preceptorship training, Dr. Clarence McClellan Cash spent only one year at medical school, yet for nearly five decades, his knowledge of medicine brought him recognition by distinguished colleagues, many honors, and the admiration and love of an entire community. He delivered more than 5,200 babies. Though he finally gave up obstetrics, he never actually stopped practicing medicine. His death on October 13, 1961, was the result of an accident. He was 97 and is pictured here in his Masonic Knights Templar regalia. (Courtesy San Benito Historical Society.)

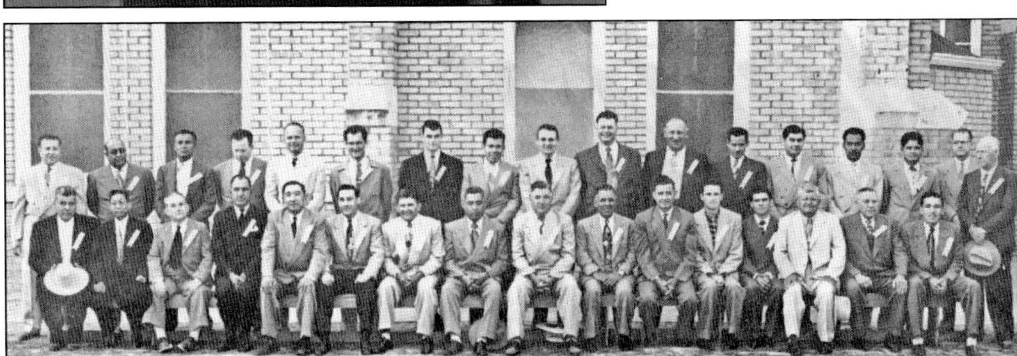

In 1952, the Knights of Columbus charter members included Tomas Aguirre Jr., Leonardo Amaya, Jose M. Avila, Reymundo G. Flores, J. A. Flores, L. L. Galvan, Cristobal Garcia, Luis M. Garcia, Felix L. Gay, Jesus E. Gonzales, A. Gonzales Sr., Rodolfo Guerra Sr., Jose M. Loya, Oscar Lozano, Armando Lucio, Guadalupe Martinez, San Benito Montalvo, N. Noyola, Donald O'Connell, Carlos Peña, Robert Perez, Felix Perez, Trifon O. Ramirez, J. G. Rodriguez, Fernando G. Sanchez, Jose Tolento, Thomas B. Tucker. Luis G. Villarreal, Frank Villareal Jr., Francisco Villareal Sr., Howard S. Williams, Enrique Zepeda, and Damaso C. Zepeda. (Courtesy Celeste Z. Sanchez.)

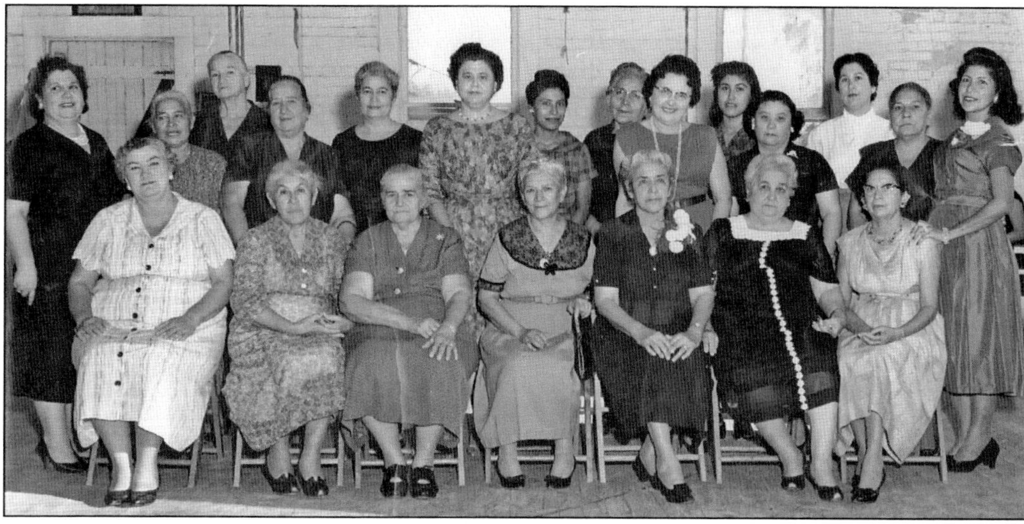

The Woodmen of the World company encouraged members to conduct projects that benefited individuals, families, and communities. These WOW women were devoted to their families and to each other. From left to right are (first row) Paula Davila, Anastacia "Tacha" Garcia, Emilia Peña, Adela Lopez, Delfina Gomez, Maria Zepeda, and Isabel Rios; (second row) Dora Zepeda Fairly, Refugia Avila, Catarina Huerta, unidentified, Eva Gomez, Consuelo Cavazos, Aurelia Bazan, Maria Bazan, Eva Sanchez, Anita Bazan Salazar, Panchita Perez, Imelda Flores, Natividad Galvan, and Elida Villarreal. (Courtesy Rey Avila.)

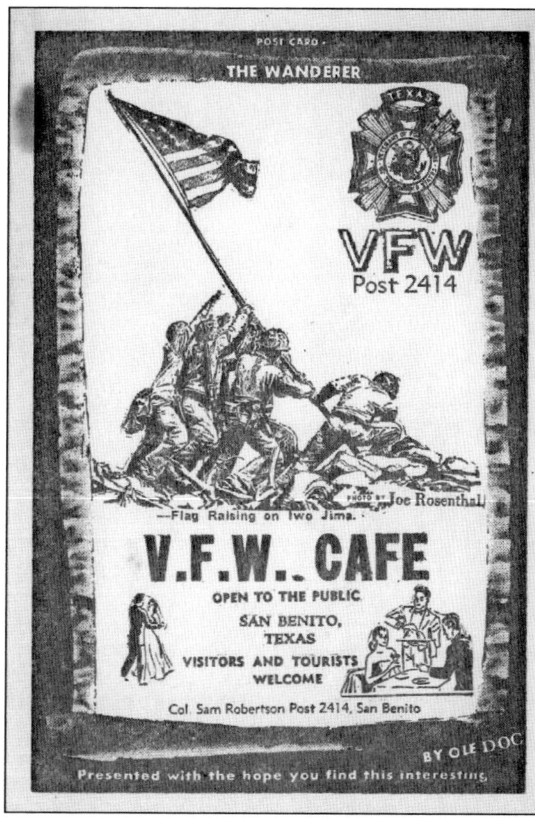

The mission of the Veterans of Foreign Wars is to "honor the dead by helping the living" through veterans' service, community service, national security, and a strong national defense. This VFW card invited the public to the Col. Sam Robertson Post 2414's café. (Courtesy San Benito Historical Society.)

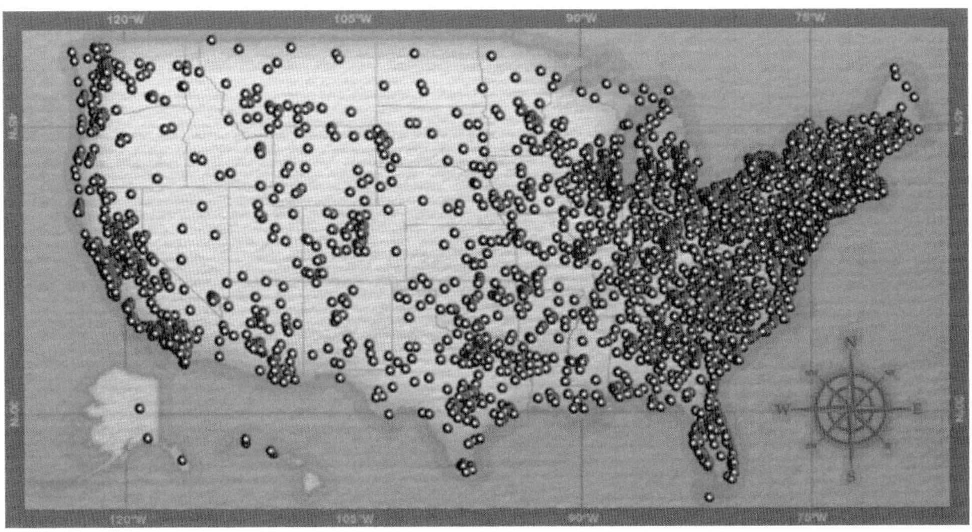

Consistent with our mission to preserve history on a local level, this book was printed in South Carolina on American-made paper and manufactured entirely in the United States. Products carrying the accredited Forest Stewardship Council (FSC) label are printed on 100 percent FSC-certified paper.

MADE IN THE USA